What Do You Think?

The 100 Best Columns of

DARRELL SIFFORD

From the pages of

The Philadelphia Inquirer

Published by arrangement with The Philadelphia Inquirer

First printing.

Philadelphia Newspapers Inc.
400 N. Broad St.
Philadelphia, PA 19101

ISBN: 0-9634709-0-6

Manufactured in the United States of America

A SPECIAL DEDICATION

One of the things that endeared Darrell to his readers was the extent to which he shared himself and his relationships through his columns — the struggles and triumphs, the pain and the joy. His love for his parents, Charlie and Hazel, and his sons, Jay and Grant, was evidenced in his life and was a matter of public record.

It is for that reason that this book is dedicated to each of them — with love.

TO DARRELL'S READERS

The bond that Darrell had developed with his readers and his sources over the years was profound. Their life stories, questions, wisdom and insights provided fuel and substance for the column as well as nourishment and inspiration to the writer.

This book is dedicated to each of you with respect and gratitude.

— *Marilyn Sifford*

Acknowledgments

First, I would like to thank The Philadelphia Inquirer for providing the opportunity and the environment that enabled Darrell to thrive as a columnist.

A few people there made this book happen. Maxwell King, the newspaper's editor, approached me shortly after Darrell's death and made it clear that The Inquirer wanted to do whatever it could to complete this work and make it available to readers. For Ken Bookman, editing this book has been a labor of love. His skill and judgment as an editor, his sensitivity to the subject matter and his creativity in putting it all together have at all times honored Darrell's vision for this collection of his columns. It was important to me to be part of the process of bringing the book to life, and Ken made me a partner in all of the important decisions. He provided guidance and affirmation that strengthened my contributions. And his concern and sensitivity to me personally have been a tremendous support during the past several months.

I would like to recognize two other people at The Inquirer — John Bull and Bob Greenberg, who worked hard to establish a journalism prize in Darrell's memory.

I wish it were possible to personally identify all of the people who have been part of Darrell's network of resources, colleagues and friends over the years. It is not, but you know who you are and I hope you appreciate the importance of your contributions to his work. On Darrell's behalf — thank you.

And, finally, I want to acknowledge the people interviewed in the columns selected for this book. Their contributions will become obvious as you read. They are:

W. Ferguson Anderson, Louis Armstrong, Edward L. Bernays, Burt Bertram, Donald D. Bilyew, Robert Bly, Philip Bobrove, William T. Carpenter, Erich and Judith Coché, Adrian Copeland, Gene Corbman, Norman Cousins, John Curtis, Jay

Efran, Duke Ellington, George L. Engel, O. Spurgeon English, Sam J. Ervin Jr., Jim Everroad, George and Sheila Ewalt, Ed Fish, Joel Fish, Frederic F. Flach, Carol Gantman, Daniel Gottlieb, David Grady, Jerome W. Greer, Larry Hall, Clark Hargrove, Raymond P. Harrison, Jerry B. Harvey, Aaron Hemsley, Phyllis Hobe, Jim Hoyme, Peter Koestenbaum, Selma Kramer, Edward H. Kuljian, Seymour "Sy" Kurland, Harold Kushner, R.D. Laing, Arnold Lazarus, Eda LeShan, Leo Madow, Leonardo Magran, J. Kent McCrimmon, Layton McCurdy, Ashley Montagu, Richard W. Moscotti, Stan Musial, Rod Napier, Donald L. Nathanson, Arnold Palmer, Maurice Prout, Kenneth Prusso, Harold A. Rashkis, John Reckless, Gilles E. Richard, Theodore Isaac Rubin, Leon J. Saul, Anne Wilson Schaef, Sabina Sedgewick, James L. Shelton, G. Pirooz Sholevar, Thelma Shtasel, Hazel and Charlie Sifford, Julian Slowinski, Erwin Smarr, Lewis B. Smedes, Betsi Smith, Jim Smith , Rose Solomon, Charles R. Starling, Fritz Steele, Rolling Thunder, Nathan W. Turner, Carl A. Whitaker and Peter Wylie.

— M.S.

CONTENTS

Chapter 2. Parents and children: The ties that bind 77

Chapter 3. Becoming masters of our work 109

Chapter 4. Feelings: Valuing our own and others'..... 147

Chapter 5. Life 101: The Politics of Living 195

PREFACE

On February 15, 1992, my husband, Darrell Sifford, and I embarked on what would have been our first month-long vacation. It was my gift to him for his 60th birthday, which he celebrated about five months earlier. Our destination? Belize, Central America, formerly British Honduras, because during the previous year, when I asked Darrell on several occasions where he would most like to go for a winter getaway, the answer was always the same — Belize.

He was drawn to the descriptions of its simplicity, its remoteness, the raw beauty of its ocean, jungles, rivers and wildlife and the prospect of being far away from Western civilization.

When I presented a calligraphed card that told him we would be away for a month, he was both dumbstruck and exhilarated. We had five months to anticipate our adventure. There would be plenty of unrushed time to experience the local environment, get to know the people and be together reading, talking, walking and enjoying the sun and the water.

Following three glorious weeks of relaxation, laughter, renewal, adventure and new friends, our fantasy was shattered. On Friday, March 6, fate intervened and Darrell drowned during a snorkeling excursion at the Hol Chen Marine Reserve — a beautiful underwater park on a 200-mile-long coral reef just a few miles from the coast of the island where we were staying.

— M. S.
July 1992

INTRODUCTION

The first time I met Darrell Sifford, he "interviewed" me. Within an hour, he had as complete a synopsis as is possible to get of who I was, where I had been and where I thought I was going. It was the beginning of a wonderful friendship that turned into love and marriage and then became a deep bond of commitment.

It was, of course, not without struggles and pain as we continued to grow and evolve as individuals, in our careers and as a couple. Our relationship grew into a true partnership that was characterized by mutual admiration, respect and support. We were both very proud of that accomplishment.

Darrell died as he lived, exploring new worlds, challenging himself to learn new things, to overcome fears, to grow, to live fully, to have fun and enjoy life, and to make a difference. He was at his peak as a writer and as a human being at the time of his death. He was strong, filled with vitality and endless plans and dreams for what was yet to come. He was a very happy man.

■

During that first meeting with Darrell, I asked him the same question that hundreds of readers asked him over the years: "How do you generate ideas for the column?" He answered simply that, "Everyone has a story, no matter who they are or what they do. You just have to find it." He was a master at discovering the stories of people, of recognizing the extraordinary in the ordinary and at presenting it in ways that provided a mirror through which readers could view and reflect on their own life experiences. Through his column, his speaking and his personal contact with people, he made a difference — over and over — in the lives of those he reached. He did it in a combination of small and dramatic ways that, taken together, form a powerful legacy.

Darrell told the story many times about why and how he decided to write the column. From 1964 to 1974, he was executive editor of The Charlotte News, an afternoon newspaper in North Carolina that closed a few years ago. In 1973, he started writing a column with two objectives in mind. First, he believed he could strengthen the paper by adding a feature with which readers could identify on a personal level. But he also wanted to put some fun and enjoyment back into his job, which had become increasingly administrative and tedious, taking him further and further from his first love since childhood — writing. He succeeded on both counts.

In the beginning, it appeared twice a week as *The Wednesday Report* and *The Saturday Report*. (Darrell would write three and four times a week later on.) He was breaking new ground in the newspaper industry by writing about subjects that many editors viewed as too soft and inappropriate for newspaper journalism. But it was an almost immediate hit with readers.

Before long, the column was syndicated as part of the Knight-Ridder News Service and its approximately 160 subscriber newspapers across the country. Gene Roberts, executive editor of The Philadelphia Inquirer from 1972 to 1990, recognized the value of Darrell's work early on and offered him the opportunity to come to Philadelphia as a full-time columnist. He turned down the first invitation. But when the opportunity came again in 1976, he was ready and willing. Darrell quickly went from being a virtual unknown to being a household name to thousands of his readers, many of whom came to think of him as a friend.

And just as important was that he loved the column and had fun doing it. He often said, "Sometimes I feel guilty for getting paid to do something I love so much. I get to talk to some of the brightest minds in the country. I have more autonomy than anyone else I know, and it's like getting paid for pursuing a life-long education. His regular readers may have noticed over the years that there was never a "blurb" in place of his column saying that he was out sick or on vacation — even during the years of his heart attacks and bypass surgery. He felt strongly that the column should always be there and that readers should be able to depend on it. It helped that he was a fast writer. He always had a stockpile of columns awaiting publication. I think the most he ever had at one time was 86. The lowest it got was 12 when he took a chunk of time to write one of his books. The motivation for always working ahead was the flexibility it gave him to do other things — write books, make speeches, spend time at the shore, visit his sons, play golf. . .

From the beginning of the column in Charlotte through March 1992, Darrell wrote approximately 3,500 columns. Thus, the 100 he selected for this book represent just a small portion of his work.

■

In the fall of 1991, Darrell and I were taking our customary seven-mile walk along Bethany Beach in southern Delaware. During the preceding year, he had submitted two proposals for books that he thought were based on good ideas and that he really wanted to write. They were both rejected by a dozen publishers. He was disappointed and somewhat discouraged about the book-publishing business, but he wasn't ready to give up.

I said to Darrell that I thought the most important book he could publish was a book of his columns. The column was the core, the heart of his work. In addition to being a powerful medium in its own right, it enabled him to build an ever-growing reservoir in his memory bank that provided a place for his book ideas to incubate and grow, a diary that chronicled many of his own experiences along the path of life and a source from which he easily retrieved material for his frequent public-speaking appearances.

Earlier, Darrell had proposed the idea for a book of his columns to a couple of agents and their response had been that publishers were not interested in anthologies, that such books don't sell. But Darrell and I knew that many readers wanted and were asking for such a book. We decided that day that if we couldn't find a publisher, we would publish it ourselves. We believed in it. It would be a fun project to work on together. It was worth the investment and the risk.

As we continued to walk, we brainstormed ideas about the format, the look and the size of the book, and the number and types of columns that would be included. It is not surprising that the vision and inspiration for the book came while we were at Bethany Beach, one of his favorite places on the planet.

Before we left for our first long vacation on February 15, 1992, Darrell reviewed his computer file of columns from 1981 to 1991 and retrieved copies of approximately 300 columns. He took these with him to Ambergris Cay, sat out on the beach one day at the place where we stayed — called The House of the Rising Sun — and selected from these the 100 columns that are included in this book. He was more excited about this project than anything he had worked on for a long time. He had planned, the following week, to make notes about how the columns came about and to comment on readers' responses. We will have to use our imagination to complete this part of his work.

■

Darrell wanted this book to be a collection of his and his readers' favorites. They have near universal appeal, are timeless in their message and provide something of substance and value to readers: inspiration, stimulation, insight, a catalyst, comfort, hope, guidance, courage, food for thought. In short, they are windows to life's realities and life's possibilities.

There are core themes that weave like golden threads through many of these columns:

¶ The importance of knowing and loving yourself.

¶ The growth that comes from taking risks, experiencing new challenges, learning new things.

¶ The importance of taking charge of one's own life and work.

¶ The inspiration that comes from nature and life, often when we least expect it.

¶ The importance of laughter and having fun.

¶ The importance of nurturing our inner child.

¶ The power of healing old hurts in important relationships.

¶ The dynamic process of personal growth at any age.

¶ The ways in which life's essence is captured in a series of special moments.

¶ The power of love and of saying the things we feel to the people who are important to us.

And you will find your own themes. One of the discoveries one makes as a writer, or as one who lives with a writer is that the reader completes a story with personal interpretations based on personal values, life experiences, feelings, relationships and decisions about what, if anything, to do with what he or she reads.

∎

To those who have read Darrell's work over the years, this book will feel like the presence of an old friend — warm, comforting, authentic, enriching, sometimes funny and healing in the same way that good memories can heal. For readers who may be discovering his work for the first time, it will stimulate your thinking, open new windows to the child within, provide breakthroughs to outdated or unhelpful ways of thinking. It will inspire or nurture that part in each of us that attempts to live a meaningful life, to know and love and accept ourselves, to say and do now the things we want to say and do with the people who are important to us. For all of us, it provides a mirror to help us reflect on and examine our own life experiences.

May his gift of these writings continue to bring insight and hope and courage to you and to those you love.

— M.S.

ABOUT THE TITLE

Darrell Sifford's regular readers will recognize the title of this book as a signature line from his newspaper column. Ending a column with the question, "What do you think?," was one of Sifford's favorite techniques for bringing together a reader and a powerful idea or experience. That technique had the side benefits of generating an ongoing dialogue between columnist and reader and of fleshing out highly charged emotional themes with follow-up columns.

CHAPTER 1

A SENSE OF SELF:
BECOMING FULLY
HUMAN

Each of us is born with unique gifts and enormous potential to become full human beings. We cannot, nor would we want to, know the particular set of challenges we will face as we travel that path. So how can we possible prepare ourselves for it? We cannot. Only by venturing into the unknown and facing the unexpected can we discover parts of ourselves that we didn't know were there — the beauty and light as well as the ugliness and darkness.

By facing the unknown, we discover our courage.

By honoring our gifts, we discover our beauty. By embracing the dark side of our nature, we take away its power.

By learning to love and accept ourselves, we are able to heal our wounds and to love and accept others.

By opening ourselves to the beauty around us, we can be inspired and lifted to new heights.

By taking responsibility for our lives, we enable new doors to open.

By going through the pain, we are able to find the joy.

The columns in this section are about all these and more — the best and the worst of life. May the wisdom in each of them speak to you and help you embrace your own experience in the lifelong journey of becoming fully human.

—M.S.

ANTICIPATING A FANTASY
February 16, 1992

Do you have a fantasy — something that you'd like to do but don't think will ever be possible? Well, for many years — ever since I was bitten by the bug that hangs around sunshine, sand and salt water — I've had the fantasy of living on an island, remote, out of the mainstream of tourism; a place where I could live the way island people live, eat their food, drink their rum, stomp my feet to their music, sail their boats.

You know what? It's a fantasy that's about to come true. No, I'm not moving to an island, but Marilyn and I are going away for a whole month, to a place that literally is not even a dot on most maps, where the sun comes up over a giant barrier reef, where the water is said to be so clear that it's possible to see down farther than anybody ever imagined.

The trip is a gift from Marilyn. She told me about it in September, on my 60th birthday, and since then, while I haven't exactly counted the days, I have lived with a conscious awareness that Something Big was about to happen to me.

Could anything be bigger than the realization of a fantasy — if only for a month? I don't think so — not for somebody who is drawn to island life as I am. We've read the books and we've gone to dinner with a few people who've been there. They've shown us their pictures and told us about the places where the locals go to gulp their beer and spin their stories, where nobody is a stranger for very long.

But even the people who've been there seem puzzled when they find out that we're staying for a month. Yes, it's different and fascinating there, but a month? There's absolutely nothing to do. I'm not sure anybody fully understands when I tell them that a place that offers absolutely nothing to do is my kind of place.

I've perfected the art of making my own fun, amusing myself, finding wonder in places and things that look ordinary to almost everybody else.

If I've given Marilyn anything in the many years we've been together, it's the ability to lose the self in tranquility, without the need for games to play, places to go, people to see.

The few close friends with whom I've discussed the trip are divided in their reaction. Some seem as excited as I am, thrilled by the prospect of solitude and comparative isolation. Others say they'd be bored stiff in a week.

What will we do — in addition to nothing? Both Marilyn and I will take along some work. She never stops thinking about her consulting business and the programs coming up that she'll design or direct or both. I'm working on a book, and I have two Dizzy Dean biographies to read for a review to which I'm committed — and scripts to get ready for the radio shows I'll tape when we get back.

How will I work? Probably I'll take a sun-faded chair to ocean's edge and sit and think and write on a long yellow legal pad. I'll listen to music on my ever-present radio, a model designed to bring in distant signals, which is a good thing since everything will be distant.

Where we're going there is no television. There are no paved roads and only a few automobiles. The apartment we're renting comes with two bicycles, and that's how we'll explore the island. We'll rent a little airplane to fly to the mainland for an excursion into the jungle.

A friend asked me, "Why on earth would you want to go into the jungle?" Because, I told him, I've never been in a real jungle before.

That's what this whole month really is about — doing new stuff, and doing old stuff in new ways. That's what life is all about — or should be.

I love solitude. I need a certain amount of it — and that's one reason why I go to our beach place as often as I do in winter, when nobody is within hollering distance. Maybe it's because I'm an only child. I grew up in a way that taught me to appreciate my time alone, that showed me that quiet was better than loud.

I don't ever get bored. If I can listen to music, take long walks, keep handy something to write on, I'm in hog heaven. It doesn't take a lot to make me happy. I like to daydream and examine my life — past, present, future. I like to ask myself questions.

What is success? A piece of it may be realizing the need to get away, to be with myself, to try to find if anything remains from my confrontation with discrepancy. You do remember about the confrontation with discrepancy, don't you?

That's recognizing and trying to deal with the gap between how we thought life would be at whatever age and how life actually is. At 45 that gap was huge for me, and at least in part the confrontation resulted in a divorce and a change in my career — from editor to writer.

What's the gap like at 60? When I look, I don't find any gap. Am I kidding myself? No, I don't think so.

Why do I work so hard? I used to be driven by demons, but, for the most part, they checked out quite a while ago. I think that now I have to confront the reality that I have only one work speed: very fast. And that gets me into trouble. I try to do too much, and I end up frazzled.

But that's the bad news. The good news is that very fast turns to very slow when I get away from the work environment. I have learned how to turn off work, leave it behind, compartmentalize it so securely that there seldom is any leakage. It takes me about 10 minutes to adjust to doing nothing, and that is for me an enormous accomplishment, perhaps even life-saving.

I've only been away from work for a month once before in my life — when I was in Louisville, Ky., at age 34. I played golf every day, and I found that it was fun although not especially fulfilling. But I was in a different place in my life then. At 34, I thought comparatively little about personal growth. At 60, I have redefined what's important.

■

One of the best vacations we ever had was a couple of years ago in Antigua. The guy who owned the hotel where we stayed, an Australian architect, took us to places that tourists never find — a back-road cafe with the best conch chowder in the world; an open-air restaurant where, along about 10 at night, steel-band musicians wandered in off the street and started jamming.

I think this trip can be like that, if we're lucky.

I was explaining with enthusiasm what we were going to do, and Herbert Benson, the Harvard cardiologist who wrote *The Relaxation Response* and other mind-body books, asked me a question that nobody else had asked:

"What are you going to do if, after 30 days, you don't want to come back?"

I told him I'd deal with that if it came up. But I didn't much like my answer. What would I do? I'm not sure. What would you do?

■

Where are we going? Well, it's Ambergris Cay, the far south end.

Never heard of Ambergris Cay? Almost nobody has — and even fewer people have ever been there. It's off the coast of Belize, in Central America, around the corner and south of the Yucatan Peninsula.

I'd send you a postcard, but I'm not sure there's any place to mail it.

5

Facing one's own death
December 23, 1990

I walked up the stairs to the third floor of the townhouse in Center City, and there, waiting for me at the door, was Erich Coché, 49, a psychologist I have known for many years and interviewed a number of times, mostly on parent-child relationships.

He smiled brightly, grasped my hand enthusiastically and welcomed me into a familiar room with a high ceiling — familiar because it was in this room that I had interviewed not only him but also his wife, psychologist Judith Milner Coché. Together, they form Coché & Coché, a practice in clinical psychology, in which they pioneered work in couples therapy and wrote a textbook for therapists, *Couples Group Psychotherapy*.

They had come to see me back in the summer because they were planning to write a popular book for couples — the title was *Intimate Investments* — and they wanted me to talk to them about making connections with a literary agent.

This was the first time that I'd seen Erich since then. He'd lost about 15 pounds, but I thought he looked chipper — and dapper, in a white cable-knit tennis sweater with red, navy and green piping at the V-neck, white shirt open at the collar, and navy slacks.

He fixed a lunch of tuna salad, served with tortilla chips and diet soda, and then we talked — about his impending death.

■

It began a year ago when Erich Coché discovered what he described as "a spot" on his back. The mole turned out to be cancerous — melanoma — and surgeons removed not only the mole but also the lymph nodes under his right arm. The nodes were clean, and doctors triumphantly told Coché: "We caught it all."

He thought that he was home free, but in August, in his words, "all hell broke loose." He felt pain in his left leg, and magnetic imaging and other tests showed multiple tumors. Doctors told Coché that his chances of survival were slim, but he consented to chemotherapy and radiation because, "Hey, I'm a spunky guy. I wanted to survive."

Over the next three months, Coché fought for his life. He used mental imagery techniques developed by Carl Simonton to try to rev up his immune system to combat the tumors. Nothing worked. "It was just one piece of bad news after another," he said.

In late November, Coché decided to stop his fight for life. "I had three or four sleepless nights, with a lot of pain. I had to face the fact that my body was telling me something. I said to myself: 'You're like a drowning man grasping for straws to stay afloat. The race has been run. You need to come to terms with the fact that you are dying. . . . Let it happen. Let it be. It's OK.'

"With that decision came a complete mental turnaround. There was a certain peacefulness. . . . It was amazing. The struggle was over."

■

Erich Coché was born in Holland and lived in Germany during World War II.

"I can remember the bombing of my town in 1944, although I was only 3. I remember crawling out from under the rubble and looking around and where there was a street before, there now was nothing. Just rubble."

His first contact with the English language was listening to occupying British and Canadian soldiers and begging for food. His formal study of English began at age 10 and, like many Germans who studied under British-educated teachers, he spoke with a British accent.

He first came to the United States in 1964 as a graduate student to study in Philadelphia. That's when he met Judith Milner, whom he married in 1966. They lived in Germany for two years while he finished work on his doctoral degree, and then they came "back to America for good" in 1969. They have a daughter, Juliette, 12.

"I love Judith so much, and I know she loves me. . . . In a good marriage, people are like members of a mountain-climbing team. They reach heights that they couldn't reach alone. This is the way it was for us. I learned so much from her, and she from me. . . . We have different natures, we came at my illness from different angles. Our expectations were quite different. I struggled until November. I think she knew in February."

■

When Erich Coché accepted death, he told himself, "OK, you've got two months, maybe three. Now here is the opportunity to say goodbye in a way that is loving and responsible."

In the beginning, he said, "I fought death at my doorstep. 'Go away!' Then, when I came to terms with it, I said, 'Well, death, I guess you won. But thanks for the extra time.' If I'd had a fatal heart attack, if I'd been killed in a car crash, I wouldn't have had the opportunity to say goodbye to people, to put things in order, at least partially finish my work on this book. . . .

"I began to look at life and death in a different way. While I was fighting to live, I focused on what I would miss if I died. I wanted to sail my boat in the sun again, play tennis, celebrate our 25th wedding anniversary in the fall, be there for my daughter's graduation and then her wedding. I had a constant argument with death, God, or whatever. . . . This was an extremely painful way of looking at it. I'd still lie in bed at night and cry. I still knew I was going to miss my daughter's bat mitzvah, but I had an additional thought: 'Hey, this was an interesting life. It was cut short, but. . . .'

"I was very ill when I was 3 months old, and doctors gave up on me, but I returned . . . and I got 49 years. I'm glad I had them."

I told Coché that he sounded like a man with not much unfinished business and minimal regrets.

"I stepped on some toes, and I feel bad, but that's life. Some decisions turn out bad. It's the existential guilt you have to live with. . . . I've had the opportunity to lie in bed at night and think a lot, and a question that came up was 'What did you do with your life?' I'll tell you that I liked a lot of what I did. . . . In a true existential sense I believe that people design the kind of person they are. If you make a decision to be tempestuous, you live with it. If you choose to be different, if you like yourself as a gentle person, then that's what you try to do. . . .

7

"When I was a teenager, maybe 14, I read a story about Alexander the Great, and somebody asked if he'd rather have a short, interesting life or a long, boring life. Even then, I knew that if I had to make that choice, I'd want a short, interesting life. I got what I wanted. . . .

"I've done a lot of fun things. I've written interesting papers, gone to court as an expert witness. I was president of the local psychological society. Teaching at Penn meant a lot to me. I've had an exciting marriage, a lovely daughter. . . . I like my 49 years, but I feel deep grief over leaving people I love. . . . I can feel sadness without being bitter about it. . . . I still have some hard times. I wouldn't want you to think otherwise. I cry a lot — mostly about people I'll leave and things I won't be around for."

What about the "Why me?" question? Did he struggle with that?

"The 'Why me?' question is destructive, not helpful at all. I knew enough not to focus on it. It's very unhealthy. . . . It causes a person even more pain. So I made a decision to focus on life — at first trying to live and then getting things in order and saying goodbye."

■

What does he most want to hear from his friends?

"Two things. One is for them to come along with me on acceptance of this rather than fighting it. I've accepted that I'm going to die soon, and I want them not to tell me to hang in there and not give up. . . . I know they mean well, but I feel they are causing themselves more pain . . . and it's not helping me.

"The other thing is that I like to hear happy stories about our adventures, about the things my friends and I have done together. I like to hear them reminisce. . . .

"My best friend from Germany is coming to visit me, and I know we'll talk about the crazy time we hitchhiked to Paris. . . . We were going through Belgium, where you can't be sure which language will be spoken, and the bargain we made was that if the driver said, 'Good morning,' in French, my friend would sit in the front seat. He spoke French but not Flemish. If the driver said, 'Good morning,' in Flemish, I would sit in the front seat. . . . Well, we were picked up in a hearse by a driver who spoke French. My friend sat up front, and I sat in back among the flowers. We talk about that and laugh."

■

Coché said he hoped to continue "at this level, working hard every day on the book," as long as he's able. How much time does he have? He's not sure — and neither are his doctors. "Maybe springtime," he said. "What will death itself be like? Will it be painful? I don't know, but I have hopes."

■

We shook hands, and I walked down the steps and out onto the street. The sun was shining, and the temperature was mild.

I walked along . . . and started crying. I cried all the way back to the office, about a mile and a half. If he could be so philosophical about it, why couldn't I?

I don't know.

I heard myself ask, "Why him?"

'WHAT THE HELL ARE YOU DOING?'
May 13, 1985

In the many speeches that I make to students every year, I constantly stress one message. It's the same message that I tried to pass along to my sons during their growing-up years.

The message: While the world can be — and often is — a friendly place in which you can succeed, it also can be hostile at times and unfair frequently. It's the prudent person who recognizes that good input does not assure good outcome and occasionally doesn't even influence outcome, and who understands that the bad guys sometimes win and that people on whom you depend don't always come through. In other words: Keep your head up and your eyes open. A little healthy paranoia never hurt anybody.

■

She was 50 years old, a professional woman who, in the words of psychiatrist Richard W. Moscotti, was "brought up to be a Girl Scout."

She had come to Moscotti for help because her life wasn't going well. In the middle of a therapy session, Moscotti decided "to teach her about herself."

"Stand up," he ordered.

She rose from her chair and looked expectantly at Moscotti.

"Now lift your left foot."

She groped for balance but managed to stand on her right foot. Again she looked expectantly at Moscotti, who stared at her but said nothing for a full 15 seconds.

Finally, he spoke. "What the hell are you doing?"

The woman's face turned red. She sat down and at long last "understood the awesomeness of what had happened" — not just in the moments before but throughout her whole life. This, said Moscotti, was "when her therapy made a breakthrough. She understood that, as a 'good little girl,' she was programmed to obey anybody in authority, to challenge nobody, to question nothing — absolutely nothing. After therapy she knew a ton more . . . and her life reflected that. Things went much better for her" after she resigned from the Girl Scouts.

■

Ah, yes, Girl Scouts and Boy Scouts. The subject is a favorite one for Moscotti, who practices at the Institute of Pennsylvania Hospital, which is the hospital's psychiatric branch.

He said during an interview that he used the labels "Boy Scouts" and "Girl Scouts" to describe people who were "brought up by well-meaning parents, who are taught the golden rule — 'Do unto others . . .' — and who make nice, ethical, moral people as they are growing up. But it provides for naive young adults, and when they get out into the real world — with sharks and barracudas of both sexes — they often are eaten up."

It's ironic, said Moscotti, that the Boy Scout motto is "Be prepared" — ironic in the sense that figurative scouts need to "be prepared to be misused by people" unless they quickly learn how to protect themselves. Unfortunately, most don't learn until later, rather than sooner, in life, and they get banged around and sometimes end up standing on one foot in a psychiatrist's office.

Moscotti said he was a Boy Scout "in both senses of the word. I was a Life Scout, which is one step below Eagle, and emotionally I was raised to be a Boy Scout figuratively." He didn't outgrow that training, he said, until he was "ground up" in a divorce proceeding and forced to admit that nice guys finish last — and sometimes don't even finish.

Moscotti said parent-taught Boy Scouts and Girl Scouts "go into the world poorly prepared for what will happen. The scout code is something like, 'On my honor I will do my best . . . .' That would be wonderful if everybody else was a scout, too. But the world is a mixture of people, and scouts are poorly prepared to understand this. As a result, they're taken advantage of, used, ripped off — and maybe their lives even are taken. . . . It's a common thing that well-meaning parents do — pass down to their children maladaptive behaviors that were given them by their parents: Be good, be nice, be a gentleman, be a lady, be trusting. . . .

"How can you be a good person and not be misused? Does facing reality mean adopting cynicism as a way of life? No, in therapy it's possible to molt in the sense of growth and modify your views of life and the world . . . and better handle the dichotomy between how you were taught the world is and how the world really is."

Parents, said Moscotti, need to "neutralize the naive aspects" of what they contribute to their children's understanding of the world. "Parents still can teach to their children the ideals of Boy Scouts and Girl Scouts . . . but they must try to be sure that the children know the real, underlying operation of the world, where, as we know, there is evil, lying, cheating and exploitation of the innocent."

What can the adult scout who is hurting do to make life better?

"When there's enough pain in life, you begin to realize that something is wrong, and you seek professional help. You run into existential problems that seem relatively without solution — problems with marriage, children, job. This is when the alarm goes off, and you think, 'Gee, maybe I'm doing something wrong here.' It's when you're disillusioned and realize that the way you've been programmed isn't working out and that you need to try another path."

Moscotti emphasized again that "the flip side of Boy Scout is not cynicism. You don't have to be that way. But you must have a sprinkling of reality in the way you approach the world. 'I have to be careful here.' That's the attitude you need. A little paranoia sometimes is a good thing — healthy paranoia, when it's appropriate to be paranoid."

When is paranoia appropriate?

"At 3 a.m. in Philadelphia, when you're walking by yourself." It's amazing, said Moscotti, how many times in life we find ourselves walking alone at 3 a.m.

THE NECESSITY OF SELF-FORGIVENESS
July 18, 1985

Is it truly possible for us to forgive ourselves for the wrongs that we have done, for the pain that we have inflicted on others, for the damage that we have caused — damage that perhaps can't ever be totally repaired?

In the opinion of Lewis B. Smedes, it's not only possible but also necessary if we are to crawl out of the trenches of yesterday and wriggle up to the high ground of tomorrow.

But it's difficult, this business of self-forgiveness. In fact, said Smedes, it's downright "outrageous."

Smedes, who is professor of theology and ethics at Fuller Theological Seminary in Pasadena, Calif., is the author of the book *Forgive & Forget*. In an interview, he said the world worked against somebody who sought self-forgiveness because "there always are people around who want you to have to live forever with it, whatever "it" is. A lot of people don't want Nixon to forgive himself. They want him to keep his tail between his legs forever" as eternal punishment for what they view as his unforgivable sin.

But, said Smedes, "for personal salvation, self-forgiveness is the only way to deal honestly with your past. You can deal dishonestly through evasion, repression, excuses or self-exoneration," but none of these has the cleansing power — or staying power — of forgiveness.

"To forgive yourself takes high courage. Who are you, after all, to shake yourself free from the undeniable sins of your private history — as if what you once did has no bearing on who you are now? Where do you get the right . . . to forgive yourself when other people would want you to crawl in shame if they really knew?"

The answer, said Smedes, is that "you get the right to forgive yourself only from the entitlements of love. And you dare forgive yourself only with the courage of love. Love is the ultimate source of both your right and your courage to ignore the indictment you level at yourself. When you live as if yesterday's wrong is irrelevant to how you feel about yourself today, you are gambling on a love that frees you even from self-condemnation," even if others are condemning you.

The self-forgiving process involves "looking at yourself in the mirror and being specific" about what you have done wrong. "You almost always will fail at self-forgiving when you refuse to be concrete about what you are forgiving yourself for."

It's not sufficient to say that you forgive yourself for being a bad person, said Smedes. "Precisely, what is it that you need forgiveness for? For being unfaithful to your spouse last year? Good, you can work on that. For being an evil sort of person? No, that is too much; you cannot swallow yourself whole."

Most of us, he said, can "manage no more than one thing at a time. . . . When we overload ourselves with dilated bags of undifferentiated guilt, we are likely to sink into despair. The only way we can succeed as self-forgivers . . . is to be concrete and to forgive ourselves for one thing at a time."

People who can't forgive themselves — or don't want to — tend to play some silly games, said Smedes.

"A lot of people live their lives to prove that they're good guys who could do no wrong." The problem with that is that it doesn't work, and on some level they tend to remain stuck in their guilt.

"I've been married for more than 30 years, and at times I've made my wife's life miserable — not because of anything she did but because I couldn't forgive myself. I always was knocking myself on the head or going around saying that I was such a good guy." Both behaviors are typical of people who haven't forgiven themselves, he said.

"I'm knocked out by some religious people. In church, they say they're sinners. But at home, if the wife says, 'You forgot my birthday,' they defend themselves. . . . They always seek to justify themselves" even if they're caught with the equivalent of a hand in the cookie jar. "When people are hard to get along with, it's often because they can't get along with themselves" because of overriding guilt about the mess they've created.

Self-forgiveness hinges on a person's being able to say and to believe that "the past is the past. I know I did wrong. I'm sorry about it. But it's not material to what I am now and how I feel now." Who gives somebody the right to take that position? "I believe that God gives us that right," said Smedes, "through love that makes it possible for us to burn our moral bridges behind us."

Smedes said that he was suspicious of "reports of overnight self- forgiveness. It's a process," and it takes time before it amounts to much — like the compounding of interest in a bank account.

Even as the process unfolds, the self-forgiving person must deal with the little voice from within that wants to disrupt the process, said Smedes. "The little voice says, 'Oh, come on. We know that you're faking it. . . . Who are you trying to fool with this forgiveness stuff?' But you've got to be able to answer, 'Sure, but so what? Yes, I lied to my wife, cheated, humiliated her. I hate myself for it, but that's not the person I am now.' And the forgiveness process can go on. Either you've uttered the greatest truth on earth or you've committed the biggest lie."

Smedes said that "to forgive yourself is to act out the mystery of one person who is both forgiver and forgiven. You judge yourself; this is the division within you. You forgive yourself; this is the healing of the split. That you should dare to heal yourself by this simple act is a signal to the world that God's love is a power within you."

THE FEAR OF CHANGE
June 18, 1991

It's a radio commercial that's been getting a lot of play for a long time — a plea from one industry for consumers not to take their business to a competitor.

Prices go up and prices come down, the stern-voiced announcer says, and there's no guarantee that the competition will be cheaper over the long run. It's wise to stick with what you've got . . . "because changing is chancy."

I hate that commercial — I really do — because it encourages people to stand pat and it never raises the reality that sometimes not to consider change can be chancy, too. Yet I think it's one of the most effective commercials I've ever heard. Why? Because it taps into a basic human fear — the fear of change.

Why are so many of us so afraid of change?

It's a subject that I talk about a lot in speeches, because a lot of organizations want to hear about managing change, meeting the challenge of change, rolling with the punches and coming out, if not on top, at least with your dignity intact.

I think that we resist change mostly for one simple reason: We want to be comfortable, and what's comfortable is what's familiar. This is why some of us stay in jobs we don't like — because they're familiar. This is why some of us stay in marriages that offer no hope — because they're familiar. This is why some of us struggle so much in retirement — because we have lost what was familiar to us for 40 years.

We're uncomfortable when a family member or a friend changes — even if we acknowledge intellectually that it's a change for the better. Somebody who has swallowed anger for years learns how to express anger. Somebody who has been a punching bag now stands up for himself or herself.

We may not like this "new" person because we have to change the way we relate. We're not so comfortable anymore, and we may even try to sabotage this person's change. "Yes, I know you're able to express anger now, but couldn't you tone it down just a bit? You'll drive all your friends away." That's sabotage — any way you cut it.

A woman marries a man who is an alcoholic. They rock along, mostly through bad times, but then the alcoholic stops drinking — and the marriage falls apart. Why? Because the woman's role is to be the helper of a person in trouble. The truth, of course, is that she has to find a new role, but this means change. Yes, there's that word again — change.

■

There are two kinds of change:

Change that we initiate. This can be unsettling, but at least it's our decision. We've considered the pros and cons and this is what we're going to do. It may be a new job, a relocation, the beginning or ending of a relationship, quitting school or going back to school — but the decision belongs to us, and we'll struggle, if we have to, to make things work out.

Change that is imposed on us, sometimes without consultation. This is the change that causes most of us the most trouble because it carries with it feelings of helplessness. Our lives are being altered — and we haven't even been asked for our input. This is when we may feel that our backs are up against the wall, but we're not entirely without options. We need to ask ourselves some hard questions: Can I do what this change demands? Do I want to do it? Can I learn something from this? What happens if I don't do it? We tally the answers — and then we do what seems best for us. By wrestling with the questions, we at least have lessened the intensity of the feelings of helplessness.

I think those of us who accommodate best to change are able to take a long-range view, to counteract our immediate feelings of discomfort with the balm of the potential payoff that's somewhere on down the road. We think of the opportunity for growth, the good things that can happen to us and those we're taking along with us on our journey.

We know that the challenge of change is to be found in the new directions in which we can move — not in lamenting what we have given up. This faith in what is to be is what sustains people during the hard times that can accompany change. Where does this faith come from? I think it comes from what psychologist Phil Bobrove once described to me as our "core of inner strength," which we may not even know is there until we need to tap into it.

■

What happens if we don't change, if we always cling with a death grip to the way things are now?

I think we calcify. It's almost like hardening of the arteries, except this is hardening of the soul, the spirit. A certain rigidity sets in, an unwillingness to even consider, let alone accept, new ideas, new ways of doing things.

A reasonable definition of maturity is the ability to accommodate to change, to deal with the ambivalence that often accompanies change, to consider all possibilities. This is also a good definition of mental health.

That's what I think. What about you?

THE VIRTUE OF SAYING NO
May 14, 1991

Meditations for Women Who Do Too Much by Anne Wilson Schaef. It's a remarkable little book, about the size of your hand, and somebody gave it to my wife a while back. Every night, before she switches off the light, Marilyn reads a meditation for the day, and every once in a while, she pushes the book at me to share a passage that she feels is especially relevant.

Here is one that hit me right between the eyes:

"One of the problems that we workaholics and careholics have is that we overextend ourselves and believe that we can and should be able to fulfill the promises we make. We want to be nice. We want to be members of the team. We want to be seen as competent and dependable. . . . We also hate to say no when someone notices us and has the confidence in us to ask us to do something. We want to be able to deliver. Yet, when we do not check out with ourselves whether we can or want to fulfill our promises, we end up overcommitting ourselves and ultimately feeling bad about ourselves, which just feeds our self-esteem problems.

"Checking to see if I can and want to fulfill a promise before I make it is good for me and good for others."

■

How about that? Did it hit you between the eyes, too? My guess is that many

14

of us try to do too many things, wear too many hats, be too many things to too many people. And ultimately — usually it's sooner rather than later — we find ourselves frazzled and weary, irritated and angry, not only at ourselves for agreeing to do too much but also at those who asked us.

All the way around, it's a bad deal, and we need to do something about it.

But what?

I think there's a relatively obscure line between doing too much to help others and not doing enough. We need to do enough things for enough people enough of the time. Call it altruism or whatever you choose, but being of service to others is — or should be — an essential part of our lives.

When we share ourselves with others, we help not only them but also ourselves. If you want to feel good about yourself, do something nice for somebody else. I guarantee that it will put a bounce in your step and a song in your heart — up to a point, that is.

That point is when we give away so much that we have an insufficient amount left for ourselves. So while it's essential that we help others, it's equally essential that we help ourselves — by saving time and energy to use as we choose, for replenishment, growth, amusement, whatever.

It's important to be able to say no to people's requests enough of the time. How much is enough? I don't always know — not even for myself . . . and certainly not for anybody else.

Some years ago, when I was president of my condominium owners' association, I discovered that when I wanted to get a tough job done quickly and correctly, I should ask people who already had more on their plates than they could handle, people who already were too busy to take on one more task. These were the people, I found, who smilingly agreed to do what needed doing. They never failed to meet my expectations, and without them my presidential term would have been much less successful.

For a long time I felt, somewhat smugly, that I had stumbled onto a great secret. Now, as I reflect on it, I don't feel very good about what I did. It now seems to me that I took advantage of what amounted almost to a character defect in some of these people — the inability to say "no."

There are a lot of these people out there. For many years, I was one of them and, in some ways, I still am. Although I'm saying "no" more often now than at any time in my life, I'm finding that it's still not enough because the numbers of requests have increased. I end up doing things I really don't want to do. I go to lunch too many times with people I really don't want to go to lunch with.

Why?

I was having lunch the other day with somebody I really wanted to be with, a guy about my age with problems about like mine, and he was saying that he felt burdened by people's requests and expectations. The problem, I suggested, was that he was "Too Damned Responsible" — too willing to help others before he helped himself. I could say this, I told him, because it's my problem, too, and a silly book proposal that rattles around inside my head at odd moments is Breaking the TDR Syndrome, which might be subtitled: How to Be as Good to Yourself as You Try to Be to Others.

On another day I was having lunch with somebody else I really wanted to be with, a psychiatrist who pounds on me, relentlessly at times, to do more things for myself and fewer things for others. If there is one thing you can say about this fellow it is that he practices what he preaches. He smiled broadly, told me that he had said no three times the day before. "That's close to a record for me," he said. I told him that I had managed "no" twice the day before. He told me that I was making progress — and I am. But it's slow.

What makes it slow? I think Anne Wilson Schaef is at least partially correct. We do want to be nice, to be members of the team, to be seen as competent and dependable. We do want to be able to deliver. Yet, for me at least, there is more. Feelings of too much responsibility are part of it. Wanting to pay back to the world some of the goodies that I have received is another part of it.

But I think that what gets me into the most trouble is my underestimation of how much time and energy things will take and my overestimation of how much time and energy I have available. Little things add up and become big things, and big things have a way of crushing what is beneath them — the optimistic people whose good intentions tend to outrun their ability to cheerfully deliver what they promise.

That's what I think. How about you?

GUILTIEST MOMENTS
December 19, 1988

In his book *Guilt: How to Recognize and Cope With It*, psychiatrist Leo Madow asks a jackpot question: What was your guiltiest moment? Then, to give everybody some breathing room, Madow answers his own question:

"When I was 5 or 6, my mother became ill, and I . . . was concerned that she might die. Our family doctor was like a god to us. Once we knew he was on the way, we immediately began to feel better. . . . He took her temperature, then handed me the thermometer, and asked me to wash it off. I carefully took it to the kitchen sink, but in the process of washing it, I dropped it and broke off the mercury tip.

"For a moment, I stood staring at my shaking hands, which had betrayed me. I was terrified. I felt guilty that I had not lived up to his expectations of me. . . . At that moment I would have given my soul to make that thermometer whole again. I didn't know what to do. Finally, I managed to take the remaining stem of the thermometer to him, and I just handed it to him. He looked at it, glanced at me with a very knowing look as if to say, 'I understand,' and said nothing. I was enormously relieved but felt terribly guilty. . . . I can still feel the shame and guilt . . . and would gladly buy him a new one, a dozen new ones, even today."

Madow, who is the senior consultant at the Institute of Pennsylvania Hospital and a training and supervising analyst at the Philadelphia Psychoanalytic Institute, commented on the incident:

"I was terrified that my destructive act would lead to punishment and the loss of love of an idealized father figure. . . . The guilt was overwhelming, despite his having clearly forgiven me. It was narcissistic guilt. I was ashamed and humiliated by the terrible thing I had done."

■

Guilt has been described as "the gift that keeps on giving," and so it is for many of us, said Madow. It can cripple us, force us to turn inward, think badly of ourselves. But the unusual thing about guilt, he said, is that it can be quite selective in terms of what triggers it.

"A kid in the ghetto may feel no guilt from ripping off somebody, snatching a purse, but he might feel terrible guilt if somebody in his gang were attacked and he didn't come to his assistance. . . . What causes you to feel guilty depends on your own standard of behavior. . . . You can have a really warped conscience. It's OK to murder, but it's not OK to be unkind to your mother."

■

Some other guilty moments in Madow's book:

A 63-year-old man: "We played golf at the club, and we had a caddy. At the end of the round, we were handed a slip which I misread, thinking it said, 'How was your game today?' Actually it said, 'How was your caddy today?' I wrote, 'Horrible!' Later I found out that the slip was to be an evaluation of the caddy. I felt guilty, believing that I might have caused him to lose his job."

A 54-year-old man: "When I was in junior high school, I sat in the library next to a girl who got up to get a book from the shelves, leaving her purse on the table. I took the purse and left the library, but I felt so guilty all afternoon that I finally looked in her purse for her address, went to her house, said I had found the purse on the street, and returned it to her. I still feel guilty as I tell you this."

A 39-year-old lawyer: "When I was a little girl of 12 and my sister was 10, my mother had gone to great pains to make Easter outfits for us. She spent months cutting and sewing. . . . When Easter Sunday came, my sister and I put on the dresses and bonnets, but we both thought they looked awful. We did not dare say anything to Mother about it. She had worked hard and was proud of her handiwork. We were sent off to church, but instead of going in, we walked around outside and avoided meeting anyone for fear they would laugh at us. . . . I, being the older, felt I had influenced my sister to misbehave, too. Ever since then, I have felt guilty for having betrayed Mother. I am too ashamed about the incident to tell Mother. She still does not know what we did."

■

My interview with Madow wound down, and he put the question to me: What was my guiltiest moment?

I had to think for a little while, not because there had been so few but because there had been so many — all of them in the distant past, all of them involving my shortcomings as a father when my older son, Jay, was in grade school and junior high. Finally, I picked one that had bobbed to the surface and refused to go away.

"I never missed a baseball game or a basketball game in which Grant played," I began. "Sometimes I'd cut short meetings or even cancel meetings, if I had to, to get to a game. . . . He enjoyed the things I enjoyed, and we did a lot of those things together, mostly sports.

"But with Jay, my interests didn't coincide with his, and we didn't do much together. One Saturday afternoon he was playing in a piano recital, and on the one hand I felt that a 'responsible' father should attend, while on the other hand I wanted to play my regular Saturday golf game. After all, a hard-working father needs his playtime, doesn't he?

"Well, I played just nine holes, came home, changed clothes and went to the recital. All the time there I was angry, feeling deprived, cheated, totally unable and unwilling to appreciate Jay's playing, which was the culmination of a lot of practice and hard work. I was so wrapped up in myself that I couldn't give even a piece of myself to Jay on that afternoon. . . . It wasn't until later in the evening that I was able to put some of it into perspective, and I felt so guilty, so ashamed for being so self-centered. I wanted to crawl into a hole."

What about you? What is the guiltiest moment you're willing to share?

SECURITY CAN BE STIFLING
August 27, 1991

What does it take to motivate people?
What works?
What doesn't work?
Well, let's see now . . .

The name of the book is *Leadership*, and the subtitle is *The Inner Side of Greatness*. The author, Peter Koestenbaum, the globe-traveling philosopher who is a consultant to some of the world's premier businesses, devotes considerable attention to motivation.

"The question of leadership effectiveness is really the question of motivation," he writes. "How does one motivate others? How does one motivate oneself? To motivate is to win the hearts of your people. How is it done?"

Koestenbaum then sets out to answer his own question with 14 points that include:

"People want to feel that their bosses care enough to open their hearts and minds to them. A person needs attention, a human openness to what he or she is doing. Employees must know that the boss is fully conscious of how hard they are trying. It is the attention and the care that motivate."

"Acknowledgment . . . must be earned, so that it is the truth and not a lie. Support must also be given — not as a technique, but with heart."

"Compensation, in the business culture, is a sign of realistic acknowledgment."

Yes, yes, I found myself saying — until I reached the 12th point:

"Security is not a legitimate motivator, for it diminishes life."

Security not a legitimate motivator? Security diminishes life?

How can that be?

It seems to me that people work better when they feel that their job is not on

18

the line every day, when they know that they have a cushion of security that allows them to try new things and make mistakes without fear that their boss will act punitively toward them.

Was Koestenbaum, whom I have known for many years, talking about security or about complacency? Or was he applying a definition to security that was different from mine?

That's what we talked about the other day when he shoehorned me into his hectic schedule, which keeps him on the road and away from his Los Angeles-area home about 300 days a year. Let's listen:

"People look for meaning and quality in life, but they often sell meaning and quality short to gain security. . . . People pursue security to abate anxiety. . . . The quest for security prevents growth. . . . The problem is that most people make security their primary goal," and eventually many of them pay an unreasonable price: failure to make the most of their talents.

Koestenbaum, who is professor emeritus of philosophy at San Jose State University and the author of a dozen books, said that "we are not well served if security is our major goal in business — or in life. . . . Security is to be found in our courage to get on with life," not in hanging back out of the belief that if we don't risk anything, we can't lose anything. Actually, said Koestenbaum, we stand to lose quite a lot: the ability to live life to the fullest.

The quest for security, he said, "keeps us stuck in jobs we don't like, in homes we don't prefer, in relationships that aren't working. It's not security we find, but a rut" that can diminish us.

Koestenbaum was at one time a tenured professor, and I asked him if that kind of security tended to lull people to sleep.

"It stops growth completely. A tenured professorship is incompatible with growth. . . . But it's a safeguard of free speech and I wouldn't suggest that we tamper with it."

Did tenure stop Koestenbaum's growth?

"It would if I had stayed. That's why I got out."

When does security become complacency?

"At the point at which growth stops," he said, and this point can be sooner for some than for others.

∎

In the book, Koestenbaum presents four leadership qualities — he calls them the Leadership Diamond model — that are essential in "expressing greatness in thought and action." The four qualities:

¶ Vision. "A visionary leader always sees the larger perspective, for visioning means to think big and new."

¶ Reality. "A realistic leader always responds to the facts, for realism means to have no illusions."

¶ Ethics. "An ethical leader is always sensitive to people, for ethics means to be of service."

¶ Courage. "A courageous leader always claims the power to initiate, act, and risk, for courage means to act with sustained initiative.

"With these qualities in mind, I asked Koestenbaum what a good leader owes the corporation.

"To fulfill the contract, to get certain results. There is an ethical obligation to do this, and a leader should leave if he can't fulfill the contract. . . . A good leader should have total commitment to the organization, but also commitment to self. One doesn't rule out the other. There is an obligation to serve the corporation, but also an obligation to serve the self."

What does a good leader owe those who work for him or her?

"The same things as a military leader — helping them get the job done, helping them grow, protecting them, making them feel good."

What does a good leader owe to himself or herself?

"Not to lead an unexamined life. To know one's potential, one's profile, one's actualization, to understand the consequences of making decisions on how one is going to live, to be successful in a meaningful way — not in a superficial way like a cheap salesman."

Are good leaders made or born?

"That's the question that I'm most often asked," said Koestenbaum. "In theory, where there's a will there's a way. But in practical terms it doesn't work that way. Some have more talents, more motivation than others. . . . The world is divided into leaders and non-leaders, and leaders have to take care of non-leaders."

SELF-ESTEEM AND RISK-TAKING
October 3, 1983

California psychologist Aaron Hemsley, who by anybody's definition is a risk-taker, says the ability to risk without debilitating anxiety stems from "the one basic thing that all risk-takers have — a high level of self-esteem. They are very confident about themselves, and they would score high if you measured them on a self-reliant scale."

How did they become this way?

That's one of the things I discussed not long ago when Hemsley was in Philadelphia to lecture at the Wharton School of the University of Pennsylvania. These days, Hemsley is a high-powered lecturer who travels the nation to deliver about 180 seminars a year on how to succeed in business by really trying and on what he calls "the psychology of maximum performance."

But it wasn't always this way for Hemsley, who for a while practiced traditional psychology — traditional in the sense that he spent much of his time around troubled, depressed clients.

It was a miserable time in his life, he said, because he feared that his clients' troubles eventually might rub off and contaminate him. That's when he decided to make the break and take a risk — by specializing in an area that would bring him into regular contact with successful people whose main concern was how to become even more successful and to realize more fully the total scope of their potential.

He never seriously considered the possibility that this new direction might fizzle, he said, and it's because he shares with other risk-takers a classic quality: "We're too dumb to know that we can't succeed — so we go ahead and do it. In a sense, a prudent person might back off, might say, 'Gee, I can't start a new business in this economy.' But the risk-taker says, 'This is what I want to do, and I'm going to do it.' The risk-taker says, 'I'll start the business now and worry about the economy later.' "

The risk-takers, in Hemsley's opinion, are more successful and more satisfied with their lives than people who play it safe, because they seize the initiative and play the game by their own rules.

For the most part, people are primed to become risk-takers by their childhood conditioning, Hemsley said. "It was the childhood experience that created their sense of confidence, their feeling that they can do it better than anybody else. It also contributed to their lack of need to conform, to consider doing it somebody else's way, by somebody else's standards.

"There's almost the feeling [that] 'I don't want to learn about doing it your way because I think my way is better.' " And while this may sound haughty, it tends to amount to a blueprint for personal and professional victory, Hemsley said.

If you lined up the world's risk-takers, you'd likely discover that a high percentage of them are first-born, Hemsley said. "This is because the first-born are raised with a lot more praise" from parents. "The first kid does anything, and everybody gets excited. He crawls, and everybody gets excited. By the time the fourth or fifth child comes along, nobody notices anything," and the result is that this child often lacks the elevated sense of self-esteem that is the foundation on which risk-taking is constructed.

The first-born child, said Hemsley, tends to get "a lot of positive feedback from parents that he's good. There are a lot of expectations" that are not disguised, and the child knows that he is expected to be better than others. In a sense he has permission to become a free-wheeler, and this is what he does when he takes risks. He thumbs his nose at the odds — because he never seriously considers the possibility that things won't work out all right in the end.

His self-esteem tends to be so substantial that he understands at some level that the worst thing that can happen is that he'll fail — and that's OK because failure can be translated into a learning experience that will speed success the next time around. People without this level of self-esteem often tend to be frozen into inaction by fear of an undertaking's failure — which they view as being the same as personal failure.

Although the role of parents is important in creating conditions for a child to become a risk-taker, other people can be involved, too, Hemsley said — peers and teachers, for instance. "Once in a while there is a teacher with whom you come in contact and get a lifetime of positive influence. I've seen a few of these, although most teachers just pass through and are forgotten, without leaving any permanent impact. . . . In the peer group there can be the recognition that you do things better than anybody else, and you get the kind of reinforcement" that makes it possible for you to shoot for the moon.

It's probably a contradiction in terms to talk about risk-taking that is entirely reasonable, Hemsley said, because "I picture risk-taking as being on the crest of a wave. . . . To some extent, it's dangerous. Any growth situation involves some risk, and if there's no risk, there's no growth. But I'm not talking about unreasonable, crazy risks. You don't run across the street without looking. That would be crazy." But on the other hand, you don't stand on the curb and look all day, afraid to make your move. That's just as crazy — at the opposite extreme.

"When you're learning to ski, you don't ski in places where you're not trained. But if you want to be a good skier, you work gradually up to better hills, and, all of a sudden, you get better. That's how it's done — not just in skiing but in everything. There's no formula that I know of to get you there. Maybe there isn't any formula" — except risk and hard work.

It's important to understand, Hemsley said, that you can't be a risk-taker and a perfectionist, too. This is because the perfectionist "can't take a risk. He has to know beforehand that everything is going to work out perfectly. The risk-taker takes the position, 'I'm going to do it now and I'll take care of the details later.' And then he goes ahead and does it."

What about somebody whose self-esteem level wasn't piled high early in life by adoring parents? Is that person forever shut out from becoming a risk-taker?

No, not at all, said Hemsley. "The question has to do with how do you change your early conditioning, and that's what we do when we go into therapy. We relearn things that we first learned incorrectly."

Much of behavior therapy has been successful in helping people unlearn the negatives and become risk-takers, Hemsley said.

"You take a specific activity that troubles you, and you learn to control your anxiety while you're engaging in it. It's like fear of flying. They teach you to relax, then they get you closer to the airplane. If your anxiety level gets too high, you stop and relax and then, when you're able, you move ahead. Overcoming fear of failure is done the same way," and it amounts to what behavior therapists call systematic desensitization to what spooks us.

MOURNING A PART OF YOU THAT'S GONE
March 22, 1981

There he was, 44-year-old psychologist Philip Bobrove, on his knees and hacking into the ground alongside a river near Harrisburg. That's where Bobrove, who admits that he has become addicted to hunting fossils, found it — the outline of a snail in a rock buried in dirt that geologists have determined to be 350 million years old.

He sat there for a minute and savored the sight of the fossil and a tiny green plant that sprouted next to it. Then a hint of movement broke the trance. Right there, in the dirt before him, a snail inched along and crawled onto the rock and directly across the fossil of its long-ago relative.

Bobrove gazed in awe at what he later would describe as "two bugs separated by 350 million years with the evolution of a flowering plant in between." And then he mumbled aloud: "Holy hell, there really is continuity."

She appeared to be in her late 30s, a strikingly good-looking woman with dark hair and, even on this cloudy afternoon, dark eyeglasses. Without an appointment she had dropped into the office to see me, as people often do, and this was what she wanted to know:

How do you cope with the loss of an eye? The ophthalmologist had just laid the bad news on her. Because of a disease that stemmed from childhood, her right eye would have to come out. No, it wouldn't be possible to replace it with an artificial eye. Why not, doctor? Because she had no ability to produce tears in that eye and, without moisture, no artificial eye could be inserted. It was as simple — and as complex — as that. She would go through the rest of her life not only with diminished vision but also with a physical blemish. How could she ever come to grips with that?

She had other questions, too: Was counseling available to help her through the crunch? Would counseling even help? She wanted to return to the job market, but would anybody hire her? What in the world was going to happen?

Not long after that she left the office, apologizing for thrusting her doubts and fears in my direction. Not long after that I telephoned Philip Bobrove and asked: "Can I come over and talk to you sometime?"

Bobrove was behind his desk, munching on a hamburger that had become his late, late lunch because of a long, long meeting that had just ended. He's a bearded, round little guy of whom I've become especially fond over the years, and the subjects we've discussed in our interviews have ranged from the obstacles that confront ugly people in a beauty-crazed culture to the lack of privacy that aggravates elderly people who want sex in the nursing homes in which they are confined.

What advice would he have for somebody who's losing an eye? Here is some of what came from Bobrove, who is associate professor of psychology in the department of psychiatry and human behavior at Jefferson Medical College:

"You mourn a lot. . . . You mourn for the part of you that is dead. It's a very personal thing. You could start a support group, meet on a regular basis and decry the unfairness of society. It might help, but eventually the buck stops with you. Nobody can get inside your skin. It's your eye. There's never been another one like it in the whole world. . . .

"Some things just are, and there's no way around them. You mourn . . . and then you get on with the business of living."

Those who seem able to do this best, he said, are those who somehow hear and heed the drumbeat that comes from within, a drumbeat that throbs so loudly and constantly that it muffles the drumbeats that sound from without.

"Few of us truthfully can say: 'To hell with you guys. I understand that you feel this way, but here I am.' We tend to measure our worth by how well we do with others, by how much they accept us. We lose sight of the reality that it's not what other people do but how we react to it that determines what happens to us. If they can't see our worth, it's their problem; if they reject us, it's their loss."

Those of us who can embrace that can defy the odds and win.

"When you lose part of yourself, you start to think more within yourself . . .

and move more within yourself and gain greater self-appreciation. You become deeper and more thoughtful. It's a popular myth, but it's often true.

"Something bad happens and you're forced to get back inside yourself. Nobody wants it. But you have to face it because it's there, and gradually it happens, if you work at it. . . . An artist loses his arms and he goes on to paint with his teeth. In the depths of depression he cries out: 'What the hell? What am I going to do — lie here and die?' Yes, some do die, but others find a way to paint. . . ."

How is it possible to get unhooked from the paralyzing bitterness?

"It seems to be a quality of a basic sense of OK-ness. How else can I put it? It's a base to tap into, but if it's not already there, I don't think it's possible to put it there. . . . You have to come to it yourself — as others have. Literature is replete with people who in despair searched their insides for something meaningful to live for. . . .

"When I was younger, I thought it could be done by group support. Now I'm older and I think that you need a place in a group, but they can't do it for you. You want them to, but they can't."

The help that can come from belonging to a group, Bobrove said, is the recognition that you're not alone — even though you, alone, must search for the core of your insides.

"I thought about that when I was digging for the fossils. Holy hell, there really is continuity. You're part of something, an entire sequence, a kind of obvious unity. This has to be tapped into on some level — either by yourself or through a group. It makes it easier to be accepting of where you are.

"When you're young and don't get a date with the girl you want, you're enraged. As you get older, you recognize that the girl is going to go with somebody who is 6-3 or rich and you say: 'Yeah, that's the way it is. I can't have what I want all the time.' And you get less angry. That's the only good thing about growing old — the sense that your anger is beginning to mellow. You don't care so much about how others judge you. You can say: 'I am who I am, and that's it.' "

Do many people have that basic core of "OK-ness" from which they can siphon strength?

"Yes, I think so . . . at least when it's done out of necessity. Sometimes the only way to tap into it is when bad things suddenly happen to you. . . . This core of OK-ness seems to transcend religion and ethnic background . . . and there may be no sense that it's even there until you have to have it."

This, Bobrove said, is "when it dawns on people that the only one who can say that you're OK is you, that the rest [of the people] don't matter. . . . If a therapist does his job well, he can [help you find the] good stuff inside. But only you truly can find it."

WHAT'S GOING ON WITH MIDDLE-AGED MEN?
February 19, 1989

The letter raised an often-asked question: What's going on with middle-aged men, anyway? Here is part of the letter: "I hope you can shed some light on my observations. I am 25, female, a bartender in the evenings. I watch people when I work because it makes my job more interesting. . . . What amazes me is middle-aged men. I believe I witness male menopause at its finest — or at its worst. . . . It's almost like a disease. Are all males afflicted with it?

"All the men are graying slightly at the temples. All of them are divorced or in a state of 'unmarriage' — pretending they are divorced or single. All of them make at least $45,000 a year. All of them drink Scotch or martinis. All of them drive sports cars or else a Mercedes or BMW. All of them try to pick up women my age. They talk about two things: their cars and their work. They are very shallow people who seem to have the social skills — at least when they're trying to interact with women — of 16-year-olds. . . .

"I love to watch these guys. They make fools of themselves. . . . Why isn't more written about male menopause? Is it a curable disease? Or does it go away when their cars finally break down? Are these guys as shallow as they seem? Do they ever find what they're looking for? Do they know what they're looking for? Do you know what they're looking for?"

■

Yes, I believe I do know what they're looking for. It's a lasting sense of peace and identity. The problem is that they're looking in the wrong places. I can say this with conviction because for some years I looked in the wrong places, too.

How does it all begin? What happens in middle age that causes a man's life to weigh so heavily on him? Let's count the spokes in the wheel.

The job isn't what he expected. The fulfillment just isn't there. He should have done better. He should have taken more risks. Whatever happened to all the grand dreams of glory? Whatever happened to the fun? At 25 he thought he was going to own a piece of the world. Now he doesn't even own his 100-foot-wide lot in the suburbs — because his wife got that in the divorce settlement.

His ability to sustain and nurture a relationship comes into question. If he's still married, he wonders why things aren't better, why the chill in the house never lifts — even in the heat of summer. What could he have done to be a better husband? How much of the fault is his? He shuffles between blaming himself too much and blaming himself not enough. What does his wife want from him anyway? If he's divorced, he wonders if he'll ever find anybody who'll accept him as he is. Can he accept himself as he is? How is he, anyway?

Whatever happened to his children, who once looked to him for answers to all questions? Daddy could do anything. But as the years fled, it seemed that Daddy could do nothing. Those golden years, so quickly lost. The regrets, so heavy as they blanket his chest at night.

Whatever happened to the man who thought that he had everything? Over and over, he asks himself: "How did I get this old so quickly with so little to show for it?" He never knew that money could be so meaningless.

What he has now is that gnawing feeling that something has got to be done. Life is meant to be lived, not merely endured. Perhaps it's time to take off the rose-colored glasses and look at himself and the world with stone-cold reality. No, that's too terrifying, too painful. Better to deaden the pain with a new sports car, a 25-year-old woman, plenty of alcohol, a trip to the Caribbean —

and a suntan in the dead of winter.

To me, the wonder is not that so many men in middle age end up in bars making fools of themselves. The wonder is that some manage to escape.

In midlife, the crisis erupts when a man enters that awful confrontation with discrepancy — the gap between what he expected of himself and what he actually got. This is the core of the crisis, the challenge of a lifetime. A man has his work cut out for him.

Often he has to be willing to scrap his life plan and draft another one. Is it time to change jobs — or even careers? Can the relationship that is sinking ever be made to float again? What would he have to do? How would he have to change? Is it possible to reconcile with the children? Is there anything he could do to open the door that they slammed shut with such seeming finality? Who is he, anyway? What does he want out of life? Is it too late? Is it ever too late?

■

People sometimes ask me if every man hits the wall in midlife. Yes, I believe so — although the speed at impact surely varies. For the man who has lived and loved wisely, the crisis can be gentle — the brushing glance of regret that comes from using up so much of the only life that he has. No matter how much he has achieved, how fulfilled he has been, he finds himself unable to pursue some of the other things that he would have liked — because he is running out of time. If he had not one but a hundred lives, then maybe . . . . This is the theme of Bernard Malamud's memorable novel *Dubin's Lives*. One life is simply not enough because there's so much to be done. It's not fair, but . . .

What's different about the men who escape the bar scene and the 25-year-old women? Why do they glance off the wall — instead of smashing into it head-on?

My sense is that they know who they are, that they're comfortable with themselves, that they know how to ask for help, that they don't try to camouflage their distress. Also, they're probably more versatile and well-rounded than many of us. They realized relatively early that there was more to life than career — and they were able to enjoy themselves and their families. This provided a tremendous buffer at high noon, when the bell was tolling and the sky was turning black.

What made them this way? My guess is that they probably had fathers who were role models of sensitivity and sensibility.

What happens on down the road to the men who in midlife sit in bars and talk about cars and try to attract women half their age?

I have a hunch that most of them eventually work through their stuff — not necessarily because they want to but because they have to. The pain is so intense that a point comes at which sports cars, liquor and, yes, even women half their age no longer are adequate as anesthetics. The men must, at last, face themselves, confront life's discrepancies, do the work that needs to be done, discover what they stand for, make peace with who they are.

This is when the sun begins to feel warm again on a man's back, when a man is reborn. There are some of us who would say that this is the prime of life.

CONFRONTING 'MIDLIFE' AT AN EARLY AGE
August 3, 1986

It came out of an interview that I had a few years ago with John Reckless, the Durham, N.C., psychiatrist who knows as much about people and their craziness as anybody you're likely to meet.

He was telling me that for a long time he held the notion that midlife crisis came "to a man in his 40s with an aging marital relationship, a man who had worked hard to acquire success, who got to the top of the heap and who became unhappy. I had the idea that this was the function of the number of years of life. I now believe that this is not true. I'm seeing more and more men in their middle 30s" and even younger who are struggling through their crises.

"I'm seeing as a patient a man who is 28 and who told me, 'I'm now where I expected to be at 55, and I can't handle it.' He's intelligent and he's dying of depression. He's aware already that it's not true that if he keeps going, one day he'll find a golden sunset and be happy. It's just not there."

The so-called midlife crisis, said Reckless, is "not an occurrence of the middle years . . . but a function of making it to the top and finding that [what you're seeking] is not there. Because men are making it to the top earlier these days, the crisis is coming earlier."

Reckless said that he hadn't changed his thoughts about what it takes to resolve the crisis, at whatever age it strikes. The solution remains coming to terms with yourself and "changing expectations so that you don't have to be the most successful or the wealthiest . . . and so that you can invest in personal relationships."

■

I told that story the other day to Harold Kushner, and he said that he had come to the same conclusion because he had seen something akin to what John Reckless was talking about. It had convinced him, he said, that crisis could arrive at any time — and that midlife really had not too much to do with it.

Was this a positive happening? If people bit their bullets earlier in life would everybody benefit?

Maybe, said Kushner. Maybe.

■

Kushner is rabbi of Temple Israel in Natick, Mass., near Boston, and he first found the national spotlight five years ago with his best-selling book, *When Bad Things Happen to Good People*. His new book, published this past spring, is *When All You've Ever Wanted Isn't Enough: The Search for a Life That Matters*, and it, too, is a tremendous commercial success.

When I interviewed Kushner at the very beginning of his promotional tour, he told me that to find lasting contentment people "have to stop defining success as money, as the thickness of the carpet, as the power to shape others, as how many people salute when we walk in the office in the morning. . . . We have to define the degree to which we have become authentically human. Only then is it possible to define ourselves as successful."

Lasting contentment, he said, comes from connecting with others in a positive way and from realizing that there is more to life than the next step up the corporate ladder. In the long run what matters is that we left a thumbprint on the world through somebody we touched, not as chief executive officer but as another human being.

When the interview was over, Kushner invited me to contact him in a few months — after the tour was finished — and he would share with me what he had learned from the reactions that he had received.

Like John Reckless, Kushner had changed some of his thoughts.

■

Kushner, 50, said that "I thought I was writing a book for people my age. But in a lot of places I went, book dealers said that they were selling a lot of my books to people in their early 30s. I didn't think people this age would understand the kinds of problems that I was talking about."

But he was wrong. What he found, as he listened to young people, was that many of them who had been on the fast track since they left college 10 years ago were beginning to have second thoughts.

"Some of them, even if the successes were still coming, were finding that the successes were not as satisfying. They were beginning to feel burned out. . . . A lot of people were finding that the successes and the promotions weren't coming as readily as in the past. At 32, they were beginning to [reach a] plateau, and this had never happened to them before."

The plateau was being reached "because of a natural funneling process. There are not enough higher jobs for those who want them . . . and everybody can't keep rising."

The result — whether people hit the plateau or were burned out from continued success — was the same, said Kushner. They began to ask themselves if this really was how they wanted to live for the rest of their lives.

"Their letters and calls tell me that they have realized that they shortchanged themselves on human values. I thought that this is something that they would realize 10 or 12 years later. I was not prepared for this" because this is the point that people traditionally reach only in midlife.

"The midlife definition is when you start to realize that you're not going to be around forever. It can be caused by the death of parents or a peer — or serious illness. But for a lot of these [younger] people it comes from a sense of futility. They have had a history of achievement, and they don't know how to cope with futility. . . . Others find that their competitive successes don't bring satisfaction, that the only kind of success that matters is to make good things happen and to share life with others."

I asked Kushner what he says to those who are disillusioned.

"I tell them that they block out time to jog and go to the gym because they need these activities to feel good. But they also need to block out time to do something cooperative and constructive — to work for a hotline or charitable organization, to do something to help others."

For 19 years, Kushner has been a member of his community's Rotary Club, and he is aware that "a lot of people make fun of Rotary. It's viewed by some as

28

a meeting of middle-aged men with cigars. There's some truth to that. But it's also very important for the mental health of a lot of successful businessmen . . . because it structures the way they work to make the community a better place. They don't do it for business contacts or commercial advantage. They do it because it needs to be done," and it provides a feeling of well-being that humans need "the same way as they need sunshine and exercise."

How do young people tend to react to his message of altruism?

"If they haven't hit the wall yet, they're skeptical. But after they've become disillusioned, they're very receptive."

Is the earlier onset of crisis a plus or a minus?

"If we're saying that young people are prematurely reaching middle age, then that's not very good. But if we're saying that they're re-orienting 12 years earlier, getting their lives in the right direction, then that's a good sign. . . . If that's what is happening, we should have 30-year-olds who end up being better parents. . . . If people get competition and careerism out of their systems before they're married and raising their kids, they'll be better parents."

These people should be able to avoid the trap that hits so many in middle age, said Kushner. "You're 47, and you realize that at 30 you should have paid more attention to your kid. So you say to your 18-year-old, 'I'm going to spend more time with you,' and the 18-year-old says, 'Gee, Dad, that's nice, but I have other plans.' "

There comes a time, said Kushner, when it truly is too late.

ON TURNING 50
September 13, 1981

Ten years ago, on a sunshine-kissed afternoon in September, I headed not for the golf course but for the office of psychiatrist Charles R. Starling. He was 47, and that meant that he was a survivor. He would be able to tell me — and others through what I would write — about the significance of turning 40.

My 40th birthday loomed like a shadow on the horizon. I wasn't apprehensive, but, good grief, society does make a big deal out of being 40. It's supposed to be a time when we realize that we won't live forever, when we're admittedly entering middle age, when our kids are getting closer to college, our parents are aging and our marriages are dulling from wear and tear.

What did Starling, my golfing companion and longtime friend, have to share with me? Why was 40 considered such a milestone?

He was glad I'd come, he said, because it had forced him to think about the 40s in ways that he didn't often have reason to do. In his mellow North Carolina dialect he began to talk:

"When you're 40, it's time to be honest with yourself. You no longer can pretend you're gonna get 'em next year. And those promises you made to yourself when you were 25, well . . . you've got to realize that some of them aren't going to come true.

"At 40 you can get little disappointments all in one great big dose. And you

29

can experience something akin to a gigantic, soul-searing kind of pain with no physical basis whatsoever.

"So you fight it and you do anything you can to avoid this pain. Even to the point of trying to fool yourself. That's why the 40th birthday is important. It's a time to decide which dreams are the impossible ones and to say: 'I'm going to be honest with myself.' "

No, Starling said, he saw no evidence that age 40 physically represented anything in life except that we were 10 years older and more experienced than we were at 30. At 40 there should be no decline in any of our functions — physically, sexually or intellectually.

But, he said, "there is an emotionalism involved in a man . . . and at 40 he may think: 'This is it. Youth is gone and I'll never be the same again.' And he can use this to explain away some of his inadequacies.

"All our lives, we've cherished some special dreams — like being president of the company or being able to beat Arnold Palmer on a given day. And we do everything in the world to keep from admitting to ourselves that it's an impossible dream. So when age 40 comes, that's what we may blame for our inability to fulfill these dreams.

"And society helps us. Hell, it's almost socially acceptable to crack up when you're 40. People look at you and say: 'Poor Charlie. The pressure finally got to you, didn't it?' If you blow up at 35, society thinks you're a crackpot. But not at 40. And we know this . . . so 40 becomes a convenient peg on which to hang our disappointments and failures."

The blueprint for healthy survival of the 40s, Starling said, was to bring the big dreams out into the open and look at them honestly.

"If you've always thought you had the ability to be a scratch golfer but at 40 you're still playing with a 12-handicap, then you ought to accept the fact that you're not ever going to be in Arnold Palmer's league. If you dreamed of being the company president and at 40 you're still a salesman, you've got to accept it — and quit kidding yourself."

This kind of candor didn't have to trigger the searing pain of disappointment, he said — "not if you really have self-respect, not if you believe you're somebody special, that there's only one person like you in the whole universe and that it's better to be you than to be Arnold Palmer or the company president."

But it isn't easy for most of us to muster this kind of self-respect, Starling said, because "we've been told all our lives that we're not wonderful or special. When you spilled milk, your mother called you a bad kid.

When you didn't want to take a bath, you were a dirty kid. When you stuck out your tongue, you were an undisciplined kid. At school, you always were measured by the performance of others. You got the feeling everybody else must be better because they're always telling you what's wrong with you.

"So you grow up thinking that way. Is it any wonder it's painful when the dream bursts? Hell, it just reinforces that notion that you're not as good as everybody else. That's why people tend to kid themselves and try to rationalize their failures."

I wrote that interview, which appeared on the day before my 40th birthday in the newspaper of which I was executive editor, The Charlotte News. That night I was at a party, and a 50-year-old woman cornered me and said:

"If you think 40 is bad, wait until you're 50. Then you'll know what misery is."

Well, here it is, 10 years later, and in six days I'll be 50. What has the last decade meant to me — and how do I feel about age 50?

Of all the stories I've ever written, the 40-year piece with Starling unquestionably had the most profound effect on me personally . . . because it confirmed what I'd pushed into the dark corners of my mind and refused to think about openly.

Being a newspaper editor wasn't really what I'd thought it would be. It wasn't much fun, but it was a goal to which I had aspired ever since I was a little kid and used my father's old Underwood typewriter to peck out copies of a neighborhood "newspaper" that I stuck behind every screen door on our street. How could I turn loose of my dream? How could I walk away from something that I had worked so hard to get?

No, it was crazy — and I should be happy with what I had. But Starling had told me in so many ways that what I was feeling wasn't crazy. I needed to pay attention to what I was feeling. I needed to be honest with myself.

My marriage was rocky, but I didn't like to think about that either. After all, whose marriage is perfect? Just cool it and don't expect too much. But Starling had said not to be cool but to be honest. If the marriage hadn't prospered in the past, what reason was there to believe that it could prosper in the future? Wasn't I beating my head against a stone wall?

Within five years I had ended the marriage and surrendered the dream. I was a writer again — not an editor. I also was honest.

If the interview impacted dramatically on me, it swatted Starling even harder. Fifteen months after we talked, he announced that he was giving up psychiatry because he'd never cured anybody. He was going to California to submerge himself in primal therapy and find out what he wanted to do with his life. He was taking the advice that he had given me. He was being honest, he said, and he thanked me for the interview.

Today, Starling is still in California. He's struggling, but his optimism is eternal that good times are right around the corner. He's not sorry that he confronted himself.

How do I feel about age 50? Will I, as the woman predicted, now find out what misery really is?

No, I don't think so. I've already experienced the misery. That came packaged with the honesty. Age 50, I think, is when those of us who bit the bullet in our 40s can harvest even greater joy from doing what we want to do with the people we love in the environment we choose. We're through with life's games, and we can aim toward things that matter to us, if to nobody else. We can be honest, without the pain of the 40s. We can accept ourselves as we are, without trying to hide the warts.

Age 50 may be the very best time of all. What do you think?

THE YEAR OF THE LAUGH
January 14, 1990

I normally don't make New Year's resolutions — they've always seemed silly and unnecessary to me — but at the beginning of 1989 I made an exception. I sat down with myself on that New Year's Day and promised that I was going to laugh more.

I was going to laugh quicker and easier — especially at myself. I was going to recognize humor even in places where it didn't normally exist. I was going to stop taking myself so seriously. Instead of being distressed, I was going to giggle at the craziness that I so often encounter out in the real world — the traffic jams, the potholes, the endless lines, the crush of people who seem in no hurry to get anywhere.

Ha! Ha! Yes, indeed, 1989 was going to be the Year of the Laugh.

■

As it turned out, I didn't do a lot of laughing. In some ways it was a good year — I learned a lot about myself and what's important — but in other ways it was not so good.

I lay in the hospital bed back in the summer, recovering from open-heart surgery, and told a visitor that I had set a goal for myself for the rest of the year: I was going to laugh more.

Well, the months have slipped by, we're into another year, and the truth is, I'm still not laughing enough. I'm beginning to wonder if I don't know how, if I'm so accustomed to dealing with life's serious side that everything else slides right past me, unrecognized and unappreciated.

How do I go about putting more laughter into my life? When I ask my friends, mostly middle-aged guys with their own scar tissue, they shrug and tell me that they don't know. If I find out, they say, I should pass the magic along to them. They'd like to laugh more, too.

■

I was having lunch with Norman Cousins, who in his landmark book, *Anatomy of an Illness*, wrote about the importance of humor in physical well-being. He told about how, when he was hospitalized with a supposedly irreversible disease of the connective tissue, he rented funny movies that primed his laughter. He never claimed that he laughed his way back to health — as many people erroneously believe — but he did claim, and still does, that laughter is good for the soul, that it can be a piece of the healing process, that it can make the sun break through and brighten cloudy days.

If there were anybody who could teach me about laughter, it would be Norman Cousins, whose new book *Head First, the Biology of Hope* continues his seemingly ceaseless exploration of the mind-body connection and its relationship to health.

What about it, Norman Cousins? My middle-aged friends and I want to know how to laugh more, especially at ourselves.

Cousins, 74, who impresses me as an extraordinarily genuine fellow, pushed back in his chair and said, "I'm not sure I can help you." Then he started laughing. That was funny, he said, because, after all, it was reasonable for me to assume that he would be able to help. But the truth — and at this point he turned deadly serious — was that we had to help ourselves, each of us, and nobody else could do much for us.

"It's not easy to make changes" in the way we view the world, he said. "Circumstances often dictate our outlook," and if too many bad things happen to us, it's going to make it tougher to laugh. But the reverse also is true, he said. If we can recognize and appreciate the good things that happen to us, then we'll be in a stronger position to find humor everywhere — even in our own folly.

Let's listen now as Cousins, former editor of Saturday Review and now adjunct professor at UCLA's medical school, talks about recognizing and appreciating the good things.

■

"I have been pursued by good luck all my life," Cousins said. "It's hard for me to deny the evidence of my experiences. . . . I had good luck with serious illness as a kid; I beat all the odds. I had very good luck in my education. My luck was especially good in my career. . . .

"Conventional wisdom says that no magazine of quality can stand on its own. But I had good luck with Saturday Review, which stood on its own. . . . Conventional wisdom says a magazine of quality can have no more than 30,000 circulation. But we had 650,000, the largest quality magazine in the country. . . .

"It's important not to be intimidated by 'experts.' Their confident predictions of what is beyond reach is, almost by definition, the point at which the beginning of real possibility exists. . . .

"I would have to deny what happened to me not to be an optimist. I am a victim of happy circumstances. . . . I was dealing with the IRS over something that accountants said couldn't be done. I represented my own case to the regional division, and I found them to be reasonable. They agreed with me in this case, which involved Saturday Review and several million dollars. The 'experts' said I was wrong, but we got a substantial refund from the IRS. Anybody who gets a substantial refund from the IRS can't be a pessimist. . . .

"Fifty years ago, nobody would say that anyone could be married to me for more than a few months. But 50 years later, I'm still married to the same woman. . . .

"I am suggesting that too many of us accept defeat prematurely, and this tends to pyramid" into a way in which we view the world — with glasses that are half empty rather than half full. "We will not win every contest, but we shouldn't assume that we are going to lose."

■

Cousins said that he doesn't laugh as much as he would like. "If I spent less time chasing airplanes and running through airports," he said, "I think I would laugh more. When I'm free of airports, when I'm with family and friends, when I have time to read, to write, to be on the golf course and the tennis court, then my quota of fun increases. I laugh more."

Cousins said that, not infrequently, he wakes up laughing from his dreams —

a marvelously uplifting experience. "I'm telling myself jokes, and I'm laughing at the jokes. The thing about this that amazes me is that one part of the brain is concealing the punchline from another part of the brain."

In his dreams "people don't get ill. They don't get killed. They don't die in my dreams. This probably has a lot to do with the fact that I'm not afraid to die."

■

It was an important conversation for me to have with Cousins, who makes a point that is so easy for many of us to forget at times. A lot of good stuff does happen to us — stuff that, when kept high in our consciousness, can brighten our outlook, lighten our hearts, prime the pump for spontaneous laughter. It's when we dismiss the good stuff, discount its importance, that we burden ourselves with the junk that drags us down and makes laughter virtually impossible.

The answer to my question — how can I laugh more? — was so simple, so obvious, yet it took Norman Cousins to point it out for me. I can laugh more if I remember that I have been pursued by good luck, too. Almost all of us have — if we're willing to stop complaining and take inventory.

Almost all of us are, to steal a phrase from Cousins, victims of happy circumstances.

Happy circumstances. That has a nice ring to it, doesn't it?

'THE HIGH VALUE OF KINDNESS'
September 24, 1989

Psychiatrist O. Spurgeon English was telling me about the woman who, as a patient, once told him: "If parents were able to be kind to their children, there wouldn't be a psychiatrist in the country making a nickel."

While he wouldn't necessarily put it quite that way, English, who is 87, is a great believer in what he calls "the high value of kindness. . . . It works wonders in promoting the growth and strengthening the personality of the growing young person. Too many parents attempt to rear their children with too little kindness."

While it's especially important in children's development, kindness is something all of us need, said English, acceptance for merely being ourselves.

As English, a former head of psychiatry at Temple University, talked, it occurred to me that what he was describing was unconditional love, with no strings attached. You don't have to do anything to earn unconditional love. It's rightfully yours, this precious gift — if people are willing and able to give it.

That brought me around to putting the question to English: How can we learn to give unconditional love?

English's response: "You have to think of making yourself into a selfless person."

I asked English to define a selfless person.

"You don't demand any reward, any return," he said. "You do something, give, and you don't expect the same in return. It makes you feel so good to be a giver. That's the only return you want. You're so sure all the time you're doing it that this is the only reward you need. To be happy, you need only the opportunity to give."

That raised a red flag for me. We've all read so much in recent times about people who become pleasers, who give and give, get nothing back, eventually become doormats. If we give and give, I asked English, aren't we at potential risk of becoming pleasers?

His response: "And what's wrong with being a pleaser? It doesn't have to be pejorative. It's OK to be a pleaser. . . . if you don't worry about coming out on the short end, if you don't worry about becoming a dry seed blown away in the wind."

But aren't you in danger of being exploited?

"No, not if you're any good at detecting phonies," he said. "Then you're in no danger of being hurt — if you have enough knowledge of human nature to distinguish phonies from genuine deserving recipients, people who will make use of what you give and who will say now or later, 'I am indebted to you for what you've done for me.' You must be willing to be acknowledged by the people you serve. . . . Abraham Lincoln was a great giver of himself even while he was a very unhappy man. He seemed to have an enormously distant vision of people who would have gratitude."

How does somebody become selfless?

"You have to believe that you can give and not be chewed up and spit out, that you will not be impoverished or injured by what you do," English said. "If you give yourself away, you have to believe that somebody will give it back. If you give money away, you have to believe that some money will come in from another source. . . . The world would be way ahead if more people learned to be selfless. People in leadership positions ideally should be selfless, but often their focus is not on what they can give but on what they can hold on to."

Must a giver necessarily ignore his or her own needs?

"No, but you have to be willing to extend yourself to help others," English said. ". . . Everybody has the potential to become selfless, but it's easier if you had role models when you were growing up, people who acted in selfless ways. If your parents were givers, it's unquestionably easier for you to be a giver."

I asked English if he thought people who always had money in the family found it easier to be givers than people who scratched hard to build their fortune.

"I don't know that anybody ever has studied this," he said, "but my guess is that people who came up the hard way and found society helpful and kind would be more likely to become generous, selfless people — instead of trying to hang on to what the family has had for generations."

It's easier, said English, to become a giver at age 18 than at 50, "when you're more set in your ways and more self-satisfied with your value system. At 50, there's a great threat of being impoverished by finances or by people who might think you a fool if you gave money away."

What's the payoff for being selfless?

"Whatever you do, you can conceptualize people, from dozens to millions, think-

35

ing of you kindly as long as you live and possibly for generations after," English said. "You're so pleased by this — and it's all you need at any time. Your reward is in the kindly thoughts that people have of you."

Do you become a giver all at once — or by stages, starting out with small steps?

"It's gradual, but it depends on how early you started," he said. "If you get to middle age and you're still a taker, there's a strong chance that you'll stay a taker the rest of your life. It's not impossible to change, but it's unlikely. You'll have a much harder struggle. You have to work like hell to solidify giving as an important part of your philosophy and value system. . . .

"It's a lot of fun to be a taker. Many people keep it up as long as others will let them. It's hard for these people to change because they get such rewards from taking."

What is the line that separates the selfless person from the person who is trying to protect his or her legitimate self-interest? For example, would a truly selfless person make a speech without a fee every time he was asked to?

"If you're doing worthwhile work, you can't be that selfless," said English. "You can't respond to every appeal because that would leave you not enough time or energy to continue your worthwhile work."

BREAKFAST NEVER TASTED SO GOOD
July 22, 1990

It had been an uncustomarily late night for me at the Delaware seashore. Normally I'm in bed by 10, but the television movie, one I'd been looking forward to, had lasted until 11, and then I'd punched on the radio, which was playing big-band music that was too good to turn off.

So it was after midnight when I finally crawled under the covers and allowed the pounding surf, right outside the bedroom window, to send me straight to dreamland.

About five hours later I woke up — as wide awake as if somebody had grabbed my shoulders and shaken me briskly.

What was it? What was going on?

I got up, washed my face, and, because the cat was growling impatiently, shoveled some food into his bowl. Then I walked out onto the terrace, and instantly I knew why my sleep had been broken.

It was a spectacular sunrise — orange, purple, yellow, blue, all of them skipping toward me across the quiet, mirrorlike ocean. If I'd slept a bit longer, I'd have missed it, and my emotional time clock hadn't wanted that to happen. I went back into the kitchen, fixed a cup of coffee and returned to the terrace. Not a soul was in sight. The world still was asleep, except for me, and I decided to take advantage of it — a world of my very own. Breakfast and exercise could wait. I was going to take my walk now, at this very moment, not at midday, as I usually do, when the crowds are thick and the noise level is high.

It was a few minutes after 6 when I walked rapidly across the cool sand and went ankle-deep into the almost-cold surf. Which way? I'd go south, past the houses set on stilts along the beach, through Fenwick Island State Park — and all the way to the tall white building three and a half miles away. That would give me a round trip of seven miles, a nice way to start the day, which, later on, would include a little work — washing windows and putting together a speech — and a lot of play — hitting some golf balls and sailing the catamaran.

The sun was well out of the water now and spreading a golden path that followed me down the beach.

Still, nobody else was around to share it. It remained my own world, a performance that Mother Nature was giving just for me. I heard myself humming "Perdido."

I walked about 300 yards, then started to run, slowly at first. When I lengthened my stride — the way I did on the backstretch when I ran the quarter-mile so many years ago — I saw in my shadow the familiar body of a teenager, arms high, pumping easily. I gulped in the salty air and thought how good it was to be alive. How very good.

I slowed to a fast walk, past the houses on stilts, into the state park. Off to my left, heading out into the open sea, were four fishing boats, their engines throbbing, neatly lined up, about 200 yards part.

I wondered what it would be like to captain a fishing boat. Did those men enjoy what they did? Or was it work for them, just another way of paying the bills, sending the kids to college? No, it had to be more than that. They were happy. I could feel it.

Some dolphins, maybe half a dozen, parted the waters about 200 yards out, their black backs humping above the gentle waves. They certainly seemed happy. How could anybody kill dolphins?

The sun quietly slipped behind a yellow cloud and, when it reappeared, it was like a starburst, with rays shooting in all directions. The Japanese flag. The Rising Sun.

I stopped to savor the beauty.

What's it all about, Alfie?

I'm pretty sure, Alf, that this is what it's all about.

A helicopter, gleaming white, with the red and blue insignia of the Coast Guard, whirled past, then disappeared to the south. Up ahead, there was a lone fisherman, in front of his pickup truck, as motionless as a statue. Maybe he, too, was thinking how good it was to be alive.

"Morning," I smiled. "How's it going?"

He smiled back. "The fishing's terrible, but I'm great. Just great." His smile broadened. So did mine.

"Nice day," I said.

"The best," he said. "I'm out here every morning about this time, but I don't see many mornings like this."

"Good luck with the fish," I said.

"It don't matter," he said. "What matters is that I'm here."

I stepped up my pace. A seagull dived and flattened out on the sand a few yards away.

"Jonathan Livingston?" I presumed. He retracted his landing gear as he flapped away.

My head was down, watching my toes dig into the sand. When I looked up, I imagined it was a dream.

Coming toward me, perhaps 30 yards away, was a deer, reddish-brown, obviously young. Without antlers, its head seemed much too small for its body. It watched me warily, but continued to approach. It was as if I almost could reach out and touch it. The eyes were brown and clear, now without any sign of fear.

"Hi!"

The deer broke into a sprint, its hooves spraying sand. I watched it move swiftly for about 200 yards, then it veered off the beach, through some dune grass, and disappeared. Wow! All those people who are asleep don't know what they're missing. A deer on the beach. Who'd ever believe it?

I reached the three-and-a-half-mile mark and turned to stare out into the ocean. The fishing boats, with their happy captains, were mere specks on the horizon.

What's it all mean, Gene?

I'm pretty sure, Gene, that this is what it all means.

I started the walk back. The happy fisherman was right where I left him.

"You won't believe what I just saw," I said. "A deer — on the beach."

His smile was awesome. "They're out here every morning, sometimes four or five of them. They live in the woods, back over there." He motioned toward the highway. "Civilization ain't hurt them none — at least not much."

"We all should be able to say that," I said.

"I think I can," he said.

I could tell that he meant it.

I was back at my place by 8 o'clock. I walked up the steps from the beach, and standing there was a man with a white beard.

"I hope you have a nice day," he said.

"I already have."

He didn't say anything else, and I like to think it's because he understood exactly what I meant.

Breakfast never tasted so good. Maybe that's because it's not flavored often enough with absolute contentment.

We really need to do something about that, don't we?

JOY OF VICTORY FROM THE ASHES OF AGONY
December 6, 1981

Back in the early fall, as I approached my 50th birthday, I wrote a column about what I perceived to be a benchmark of midlife contentment, and the sum of it amounted to this:

Separate the possible dreams from the impossible dreams; pursue the possible but turn loose of the impossible. No greater virtues exist than the honesty that is required to do this and the willingness that is necessary to make the changes

— occupationally and professionally — that are essential in the march toward happiness and fulfillment.

I ended the column this way:

"Age 50, I think, is when those of us who bit the bullet in our 40s can harvest even greater joy from doing what we want to do with the people we love in the environment we choose. We're through with life's games, and we can aim toward things that matter to us, if to nobody else. We can be honest, without the pain of the 40s. We can accept ourselves as we are . . ."

The response to that column was enormous — and much of it came from people who recounted the obstacles to change in their lives, who offered a thousand and one reasons for staying stuck exactly where they are now. I'd like to share with you part of one letter that raised some especially interesting questions:

"At 45, I can relate to the struggle. I envy the man whose dreams never burst but continue until senility. How many of us can adjust to the reality of our lot in life and our goals? It's certainly easier for the professional to pick up sticks and start again; after all, he has recourse. But just ponder the fate of the ordinary working man who is 'lifestruck' in his 40s. How many options can he really play? His prior years of occupation, family and personal commitment are not easily abandoned for new horizons. Honesty, in its purest definition, is a luxury that he hardly can afford.

"Misery at 40 or 50 cannot be dealt with intellectually. Ignorance is bliss and lofty dreams of self become salvation — much like the nice dream you have and when you wake, you try to return quickly to the dream. Those waking moments are the ordinary man's real potential misery. Take away the ordinary man's dreams and you take away the man. . . ."

Well, what do you think? Is honesty about self and life a luxury that "ordinary" people can't afford?

Can self-deception, through clutching onto impossible dreams, ever be a road to happiness?

I took the questions to Maurice Prout, a psychologist who is head of behavior therapy at Hahnemann Medical College and Hospital, and dumped them in his lap. Well, Doctor, how does all of it look to you?

In a nutshell here's what he said:

Most of us have but two choices when we become mired in life's potholes. We can hide the disenchantment under a rock or we can "come into the arena prepared to do battle." Both have painful consequences, but the thing about hiding it under a rock is that it doesn't change anything and inevitably the disenchantment crawls out again — in the same form or in disguise. On the other hand, doing battle in the arena may leave us bloody and battered but at least we've gotten your licks in and hopefully learned a thing or two.

What separates those who hide it from those who attack it often comes down to this, Prout said: The hiders feel that they don't have the resources to fight and that they can't endure major change; the battlers have the "underlying notion that they can survive — or else they wouldn't be in the arena."

Can a hider become a battler? Or, in Prout's higher-sounding language, "how can somebody get the resources to manage change?" Well, he'll back into his answer to that. Be patient, won't you?

It's difficult, Prout said, for most of us to be brutally honest in the "situational areas of our lives — work, family and the questions of who we are, where we're going and is it worth it. Honesty may be rather tough to take in substantial doses all at once. I suspect that it has a way of overloading the circuitry." So even those of us who are the battlers don't put on our Victor Mature masks and go charging out after all of the lions. No, we bang on them a few at a time, and then we go after a few more. Eventually, if we're lucky, the lions are down, and we're still standing.

If you decide that your work situation holds no promise or that your ailing marriage can't ever be fixed, the confrontation that results from your honesty is not going to be pleasant, Prout said. "It creates anxiety and depression . . . and stirs up amounts of dust for ourselves and those around it."

But the thing is, Prout said, most of us adapt to some extent to whatever course of action — or inaction — we choose.

For some people — perhaps the letter writer — the very thought of major change is overpowering and out of the question, and to make peace with themselves and their situations they have to "settle for less or change their perception of their needs. . . . Staying in an unrewarding job or a bad marriage is not as painful as getting out. There's a more comfortable kind of discomfort in staying in. To take a substantial risk with big pieces of yourself — job or marriage — well, this kind of change requires you to go into crisis, with anxiety and depression, physiological signals and psychosomatic distresses."

But out of the ashes of agony, Prout said, can emerge the joy of victory — the notion that you have taken on the lions and defeated them. This brings to life a full-bodied flavor that is not familiar to many of those who settle for less than what they want — because they're afraid or because they don't have the resources to survive change.

"If you view change as a threat, you try to cover up the situation or deny it and convince yourself that it's not as bad as you thought. If you view change as a challenge that you can manage, you go into the arena prepared to do battle."

Prout doesn't view the resources to manage change as biochemical in origin. "I say that they're pretty much learned phenomena. A lot of it depends on how you've managed crises in the past. Were you successful? Or even if you had many battles and losses, did you still have the notion that you learned from them and that you were better off for your wounds?"

It's important to "know you can fail and still survive. Most of us are brought up with the notion that failure is the worst thing we can do. And that dampens our desire to take risks. But we tend not to focus on the flip side — that we can learn from our failures. You can't succeed in the ring until you get in and lose a number of times. . . . You can't learn until you make errors."

Prout said that the letter writer "sounds like a guy locked into security. Most of us hit that at one time or another. We go through a period of envy for everybody else. Our rationalization sustains our stuckness . . . but later some of us realize that we can't swallow it any more. That's when we decide what needs to be changed, check our resources and then take a risk."

Those of us who "get locked into a standard of living and feel we can't take risks" have a lot of company, Prout said, ". . . but the questions are: What do you want out of life? What makes you happy? Often making money at what you don't enjoy doesn't do it."

Does the "professional," as the letter writer suggested, have the inside track to happiness? Does he have more options? Can he afford honesty?

"I don't think that professional people necessarily find it easier to make transitions. I find people who are well educated and terribly dissatisfied with what they do. If they're overly conscious of security, they may not make changes. They even may envy the blue-collar worker. They're in a stuck, stagnating position. They feel it, but they can't manage it.

"Some say that the grass always looks greener on the other side, and to some degree that's correct. It depends on how we perceive solutions. Are our resources zapped — or were we taught always to look at the bleak side of things? Do we feel dried up, with no vitality? Do we say that we only have to put in another eight years until retirement — and so we'll continue doing something we don't like? Time is the richest resource we have and to [throw it away] is not wise. That's when we end up walking the land without any blood in our veins. That's when we become the living dead, the victims of stuckness.

"To take a risk is tough business, leaving something that's solid even if it's irritating. To let go puts most of us on shaky ground. Most of us encounter shakes . . . but then some of us go on with change despite the shakes — because we have the notion that we've been there before" and that we can survive.

THE WARRIOR'S GLORY: THEY LIED
January 26, 1986

They said "You are no longer a lad."
I nodded.
They said, "Enter the council lodge."
I sat.
They said, "Our lands are at stake."
I scowled.
They said, "We are at war."
I hated.
They said, "Prepare red war symbols."
I painted.
They said, "Count coups."
I scalped.
They said, "You'll see friends die."
I cringed.
They said, "Desperate warriors fight best."
I charged.
They said, "Some will be wounded."
I bled.

They said, "To die is glorious."
They lied.

— From *Battle Won Is Lost* by Phil George

Psychologist David Grady knows a lot about bleeding and dying. He first read the poem five or six years ago, and "it really struck home with me. It's a training material I use. . . . It's as generic as you can get in the individual response to being a warrior. . . .

"A primary rite of passage for males to come of age is to become a warrior. It was no different for the 19-year-olds in Vietnam. We went to war, and we were reinforced for it — through GI Joe dolls and every other way. It's in society's interest to glorify warriors. There'll always be wars, which means that there'll always be the military — and, unless we have a mercenary army, society always will need to indoctrinate young males with the notion that part of developing as an adult is to be a warrior.

"I volunteered for the Marines, and I volunteered to go to Vietnam — partly because I thought it was important and partly because I wanted to find out about myself in the crucible of war. Could I hack it? I went there to learn some things about myself."

What he learned, said Grady, was that killing was "so senseless — no matter who was killed. Survival was the only issue. My goal, as a sergeant, was to get as many of my people to survive as possible."

■

"My unit was in the field all the time. We set up ambushes . . . I remember one night with no moon, absolutely pitch black. I thought 'This is great. We won't have any contact unless somebody steps on top of us.'

"That night we had a sniper with us . . . and he had on his rifle a starlight scope, an infrared thing through which you could see everything. . . . . I wanted to look through his scope. We were on the crest of a hill, overlooking rice paddies. I looked through the scope, and I spotted one Viet Cong with a rifle over his shoulder. He was holding it by the barrel, bopping along and probably feeling safe in the belief that nobody could see him.

"I followed him on the scope across the line of fire — for 300 or 400 yards — for what seemed like an eternity. I had to decide 'Do I blow him away?' All kinds of thoughts ran through my mind — from 'I wonder if he believes in what he's doing?' to 'Will some Americans die if I don't shoot him?'

"I was 20 at the time . . . I considered it for a few seconds, and I chose not to shoot . . . and he walked out of sight. I thought about it later, that I'd done the right thing . . . I liked my reason: I had to be in war, but I didn't have to be a killer. I killed when I had to, but mostly I had no choice. It was to save myself or my friends . . . and it always happened in a flash. . . . Here, I had time to consider. I had a choice. . . . "

■

Grady was in Vietnam for 222 days and was wounded twice. The first time was from shrapnel from "one of our artillery rounds. It killed half of us, including my best friend."

42

The second time was from a hand grenade that "went off next to my left foot. . . . I was in and out of consciousness for a couple of weeks. I found out what happened when I was in Japan. . . . A Navy doctor said 'I'm sorry, but we can't save your leg.' I said 'OK, but can you take it off now? It really hurts.' They did save one leg . . . both were a mess. . . .

"For a long time, I expected that life without a leg meant that I could do all the things I'd done before, but without one leg. That, I found out, was not true. I'm still learning about life without a leg."

■

David Grady, 38, is a senior staff psychologist at Friends Hospital in Philadelphia, and over the years he has worked with many war veterans and others who suffer from what now is known as post-traumatic stress disorder (PTSD), which is listed in psychiatric manuals as a specific diagnostic category.

"Anyone who goes through combat has some residue. . . . Some deal with it on their own. With their social supports — family, wife, buddies — they have opportunities to process what happened and to get distance from it in a healthy way."

But many don't deal with it on their own. "A veteran fears that he can't share it with his wife. The fear is that if she hears about what you did, she'll never see you again as the same person. . . . In therapy, you need to recognize that if she wasn't there, she can't realize what it was like. But she can hear, and you can talk. . . . What happened speaks to who you were then in that situation — and not necessarily to you are now. . . . You have to give up some of the identification with who you were and what you did then."

There are, said Grady, two major types of combat trauma that increase a soldier's risk of developing significant problems:

One is involvement in "abusive violence. A large amount of violence is asked for in war. But other violence is not necessary because a war is going on — wanton killing, torturing of the enemy or civilians. At the moment, it may seem like the thing to do, but you get out of the war zone and you wonder if you had to do it."

Example: "This guy had as much combat experience as anybody I ever knew. He was in the same regiment with me, a squad leader, who was out on patrol one night. . . . They decided to go to a local village, find some women and have sex. They were in a hooch with the women, and they heard a noise. They went outside, saw movement, and some of them started shooting. . . . Then they went out to check and they found that they'd killed a woman and two children, who had been sneaking around in a free-fire zone. They weren't supposed to be there, and they'd been heard by Marines who weren't supposed to be there. . . . The Marines threw the bodies down a well in the village, then left.

"None of this ever came to light . . . but the squad leader was fundamentally changed by the experience, and to this day feels responsible — for not being in control, for not burying the bodies. At times his guilt is overwhelming. . . . He's tried alcohol to numb the guilt. This is a man who was wounded six times, who was highly decorated and who can't overcome this incident of abusive violence as he now sees it."

The other is the loss of somebody close — and a resulting sense of feeling responsible for the person's death.

Example: "He was a tank platoon commander, and his tank was hit by a rocket, which went through 13 inches of steel and exploded when it hit the air pocket inside. The tank blew up. . . . He was up top, sticking out, commanding a column of tanks. He jumped out and pulled the top gunner with him. But he couldn't get back for the driver and the other gunner. They burned up . . . and he's unable to come to grips with it. He couldn't realize that he'd done all he could do, that he'd acted on instinct, that he'd saved one person, that he was not responsible" for the two deaths. The man's reaction was to "seal over all feelings, to withdraw to himself, never get close to anybody."

■

Sometimes, said Grady, PTSD is triggered by an event years after exposure to trauma.

"After Vietnam, this guy had gone to law school, had practiced successfully for many years. Seemingly he had no residue from the war, no problems. He married, had children. He was doing great. Then one day he was driving back to Philadelphia from Atlantic City, and there was a huge fire along the expressway. . . . Smoke was blowing across the road. It was hard to see, but as he approached, he saw that there'd been a multi-car collision. . . . He pulled over to help and pulled from one car a little girl, who died in his arms. . . .

"He flashed back to Vietnam. He had called in an artillery strike, but it was off target and hit a village and killed many civilians. After the attack, he ran to the village and pulled from the rubble a little girl, who died in his arms. . . .

"Here, on the expressway, with the fire, the smoke, it was like war all over again. He was overwhelmed. He spent the next year and a half without talking to anybody. He'd go to his office and sit. Eventually, he had problems with the bar association because he wasn't representing clients. He wouldn't answer the phone. He just sat there. . . . He sought help and started to get a handle on what happened. This freak experience had brought it all back to him."

■

PTSD doesn't happen only to combat veterans, said Grady. It can happen to anybody who has been exposed to something he or she can't handle — rape, abuse, a critical automobile accident.

"Victims undergo a change in the way they understand the world and themselves. They become aware of how vulnerable they really are in life. Mostly, we don't allow ourselves to deal with our vulnerability, but the victim experiences it. . . . The victim gets in touch with the evil, the hurt, the suffering. . . . The message is that the world is not as safe as we need it to be. The question always is 'Why me?' And it's not hard to find reasons why you may deserve it. There's often anger at self for not preventing it. . . .

"There's a search for meaning. You and the world look different, and you've got to reorganize things. . . . You never can forget it, but you can begin to put it aside and get back some hope, put some distance between you and the event."

■

For combat soldiers the nightmare can go on and on.

"At 19, you're given life-and-death power. You're told to kill. No matter what the training has been, when the stuff hits the fan in combat, anything can happen. Combat is the most unpredictable, primal experience known to man. . . .

"I was in an area where most of the casualties were from booby traps and mines. The villagers knew about them. . . . Many of my friends were killed. That doesn't make you feel warmly toward the local people. Why didn't they tell us? We were there supposedly to help them. The answer, of course, was that if they had told us, they would have been killed by guerrillas.

"But at the time . . . well, some people lose it at times. There's a lack of control on carnage in war. And after the war, you're left with who you are, with the loss of control. . . .

"What it comes down to eventually is your relationship with self. You have to be able to forgive yourself, entertain the idea that things were different then. . . . You have to wash the blood of the enemy off your hands . . . and the blood of the men you loved. It's acceptance . . . the final step is acceptance. You have to accept what happened. It happened, so don't fight it. . . . The biggest tragedy is to go on and to be hurt by what happened many years ago — and to hurt others."

REFLECTIONS OF A GENTLEMAN
December 24, 1991

It was early in the morning — not quite 7:30 — and I'd dropped off my Mighty Miata at the suburban agency for its 15,000-mile checkup. I walked almost a mile to the bus stop, and waited in the chill for transport into the city.

When the bus stopped, it already was crowded, but I managed to find a seat near the front, behind the driver. By the next stop, every seat was filled, and then people who boarded had to stand.

I felt uncomfortable, sitting there, while the female passengers stood. I started to stand up and give one of them my seat. But then I sat back down, still feeling uncomfortable, but this time for a different reason. No, this wasn't 1940, and I wasn't in my little hometown in the Midwest. This was 1991, and I was in the Big City.

The two were separated by more than time and distance. Now I didn't feel uncomfortable. I felt sad. So much had changed.

■

When I was growing up, I was taught — not just by my parents but by what seemed like the world — that a male immediately and willingly surrendered his seat on a bus to a female if no other seat was available.

I asked Dad why, and he said it was a sign of respect. A man should respect a woman, and this was one way to show respect. It was a lesson that I internalized quickly and deeply. Once when I was maybe 14 and taking my girlfriend home from a movie on the bus, I gave my seat next to her to a woman with a big package. Eventually, a seat opened up at the back of the bus, and I sat there, about 15 rows from my girlfriend, who subsequently told me that she was both pleased and distressed by my action.

"It's nice that you gave your seat to that woman, but I felt abandoned when you sat way back there. Couldn't you have stood next to my seat?"

I apologized. Back in those days I apologized a lot. It was something that I was taught to do. Polite people were quick to apologize if they messed up, and sometimes they even apologized if they hadn't messed up. I never understood that, but I didn't press it. After all, polite people weren't pushy.

When I was grown and out of the Midwest and into the South, I retained my politeness. Occasionally, somebody even called me a "Southern Gentleman," which I always took as a compliment, whether it was intended that way or not. I opened doors for women, pulled out chairs, walked on the street side of the sidewalk. I said "Yes, Ma'am" and "No, Ma'am"and if I didn't understand something, I said "Beg your pardon?" I never put down my coat to help a woman across a rain puddle, but it's something that I might have considered. That's how straight I was.

Then I left the South and came to the Big City in the Northeast. Times also changed. Politeness was out. People tended to react to it with suspicion or ridicule. Or they tried to take advantage of it.

If I let other people get on the elevator ahead of me, I found there was no room left for me. It was the same thing on the subway. The meek might inherit the Earth eventually, but they surely wouldn't make it onto the subway. I learned to push and shove and step on toes and if somebody snarled, I snarled back.

If I opened a door for a woman, I had to be prepared for a rebuff. "Really," the woman would say, "Do you think I'm incapable of opening my own door?" A lot of women said that. They really did. And eventually I came around to their way of thinking. "Forget it, lady." Occasionally, I still open doors, but mostly it's for men, who always seem appreciative. Not a single man ever said to me "Really, do you think I'm incapable of opening my own door?"

On the subway, after all the shoving and snarling, I never seriously considered giving up my seat to anybody — except once. That was to a woman who was carrying a big box and who looked to be eight and a half months pregnant. She seemed grateful, but the man standing next to me shook his head in what I took to be a gesture of dismay. Was I a rube who didn't know The Rules?

I learned The Rules. That's the sad part of it. I really did learn The Rules. When I came to Philadelphia 15 years ago, I was appalled by the behaviors that I encountered in so many people so much of the time. Then one day I realized that I had become one of them. I had assumed as my very own the behaviors that had been so abhorrent to me. To paraphrase Pogo: I had met the enemy, and he was me. Whatever happened to that Southern Gentleman?

■

The memories, recent and distant, washed over me. I sat there on the bus, thinking, wondering why I automatically had started to get up to surrender my seat to a woman. The answer, of course, was that I seldom ride the bus. Subway, yes. Bus, no. It's an unusual experience for me, and I was reacting as I would have back in the old days, when I was younger and when I often rode the bus.

The bus was packed now as it wound its way toward the central business district. I looked up and there was a woman, gray-haired, with rimless glasses. For an instant I thought she looked like my mother, the way I remember Mom from when I was a boy. Was the woman on her way to work? Mom worked retail for many years and, when Dad wasn't around to drive her, she took the bus, which stopped a block from the house.

I didn't make a conscious decision. I just got up and invited the woman to take my seat. At first she seemed not to understand what I was doing. Then she smiled and sat down.

"It's going to be a long day," she said, "and I'll be on my feet a lot, so I really appreciate the chance to sit down. Thank you."

I smiled back at her. I wanted to ask if she worked retail, but I didn't. I got off the bus before she did and I told her that I hoped she had a nice day.

I stood on the sidewalk and watched the bus disappear into traffic. The day barely had begun, but already it had been nice.

KINDERGARTEN FOR GROWNUPS
March 24, 1991

First there was a telephone call from Betsi Smith, who teaches kindergarten in the Abington Friends Lower School in Jenkintown. Would I like to join some other adults in her first "Kindergarten for Grown-ups"?

Yes, indeed, I told her. I couldn't think of many things I'd rather do. Just think of the possibilities a day in kindergarten would raise for contacting my inner child, the too-often-neglected little kid who lives somewhere within me and who, despite all the stuff I've laid on him, still knows how to have fun.

Then there was a form letter:

"I have carefully selected 10 of you, several in the field of education. Others include a musician, two homemakers (one of each gender), a chemist, a writer, an instructor of physics, a law student and a nun from a local parish. I feel I know each of you well enough to trust you will come ready to play, share and generally nurture that 5-year-old who lives, though often hides, in all of us. . . .

"With few exceptions, you will not be acquainted with the other 'children.' We will be using first names only and for one sweet morning it will not be important to know the others' backgrounds, careers or stock holdings. . . . Wear comfortable clothes and bring along your favorite mug (for hot cocoa), a show-and-tell item or story you cherish, your blankie and pillow, your willing child spirit."

And then, finally, there was my day in kindergarten. Wow!

■

Betsi Smith invited me to bring along a friend, and I asked Bob Katz, my cardiologist, who, better than almost anybody I know, has managed to hang on to his inner child and make instant connection with him when the going gets tough and he needs relief in a hurry.

Katz and I were the first children to arrive, wearing bluejeans and carrying our cocoa mugs and blankets. We made out our name tags — "Bobby" and

"Darl" — and then, as the others wandered in over the next 15 minutes, we listened as Smith, who has been a teacher for 22 years and who has two sons, explained how we would spend the morning.

In the beginning there would be "choice" — when we'd have the opportunity to do whatever we wanted — model with clay, fingerpaint, build with blocks, play games. Then we'd get in a circle for show and tell. Then we'd listen to a story and drink cocoa, and, finally, we'd take a nap.

It was time for "choice."

Bobby and many of the other children rushed to fingerpaint — mostly for the opportunity, it seemed to me, to get their hands all messy and sticky. I went straight to the modeling clay, put on a tiny apron and sat in a tiny chair at a tiny table. I closed my eyes.

"OK, remember when?"

It was almost as if it happened by magic. I was a little kid again, building a model airplane, a fighter-bomber. I shaped the fuselage out of green clay, the wings and tail assembly out of yellow clay. I examined it carefully. It wasn't bad — although my models were better when I was a little kid. I picked it up and took it over to Bobby, who had red paint up to his elbows.

"Bobby, will you paint a star on each wing?"

He smiled and with a forefinger made something that looked like a star to anybody who was willing to stretch the imagination.

I put the airplane back on the table. Then I made a picture book — with my very own pictures of Mommy and Daddy, a car, truck, chair, desk, cat, dog and a glass with a cherry at the bottom. Betsi Smith hadn't said much about my airplane. Quakers, after all, aren't into warfare. But she was ecstatic about my picture book.

"Oh, class, look at Darl's picture book. Isn't it nice?" She clapped her hands and the other children joined in.

It happened every time she held up somebody's project. Applause. Talk about positive reinforcement. Nobody said it wasn't good enough. Nobody said it was silly or inappropriate. Nobody said they could do it better. There is much to be said for positive reinforcement, and it's a shame that Corporate America, somewhere along the line, drifted away from it. And spouses, too. And parents. And . . .

Somebody made a fingerpainting of a flower with the word love under it and then sprinkled glitter into the soggy paint.

"Oh, class, look . . ." Ah, cheers, applause — and acceptance and recognition, without any qualification whatsoever.

Bobby moved to the chalkboard and carefully crafted an abstract drawing of the piano keyboard — he takes jazz piano lessons — with notes floating up and out of the drawing.

"Oh, class, look . . ." Applause.

A kid named Ed asked me to play marbles. With chalk he drew a ring on the playroom's carpet and dropped some marbles in. I hadn't shot marbles for 50 years, but . . . the old touch came right back. I didn't hit anything — except Ed's knee on the other side of the ring — but I had incredible velocity.

"If I ever make contact, I'll be unstoppable," I said.

"That's a big if," Ed said.

Bobby wanted to join us. He took a black marble and shot it . . . butterfingers.

That's a wimpy way to shoot, and, when I was a kid, I always looked for guys who shot butterfingers because they couldn't generate any velocity, and, in a big ring, they were out of it right from the beginning. So there was Bob Katz, the cardiologist who helped save my life, and he was shooting marbles butterfingers. What disillusionment.

"Bobby, I wish you hadn't asked us if you could play," I said.

"Shut up and shoot," he said.

It was show-and-tell time. I read a passage from my treasured Zane Grey book, *The Red-Headed Outfield*, copyright 1920. Almost nobody knows it, but before he wrote westerns, Zane Grey wrote baseball books for boys. I finished the reading and — applause.

Bobby read a poem. A woman showed a plant she had nurtured from a sprout. Another woman showed a purple stone. Two women displayed teddy bears. A man produced a blanket that had been with him from childhood — when he was in a Japanese prisoner-of-war camp in the Dutch West Indies.

We sipped our cocoa. We sang a song about a woman who ate a fly, then the spider that chased the fly, the mouse that chased the spider, the cat that chased the mouse, the dog that . . .

Betsi Smith asked us to close our eyes and drift along with the mental picture she was painting:

"You're walking in your favorite place and all of a sudden you see steps that descend. You go down the steps and there's a body of water . . . and a rowboat there waiting for you. You get in the boat and begin to row. . . . You see an island and, as you get closer, you see a small child on the island. The child is turned away from you. You get out of the boat and approach the child and, when the child turns around, you know that the child is you — when you were 5 years old. The child cries, 'You never play with me anymore.' You rush to the child, and the process of getting reacquainted begins. . . . "

What a wonderful story. What a powerful image. What an essential message. I looked around the room, and a woman seemed to be on the verge of tears. I understood why.

It was nap time. Betsi Smith turned out the lights and put on quiet new-age music, as we stretched out on our blankets. She came around to each child and asked, "Would you like me to cover you up?" She gave me a choice of three stuffed animals to snuggle with. I chose what looked like a penguin. "Oh, that's the mommy," she said. I went to sleep. I actually went to sleep.

When I awoke, it was time to go. Bobby had to get to his jazz piano lesson. I had a midafternoon appointment. Suddenly, we were adults again, looking at our wristwatches and pocket calendars.

We gathered up our stuff and Betsi Smith invited us to come back anytime we wanted, anytime we wanted — or needed — to be kids again.

Bobby didn't want to leave.

"Come on, Bobby, act your age," I admonished. "You're a big boy now."

"Shut up . . . and where do you get off calling me butterfingers?"

We walked out into bright sunshine, got into my car and put on a big-band tape for the drive back into the city.

"What do you think?" I asked.

"I loved it," he said. "Let's do it again."

I loved it, too, and I'd like to do it again. There was something about this experience that was powerful enough to allow me to give up power without feeling stripped. I was a little kid again. The world was not competitive. I was accepted — not for what I did but for who I was. People expected nothing from me and, because they expected nothing, I felt eager to give them everything: unconditional approval.

It was a look at life the way it used to be — uncomplicated, cheerful, growth-producing. For a few hours business was not as usual because there was no business — except having fun. What a change. What a treat — like a big red sucker that lasts half the day.

It was glorious. Really.

HEEDING LIFE'S BEACONS
July 9, 1991

Wise men tell us that, as we go through life, we will encounter from time to time beacons that will offer information on how we're doing — whether we're gaining ground or losing ground or standing still. The trick, we're told, is to recognize these beacons when they appear, pay attention to them, and act on what they tell us by making whatever life adjustments are called for.

I think that for many years I ignored many of the beacons — sometimes because I didn't see them, sometimes because I didn't like what they were trying to tell me. But the other day when a beacon appeared, I paid attention, and I want to share the experience with you — one of those peak moments that from time to time happen to all of us, if we're lucky.

■

I'd been on the driving range for more than an hour, hitting golf balls and grumbling to a friend that "my problem is that I'm hitting it like a writer — not like a golfer." He said, "It can't be that bad," but after watching me hook a few more drives he remarked, "Yes, I see what you mean."

He and I were going to play nine holes after we finished at the driving range, but he had to leave early, and so I had a choice. I could hit more golf balls — and presumably grumble more — or I could play by myself, six holes, and then quit, since my house is beside the sixth green.

I decided to play by myself.

I squinted down the fairway, into the late-afternoon sun that exploded like an orange ball through the trees. I teed up my ball, and there they were, coming out of the shadows, a man and a woman, playing ahead of me, two-thirds of the way to the green. I watched the woman swing and, oh, heavens, she hit the ball about 20 yards. The man didn't hit his ball much farther. It was going to be a slow round — but maybe they'd wave me through.

I hit my tee shot down the middle and then hooked a 7-iron onto a mound to the left of the green. The couple had putted out and moved to the second tee, across the road. I wedged the ball 10 feet from the hole and 2-putted for a bogey. I walked across the road, and the couple had just left the tee. Now, for sure, they'd ask me to play through.

But they didn't ask. They seemed unaware that anybody was behind them. The woman was lining up her second shot. Thud! Another 20-yard boomer.

In my previous life, this would have driven me crazy. I'd have yelled at them and asked if I could go ahead and hit. I'd have fumed. But instead I watched a duck paddle slowly across the pond that wraps around the tee. He had a shiny green head, almost metallic, and it glistened in the sunlight as he climbed out of the water and waddled across the tee, right in front of me.

"Hi, duck."

"Quack."

It was quiet, peaceful, serene. I felt happy, lucky to be alive. I went up the hill after my hooked tee shot, and when I looked back, I was almost overwhelmed by the beauty of what I saw — the long shadows that blended into the water, the brilliant green of the freshly cut grass, the exploding flowers in a rainbow of colors. I waited for the couple to move out of range. I heard myself humming. I hit a practice pitch shot. I hummed some more.

I played that hole and then another. It was getting darker. Did it matter if I played six holes? No, it didn't matter. If daylight ran out, I'd just walk home. I stood on the fourth tee and looked into the wooded field to my right. What was that? Movement. A deer. Then more movement. Another deer. And, finally, a third deer.

They were coming in my direction. Didn't they see me?

I remained motionless. Now the distance was down to 50 yards, and still they walked toward me. I could hear the sounds their hooves made as they moved through the grass. They were out of the field now and on the golf course, in front of the tee, no more than 15 yards from me.

Two of the deer continued to walk, but the third one stopped and looked directly at me with big brown eyes. He — or she — jerked in what seemed to be a reaction of surprise but didn't bolt. It was incredible, like on the beach last summer when I unexpectedly came upon a deer in early morning. The third deer moved off to join the other two, and then they galloped into some trees a hundred yards away.

Isn't nature grand?

I looked up and there was a hot-air balloon, red and silver, low enough that I could see the person in the gondola wave at me. I waved back.

Could anything be better than this?

My tee shot disappeared into the dusk. Not a bad shot, but what difference did it make? I played out the hole and then talked to a goose on the next tee. The goose — he or she — looked up long enough to acknowledge my presence and then went back to rooting around in the grass.

"Hi, goose."

"Honk."

It was too dark to finish playing. I walked home, humming, happy, satisfied.

■

That was the beacon, my awareness of the mega-change in my attitude and in my behavior. It wasn't an act. I hadn't willed it. It just happened.

Why? I thought about that for a long time. If I go to the golf course to play golf, I become furious if I get behind slow players. But if I go to the golf course to enjoy the experience of being there, if I immerse myself in the moment, I can get back something that is far more meaningful than any score I could post.

What I can get back is myself, Darrell, the boy, whose eyes were wide with amazement, curiosity and thanks as he viewed the world, who appreciated what was, instead of lamenting what was not.

It was a profound reality check, my beacon, and like so many good things, it came when I least expected it.

How about you? Any beacons?

'JUST:' A LOADED WORD
September 18, 1984

A long time ago, when I was a journalism student, I believed almost everything that big people told me. Then one day, I executed what for me was a major rebellion. I suggested to a journalism teacher that he might be standing in a ditch.

What prompted such out-of-character behavior?

The teacher was lecturing on the evils of "loaded words" — words that imply far more meaning than the writer usually intends. Words like:

Admit. Did the fellow admit it — or did he say it? Admitting something tends to convey that the fellow was backed into the corner because somebody had the goods on him, and he had no choice but to come clean.

Deny. Did he deny that he was there — or did he say that he was not there? There's a world of difference in meaning between the two words because, in the minds of many, deny suggests that the fellow is trying to hide something.

Leer. If he really leered, it's OK to say so, but how can you be sure? Maybe that's how he always looks at people. Anybody who leers is usually thought to be evil to the core — so be careful.

Refute. Did he really refute it — or did he disagree with it? When somebody refutes something, he proves that it's not true. This is vastly different from claiming that it's not true.

Just. This can be — and often is — a term of "deprecation," and unless that's what the writer means, he should stay away from it because . . .

Hold it, hold it, teacher. I don't agree with that. "Just" isn't loaded — not like those other words. What's "deprecation" got to do with it anyway? You're just trying to show off. Ah, ha, how do you like that? Just trying to show off. Pretty good, eh?

Oh, the rigid righteousness of youth. Now that years have passed and gray hairs have sprouted — and now that I'm tuned in to the ramifications of "depre-cation" — I understand what the fellow meant. I agree with him. Boy, do I agree with him. "Just" is a word that should be banned from everybody's vocabulary — even from the language.

■

A long, long time ago, when Og the cave man took his wife, Ogga, to the plan-et's first cocktail party, it is probable that somebody came up to her, swirled his drink nattily and asked, "Tell me, Ogga, what do you do?"

It's also highly probable that Ogga answered, "Oh, I'm just a cave wife."

While it's not recorded in history books, this undoubtedly was the beginning of what later became, "Oh, I don't do much of anything; I'm *just* a housewife and mother."

Does the woman mean that she's just rearing tomorrow's leaders? Yes, unfor-tunately, that's exactly what she means. She is deprecating herself up to her eyeballs — and she couldn't announce it with more vigor if she pinned a sign on her blouse: "I don't amount to anything." Did you ever hear anybody say, "Oh, I'm *just* an astronaut"?

■

I had agreed to speak at a family forum meeting that was being held in an auditorium at Temple University, and the advance literature had identified me as editor of my newspaper's family department.

I arrived for the speech, and the first order of business was to tell the chairman, "Hey, I'm not editor of the department; I'm a columnist in the department."

The man nodded his understanding, mounted the platform and, in introduc-ing me, said: "Mr. Sifford tells me that he is not editor of the department but just a columnist."

Would you call it overreaction if I told you that I began my speech this way: "No, damn it, I'm not *just* a columnist in the department; I am a columnist in the department"?

The man's expression told me that he didn't have the slightest idea of what was going on — except that I suddenly had gone mad for no apparent reason.

■

Ring. Ring. Ring.

It was later that same afternoon, and I was at home in the condominium, working on another speech.

"Hello."

"Is this Mr. Sifford?"

"Yes, madam, this is he."

"My husband is having a problem, and he has agreed to see you. You're the only therapist that he trusts enough to see. What are your office hours?"

"Madam, I don't have office hours. I mean I'm not a therapist. I'm a writer, and sometimes I interview therapists."

"You're not a therapist?"

"No, madam, I'm not."

"You're just a writer?"

"No, I'm not *just* a writer. I am a writer."

53

"Well, I don't know why you're so uppity about it. You probably wouldn't have been a good therapist anyway. I'm glad my husband didn't come to you."

"Goodbye, madam."

■

Ring. Ring. Ring.

Next day, 10:30 a.m., at the office. Yes, I really do have office hours, but they're hours for writing, not for dispensing therapy — except to myself.

"Hello."

"Mr. Sifford?"

"This is he."

"Look, I need to ask you about something. I'm just a reader, but I wondered if . . ."

"Please don't say that you're *just* a reader. I need you. You're not *just* a reader to me; you're a very important person."

"I am?"

"What can I do for you?"

"Why do you think I'm so important?"

"It's a long story. How much time do you have?"

■

And so there you have it, the straight-from-the-horse's-mouth story of why I have declared war on "just," why I am trying mightily to keep it forever out of my writing and out of my language. Yes, I am somewhat crazy about it, and occasionally it shows in my behavior.

Just (oops!) the other day we had some folks over for brunch, and I overheard part of a conversation between two of the guests who didn't know each other:

"What do you do?

"I'm a psychologist."

"A department chairman, perhaps?"

"No, I'm just a therapist."

I couldn't control myself. "Whadda you mean — just a therapist? What's the matter? Don't you like yourself?"

The two guests exchanged glances that silently agreed, "Yes, sometimes he acts a little strange, but overall he's a decent enough fellow."

The psychologist squared his shoulders and spoke to me, "I said what I meant to say. I'm a little down today, and I'm feeling like I'm just a therapist. Is that quite all right with you?"

I refilled his bloody Mary glass and carried some empty bottles to the trash chute. Being righteous and standing up for what you believe surely can offend some people, can't it? It just doesn't seem right.

Oops, again. But I'll keep trying.

'LOCALS' AND 'COSMOPOLITANS'
March 12, 1984

The year was 1962, and at age 30 I was faced with what I considered the first crisis of my career: I needed a change, and in the newspaper business change almost always means relocation.

I was managing editor of the newspaper in my home town in Missouri — the place where my lifelong friends and my parents lived, where my kids could walk to the neighborhood school, where I had built what I thought was my forever house, where the golf course on which I played forgave my scattergun shots.

I struggled with the decision — even though intellectually I knew that it was a choice between staying and risking stagnation and leaving and risking growth. Why did I struggle? Because I was afraid, afraid that I wouldn't be able to make new friends, wouldn't be accepted, wouldn't be good enough to prosper in what I considered the fast league of journalism in Louisville.

Although I didn't know it at the time, I was a classic example of a Local.

■

The year was 1966, and at age 34 I was faced with what I considered the second crisis of my career: I needed another change.

But this time there was no fear and very little uncertainty about moving to another city. Yes, it meant leaving a second "forever" house, but there always would be another — and new friends, too. I went to Charlotte without missing a beat, and 10 years later, when it was time to pull up roots again, I steamed north to Philadelphia — with feelings not of anxiety but of anticipation.

Although I didn't know it at the time, I had become a classic example of a Cosmopolitan.

■

I heard about Locals and Cosmopolitans not long ago from my wife, who had participated in a seminar directed by Fritz Steele, the widely known organizational consultant who has written half a dozen books on how to make the wheels turn more smoothly in the wonderful world of big business.

Yes, Steele was saying, there really are two kinds of people, Locals and Cosmopolitans, and one way to distinguish them is to examine their attitudes toward work. The Local tends to ask, "What can I do for the company?" and "Am I right for the job?" The Cosmopolitan asks those questions, too, plus two more: "What can the company do for me?" and "Is the job right for me?"

What it all added up to, said Steele, was that Locals and Cosmopolitans had opposing philosophies that, in fact, extended far beyond work and shaped entire approaches to life.

For reasons that I never understood, the terminology wrapped itself around me, and I began to apply to people I knew either the Local or the Cosmopolitan label.

When I shared the concept with some therapists, they immediately understood it and embraced it — even though they said that they'd never heard of it before. During one interview, a psychologist even started peppering his stories with Locals and Cosmopolitans because, he said, the terms succinctly described mindsets that everybody could grasp.

"The Cosmopolitan person is the first to order at a restaurant — without waiting to see what anybody else orders," the psychologist said. "The Local waits" — as if he needs permission to order lobster or something else that's expensive.

Yes, there's no doubt about it, Fritz Steele, you've really started something.

The fact is, said Steele in an interview, he really didn't start anything at all. The terms Local and Cosmopolitan come from "traditional sociology . . . and they must be 40 or 50 years old. They're so common in beginning sociology that they're taken for granted," and nobody is quite sure who first plugged them into the language.

"As I use them, they describe how people behave in the organization," said Steele, who is a principal in the Portsmouth Consulting Group of Portsmouth, N.H., but who works out of Boston.

The Cosmopolitan, he said, is "willing to take risks, to assume unpopular stands. If he's asked to do something that he considers unprofessional, he's willing to say: 'No, I won't do that.' On the other hand the Local tends to say: 'OK, I'm the employee, and my first job is to obey. I'll do it.' What we have here are two very different notions."

Why Locals and Cosmopolitans behave so differently can be traced at least in part to the foundation of self-identity, said Steele. Like almost everything else, much of it can be attributed to parenting. "The Local gets his identity from a sense of belonging . . . to a community. He has the experience of being rooted. 'This is my home; this is my tradition.' From this he builds his identity, and 'who I am' is to a great extent 'where I am.' "

But the Cosmopolitan is "clearly passing through. 'I'm here now, but I may need to change later.' He's had practice moving, and he's probably more confident of his ability to make new friends." His basic identity is built on what he can do — not on where he does it.

It must be emphasized, said Steele, that Locals and Cosmopolitans come in all shapes and sizes, that one is not inherently better than the other. They tend to be equally well educated, and the issue, he repeated, is "how I get my identity" — not "how competent I am."

It seems obvious, said Steele, that personality "plays a part. The Cosmopolitan feels more secure. He gets his strength from himself . . . and, as a result, he's not pushed into as many corners. He may like it where he is, but he can stand to leave" if the ball isn't bouncing in his direction. The Local often will bite his lip and stay, but "a Local can get fed up, too, and at times take risks. At this point, the difference may depend on how he feels about moving. He may be more uncomfortable" than the Cosmopolitan — although outwardly they can appear to be in lockstep.

It's possible, said Steele, for somebody to remain in the same city for a lifetime and still be a Cosmopolitan — if he stays because he feels that he's getting what he wants from the organization. But he could leave, and he never forgets it. Conversely, a Local could remain a Local through several moves — if he retained the fundamental mindset that he was owned by the organization.

Is there a blueprint for a Local to follow if he wants to become a Cosmopolitan?

Yes, said Steele, and it centers on "becoming aware of your strengths and what you can do, with realizing that new bonds can be built somewhere else, with believing that nothing is a total disaster, that change is not catastrophic."

Are Locals and Cosmopolitans about even in number?

Nobody has run a head count, but Steele's guess is that Locals are in the vast majority, probably 80 to 20 over the Cosmopolitans.

WHAT IS A HERO MADE OF?
March 9, 1982

He was only a year or two out of high school, but now here he was — a Navy frogman on a scouting mission along a desolate stretch of Vietnamese shoreline.

The scouting party had not expected to encounter the enemy, but the crackling of rifles and the whine of machine-gun slugs murderously announced the ambush. Death was all around, and the young frogman charged blindly back toward the water, running, turning to shoot, running. He was a magnificent swimmer and if he made the water, he could swim the 500 yards out to the ship from which the party had been launched.

As he fired a final burst, he saw the young lieutenant topple into the sand a hundred yards back up the beach. He had fallen the way a dead man falls, and the frogman instinctively wanted to retrieve his body.

"It just didn't seem right to leave his body out there," the frogman said later. So he put down his weapon and dashed back up the beach, dodging bullets that kicked up sand all around him. He reached the bloody body, seized it in a fireman's carry and started running again toward the water — through an indescribable hail of steel. Only when they were at water's edge did the frogman become aware that the lieutenant was not dead. He was critically wounded, but he was alive.

The frogman bound the lieutenant's arms around his neck and began to swim mightily through the icy water as the Vietnamese, from the shoreline, peppered gunfire toward them. He swam and swam . . . and finally he reached the safety of the vessel.

The frogman had saved the lieutenant's life, and he had become a classic American war hero. He was invited to the White House, where the President looped the Medal of Honor over his head. Then he came home to rural South Carolina, which is where I interviewed him.

No, he said, he didn't consider himself a hero. He was just doing what needed to be done. The lieutenant, he was sure, would have done the same thing for him.

I asked if he hadn't been concerned that he would be killed trying to rescue what he thought was a dead body.

No, he said, he'd not even thought about death. It never entered his mind.

The wire services hummed their stories about a hero on the afternoon of January 14:

"A middle-aged passenger on a downed Air Florida jet repeatedly gave up a lifeline thrown to him in the ice-clogged Potomac River so five other persons might live. . . . And while the others were carried to safety, the unknown hero quietly slipped beneath the water. . . . 'I've never seen anybody with that commitment,' a paramedic said. 'He gave the ultimate. He was a true gentleman and a hero in my eyes.' "

What is a hero made of? Why is he willing to jeopardize himself for the sake of others? Is he even aware of what he is doing?

I took my questions to Dr. Adrian Copeland, who is clinical professor of psychiatry and human behavior at Jefferson Medical College. Here is some of what he said:

Not uncommonly, heroic behavior results from a bargain that a person strikes with himself without being aware of it. "He gets something back from the group, perhaps admiration. If his life has been devoid of admiration, if he's been neglected, one of 13 children whose mother abandoned them, well, here's a chance for him to get admiration . . . by running faster than anybody else, by shooting more of the enemy — by doing whatever the situation calls for.

"It's a tradeoff: admiration in exchange for personal sacrifice for the good of the group. And people do it in the way they know best. If it's an aggressive person in wartime, he destroys others — and the group pays him back in admiration. He's willing to pay the cost, which is personal jeopardy, to get the admiration."

It's also not uncommon, Copeland said, for heroic behavior to be thought out beforehand to some extent. "You take that guy [Lenny Skutnik] who leaped into the Potomac River and pulled out the woman after the plane crash. Why did he do it? Perhaps it was the recognition of his strength and how this related to the size of the task. Perhaps he felt he could do it. He was in good shape . . . and a strong swimmer. Perhaps he felt that he could spend 43 seconds in the icy water without particular risk to himself. That's heroic behavior with calculated minimal risk."

What about the still-unidentified passenger who kept passing the lifeline to others? Was it possible that he miscalculated his ability to survive and paid for the error with his life?

We'll never know, Copeland said. "Was he willing to sacrifice his life because he had terminal cancer and was going to die anyway? Did he pass the lifeline because he was a powerful swimmer who thought the risk to him was minimal? Was he looking for praise and adoration" and a chance to break out of what he perceived as a dull life?

It's a fact, Copeland said, that many of us search for opportunities to seize "our finest hour . . . so that we can look back 35 years later and tell our grandchildren about it."

It's also possible, he said, that the man in the water — or any hero, for that matter — could have thought that everybody else deserved to live more than he did. "Some see themselves as dispensable and think that others are more important" — and their heroic deeds can be a manifestation of this downgrading of themselves.

Why people become heroes is exceedingly complex, Copeland said, and to a great extent it's not really important because "in our system we are less concerned with motivation for behavior and more concerned with behavior. The man in the water was laudable even if he was sick and going to die next week from cancer."

But, Dr. Copeland, don't life-jeopardizing heroics run contrary to man's burning instinct for self-preservation?

The survival instinct is important, he said, but not necessarily survival in a physical sense. "You have to deal with the transcendental idea," where a mother who runs into a burning house to save her child may be willing to sacrifice her body so that her spirit can continue to live in the child. In World War II, the Japanese kamikaze pilots were willing to sacrifice their bodies to be "venerated in heaven and by their country. The spirit transcends the body. . . . Yes, we talk about the preservation instinct, but for some it means the preservation of the spirit in a transcendental way."

Some people become heroes, Copeland said, because they have "a naive sense of omnipotence. This is characteristic of the adolescent phase of development, but usually it's eroded with the passage of time. It gets whittled down with experience." But some people carry feelings of omnipotence into adulthood, and "they think nothing bad will happen to them. They think they can do [dangerous things] without getting killed. Maybe this stems from overestimation of capability, but feelings of omnipotence could prompt this."

It's possible, he said, that the Medal of Honor winner I interviewed had felt omnipotent — or maybe he simply had confidence that he possessed physical stamina that was more than equal to the task. The reasons, Copeland repeated, don't really matter.

Is hero worship realistic?

Yes, it is, Copeland said. "It's realistic to worship at the shrine of altruistic behavior. In America, we don't have the philosophy of the Chinese that life is cheap. Here, God is love; altruism is primary; we're taught to love our neighbor. Kids grow up with that philosophy. It's almost genetic. You may not ever explain it to your kids, but they know it anyway."

As a result, Copeland said, hero worship is inevitable. And it's not bad. No, it's not bad at all.

REMEMBERING MY 'FIELD OF DREAMS'
July 15, 1990

It was a Sunday afternoon, bright sunshine, no wind, almost 90 degrees, and I was half an hour early for the faculty meeting that was launching the 33d annual St. Davids Christian Writers Conference at Eastern College. My assignment: to teach five segments on nonfiction writing during the week.

I'd been to Eastern College in St. Davids, about a 40-minute drive from Philadelphia, a few times before — to lecture to clergy people who were enrolled in a doctoral-degree program — but I'd never had time to walk around the campus. Today I had time . . . and so I walked.

Over there, right down that path, was a footbridge that crossed the end of a pond. That looked like a good place to walk. Golly, look at those two white swans . . . and listen to the water as it trickles out of the pond, goes down over the rocks and into a creek. What a sight. What a sound.

The path meandered around the pond and then up some wooden steps, and then . . .

On the left were four tennis courts, two of which were occupied by women players. On the right was — a baseball park.

I walked down the embankment along the first-base line and examined the field. The bases were in position. And the pitcher's rubber, atop a mound that was elevated at least 18 inches. The outfield was enclosed with a chain-link fence, six feet high. The signs showed that the leftfield line went 326 feet, right-field 322. The long part of the park was right-center, 370 feet.

It was, by appearance and dimension, a real baseball park, with real grass that now was in need of mowing.

The white heads of clover blooms dotted the outfield and the infield, too. "A good park to bunt in," I told myself. "They'd lose the ball in the clover."

I walked over to a folding chair at the end of the players' bench and put my briefcase on it. Then I went to the plate, positioned myself with an imaginary bat, waggled it a time or two, and looked up at the mound. It seemed incredibly close, almost on top of me. "That can't be 60 feet." I stepped off 20 paces. It was 60 feet.

The outfield looked close, too, even out at the 370-foot sign. "It's from playing golf," I told myself. "That's a good shot with a baseball, but in golf it's only a wedge." I had forgotten what a baseball field felt like — because I hadn't been on one for 15 years, since the end of my son Grant's pitching career after a car accident.

But how could I forget?

After all, for so many years baseball was my life — through three American Legion seasons and then into semi-pro play that went through college and two years beyond. How could I forget?

I walked down to third base. I'd played a year there in a championship season when we had somebody else who could play first base, my position, but nobody who could play third. I stood there, crouched, looked to my left, and there was Russell Desseaux, the shortstop, red hat pulled far down over his eyes. When the game was on the line, you wanted them to hit it to Russell, who ate ground balls the way the rest of us ate Wheaties — with gusto.

"Soft hands," he told me. "You got to have soft hands to pick up ground balls."

Russell's hands were soft.

Crack!

I lunged for the smash to my left, but I wasn't quick enough. The ball was past me and into the outfield. That's two runs for sure, and we're going to lose . . . but there was Russell, deep in the hole, backhanding the ball, setting his right foot and throwing a rocket to first base. The game was over, and we'd won. Once again, we had won.

I looked again, and Russell was gone. Whatever happened to Russell?

I walked into the outfield, toward the 370-foot sign, turned around and looked back at the plate.

Crack!

The ball was screaming into the gap. That would score two, maybe three, runs. It would be an uphill fight from here on because nobody got many runs off the guy they had pitching.

Leon Green seemed to be moving before the batter ever hit the ball, moving into right-center, swiftly, decisively. Leon never ran. Rather, he glided, but he always got there, usually with time to spare. But now there was no time. He was straining . . . and he and the ball arrived at the fence together. The ball disappeared into Leon's big brown glove. He hit the fence, fell down, bounced up and came running in, white teeth gleaming against his suntanned face. Leon, why did you have to die? You were so young.

I stood at first base, now covered by shadows, my position. So many seasons. So many chances. So many . . .

Crack!

I turned to my right, but the ball was past me. "I should of had it."

"Rockin' chair!" screamed a voice from the grandstand. "Get him a rockin' chair! He can't move!"

I came to bat in the next inning, and the voice sounded again in my ear. "Rockin' chair!" The crowd picked up the chant: "Rockin' chair! Rockin' chair! Strike out rockin' chair!"

On a 3-2 curveball I struck out. "Rockin' chair! Rockin' chair!"

I went back to the plate, past my briefcase on the folding chair. I stood in the batter's box and examined the pitcher, tall, slender, maybe 35 years old. Three years ago, they said, he was in the White Sox organization, Triple A, but now here he was in . . . What was the name of that town anyway?

The first pitch was a fastball, thigh high, and I took it. The next pitch was in the same groove, and I drove it over the centerfield fence, a three-run homer.

The next inning, the 35-year-old pitcher singled. I came over to hold him on the bag, and he squinted at me and said, "Kid, you got trouble." I said, "Looks to me like you got trouble. You're behind, 3-0." He said, "Nobody takes me out of the park like that."

The next time I came up, he hit me with a fastball on the left shoulder. The time after that, he stuck the fastball in my ribs. Oh, man, does that hurt, but you don't rub it. That's part of how the game is played. You don't rub it, no matter what.

Ninth inning, score tied, 3-3, bases loaded. I'm up. Well, for sure he won't hit me this time. He struck me out on three curveballs.

In one game, I got two doubles and a home run off a pitcher who once was with the Washington Senators, and after the game he told me, "Kid, you're a hell of a hitter," but I wasn't — not against good curveballs.

I played until those curveballs got me. It was awesome, trying to stand in there for a tight pitch that exploded down and away, dropping right off the table.

I quit and took up golf.

■

I sat down on the folding chair. Birds chirped in the trees beyond the outfield fence. Shadows lengthened across the infield.

Thud. Thud. It was the women on the tennis court, pounding the green ball.

I looked back at the baseball field, and I saw all of them, the faces, young, smiling, just kids. All of us, just kids — Russell, Leon, Bus, Hugh, Frank, Wyman, Auggie, Mel, Kenny, Marty, Eddie, Richie, Connie. It was my Field of Dreams, come to life, just a stone's throw from the pond with the two white swans.

Crack! The ball was screaming over the bag, hooking from the lefthander's bat. I went after it, headfirst, and it stuck in the top of my Elbie Fletcher-model Trapper's mitt. I was on my knees, 20 feet behind the bag, and Connie Buersmeyer was off the mound and running toward first. I gave him the ball at his belt, quick enough by half a step.

We win! Again. We always win the close ones. That's what it takes, winning the close ones, to make a championship season.

■

A long time ago, in the days of black-and-white television, I watched a show that featured oldtime sports heroes who narrated film clips of their greatest moments. I poked fun at how they could remember every pitch they ever hit or threw, the count, the inning, the score. How could they remember . . . after so many years? Why didn't they get on with their lives and stop living in the past? Why didn't they grow up and accept reality? They weren't kids anymore.

I sat on the folding chair and thought about that. I don't live in the past. I've surely gotten on with my life. Yet . . . incredibly, I, too, remember the pitches, some of them, the count, the inning, the score.

It's all up there, engraved forever in the brain, and all it takes to unlock the door is the right key. This ballpark — this marvelous ballpark beyond the pond with the two white swans — was for me the right key on a Sunday afternoon with bright sunshine, no wind, almost 90 degrees.

Not kids anymore? Who do I think I'm fooling?

We're all kids, and, if we're lucky, we always will be.

I walked back to the building for the faculty meeting.

"Where you been?" somebody asked.

"Over there."

"What have you been doing?"

"Remembering."

THE MISSING DAY IN MY LIFE
September 17, 1989

Friday, June 16, 1989. It's a missing day in my life — the day I underwent triple-bypass surgery after suffering a heart attack two months earlier.

They had told me that the day would be pretty much a blank for me — and they were right. I shaved and showered before 6 a.m., gulped a pill and took a shot that, they said, would put me in the proper frame of mind. Then I hopped on the gurney to go to surgery.

"Good luck," said a white-jacketed man who patted me on the shoulder.

We were in the surgery room.

"It's time," somebody said.

"OK."

"See you later, Mr. Sifford."

"Goodbye."

■

Somebody was softly shaking my shoulder.

"OK, Mr. Sifford, time to wake up. Can you hear me?"

I couldn't talk because I had a tube down my throat. I nodded. I knew that I was in the intensive care unit not far from the surgical suites — because that's where they had told me I would be taken.

Everything looked dark to me.

Later, I found out that almost 10 hours had passed since the man in the white jacket had wished me good luck.

What happened during the surgery? What exactly had they done to me?

It was something that I felt a powerful need to know more about. They had explained it to me, beforehand, in all the detail that I had requested. They had drawn for me pictures and more pictures. They had shown me a film. But I needed still more. What I needed was the opportunity to experience what had happened to me, to hear the sounds, smell the odors, see the masked faces and the gloved hands.

Especially, I needed a wide-awake encounter with The Saw — which in my pre-surgery dreams I had envisioned as a giant circular saw by Black & Decker. It was going to descend upon my bare chest and split my breastbone. The Saw became the centerpiece of my fear. The surgery was long ago finished, and the chest incision had healed completely — but the memory of the dreams was as fresh as ever. I needed to come to terms with The Saw.

On the morning of Wednesday, August 16, I had the opportunity. The surgeon who had operated on me, Clark Hargrove, invited me to put on a green surgical suit and stand beside him at Presbyterian-University of Pennsylvania Medical Center while he performed two open-heart operations. I'd witnessed surgery up close before, but never anything like this.

■

Hargrove is 42, a North Carolina native who had been described to me by cardiologist Bob Katz as a "lean Rhett Butler." He wears a handlebar mustache that gives the impression that he's smiling all the time, and it would be safe to say that his appearance probably is at odds with many people's preconceived notion of what a heart surgeon looks like. A former patient told me that Hargrove "looks like he should be singing to you instead of operating on you."

But operate he does — about 250 times a year. "It's as many as I want to do," he said. "If I did more, I wouldn't be able to keep up with the patients. It would become an assembly-line procedure, and to me that's not medicine."

Before and after my surgery, Hargrove spent as much time with me as I asked for to answer my questions. I wanted to know about The Saw. "No, it's not what you think it is," he said. I wanted to know about the blockage in the right artery that had forced my heart attack. Hargrove had promised that he would, if he

63

could, take it out.

"Did you get it out?" I asked.

Yes, it had popped right out after he slit open the artery, he said. It was a perfect mold of the inside of the artery, about 2.5mm wide, two inches long, and "it looked like a piece of yellow concrete."

"But I've been so careful about my diet for so many years," I said. "When could the concrete have begun to form?"

His answer chilled me. "Maybe when you were 10."

■

The man on the operating table is 53 years old. He's had a heart attack, and he's going to receive a triple bypass.

His body is draped in a green blanket that has a plastic-covered slot right over the center of the chest, where the incision will be made. Hargrove stands on the left side of the patient, and the surgeon who is assisting, Bob Villare, stands on the right side. At the bottom of the table is certified physician's assistant Ogden Gorham, who already has begun removing a 2-foot-long section of leg vein that will be used to bypass the blocked sections of the coronary arteries.

Hargrove and Villare adjust the overhead lights, ask nurses to plug in the doctors' fiber-optic headlamps.

"May I start?" asks Hargrove, seemingly to nobody in particular. "Knife, please."

The incision is made through the plastic slot with bold, swift strokes, and the wound is sponged clean of blood and cauterized.

"Saw, please."

Here it comes, The Saw. It looks like a huge stapling gun, silver colored, with a blue cord snaking out of the bottom. The vertical blade, which cuts by oscillation, looks almost too fragile for the task at hand. Hargrove hooks the blade into a notch at the top of the breastbone, and The Saw whines to life. With a steady pull, Hargrove guides it downward to the tip of the breastbone. The cut is almost a foot long, through half-inch bone, and it is completed in less than 10 seconds. Neat. Tidy. Not really the stuff of which nightmares are made, but, it's enough to cause me to wince.

Hargrove wonders where the perfusionist is — the person who operates the heart-lung machine that will do the heart's work during the operation.

The retractor is placed over the wound, and the chest is ratcheted open, revealing the pericardium, the sac that surrounds the heart. Hargrove cuts through the sac, stitches up two sides of it to the chest wall to form a cradle that lifts the heart and puts it in a better position for Hargrove's work.

The heart — the symbol of life and love — is pumping away, creating ripples in its exterior of purple, yellow and white. It is about the size of a clenched fist.

"Go on bypass, please."

The lines from the body to the heart-lung machine turn red, and the heart, now empty of blood, goes flat, like a punctured balloon, reduced in size by about two-thirds. By now the body has been cooled to about 80 degrees, creating a sort of suspended animation to reduce metabolic demands.

Ogden Gorham has the vein out of the leg, and "it's a beauty." But the internal mammary artery in the chest, which would have been used for the third bypass, is "not any good. It looks diseased," says Villare. They'll have to make all three grafts from the leg vein. "In about 5 percent of cases you can't use the mammary artery," says Villare. "This certainly is one of them."

"Let me have my glasses, please," Hargrove says.

Eyeglasses with built-in magnifying lenses are set on Hargrove's nose for the delicate work that is to come.

The heart arteries are tiny purple rivulets that meander down the heart. Hargrove punches a hole in an artery, above the point at which the angiogram revealed the blockage. He's working from memory now. Swiftly he sews in a piece of leg vein, six or seven stitches on each side.

Fluid is pumped into the bypass to check for leakage. It spurts out. There is a leak.

"I need to make another stitch."

The stitch breaks.

"Shoot." Hargrove puts in another one.

Now the bypasses are all sewn in, and the drainage tubes are forced into position. "Some people say the worst part is getting the tubes pulled out," Hargrove says to me. "Did you think so?"

"No, the guy who pulled them out did it very quickly, with one big jerk. There was some momentary discomfort, that's all."

The pericardium is stitched back together. The retractor is removed, and the breastbone is wired together with stainless steel.

"Will the wires always be there?" I ask.

"Well, I could take them out, but nobody ever asked me to." Hargrove's eyes tell me that he is laughing behind the mask.

The wires are twisted, cut off and bent down so that they won't puncture the skin. Then the stitching begins through the layers of skin.

About two hours have passed. It's all over now.

■

I go with Hargrove to see the patient on whom he operated earlier in the morning, and then we walk to the dressing room, where I take off my surgical garb and put on my business suit.

"Did it help you — to see all of this?" asks Hargrove.

"Yeah, especially The Saw . . . It helped me to see how good you guys are at what you do, how quickly you work, how much confidence you seem to have."

"Well, we do a lot of it."

"You ever get tired?"

"Yeah, if I do three in a day, I'm really exhausted. I take off the glasses and it's like I'm blind for a while."

We shake hands, and I walk out into the sunshine.

It has been a very good morning for me. I now know what happened. Those hours aren't blank any more. It's a good feeling.

I have the urge to go back, hug the 53-year-old man and tell him that I'm sure his recuperation will be as rapid and complete as mine.

I didn't do it, but I wish I had.

65

'ONE HUMAN TO ANOTHER'
December 29, 1988

R. D. Laing, the Scottish-born psychiatrist, was telling me that his approach to treatment is not drugs or traditional psychotherapy but simply "one human to another. . . . Things go wrong in life, and we've got to move into a zone of understanding about where the estrangement comes from. I address myself to that."

Laing, the author of more than a dozen books, is a controversial figure in psychiatry, in part because he makes fun of some things that other people take seriously.

Example: Diagnostic manuals, in Laing's view, tend to put stigmatizing labels on people — and do nothing to help the therapist understand the problem.

Another example: Formal psychotherapy very often "creates the situation it's supposed to be curing" by putting the patient on the defensive and erecting a barrier that makes effective treatment impossible.

Laing said that much of what he did in therapy was "like being a mediator. There's nothing particularly medical about it. I'm using informal common sense. . . . What do I do when I don't know what to do? Doing nothing is doing something. Not replying to a question is a reply. Silence can be as much a statement as words. When I'm at a loss, I play it by ear into the unknown.

"There's often a breakdown in communication, a breakdown in ordinariness. Togetherness gets shredded . . . and I help them look for a way to get stitched up again. . . . I can't find any general satisfactory words to describe what I do. You've got to get to know the people, spend time with them."

Sometimes, said Laing, the quality of the time is more important than the quantity.

"This father came to see me a number of years ago, and the problem was that his 7-year-old daughter had stopped talking. She never had talked much, but she had stopped talking completely three months before. . . . Let's see now. . . . If you looked at [a diagnostic manual], you'd have to say that she was suffering from mutism. That's a funny way of saying that she's not talking — can't or won't talk.

"So I invited her to come and meet me. I hadn't any special plan. She came into my office and sat on the floor, with her legs crossed. I asked her 'Would it be OK if I asked your father to leave us for a while?' She didn't say 'no' so I asked the father to leave.

"Then I sat on the floor, too, facing her, and I thought she looked like a miniature Buddha — composed, motionless, silent. . . . I reached out and touched the tips of her fingers with my fingertips. Now we were sitting with our fingertips together, and I shut my eyes. I don't know if she shut her eyes, too, but I rather think she did.

"We moved our fingers together for a time, perhaps 40 minutes, a kinetic dance with our fingertips. It was very important to me, not to lose touch. . . . Then I opened my eyes, and put down my hands. I said to her, 'Is it OK if I asked your father to come in and take you away?' She nodded, and I got the father, and they went off together. . . .

"He told me later that as they were walking hand in hand to the car, he asked, 'What went on with you and Dr. Laing?' She then spoke her first words in three months: 'It's none of your business.'

"That was it. She started talking . . . and I didn't see her again for 10 years. . . . The next time was in London, when she looked me up to say hello. Today she has a graduate degree in philosophy. She's not a woman of many words, but she speaks well when she cares to. It's just that she doesn't feel like speaking as much as others."

What happened during those 40 minutes of the fingertip dance?

"I don't know. I venture to speculate that our tactile contact . . . formed some sort of bridge" that brought her back from her own world into the ordinary, everyday world. "I felt it was very moving. I cried a bit when she left. There was nothing sexual, nothing intrusive about it. But somehow it seduced her back into ordinary discourse again."

■

When Laing's son, Max, was 9 years old — he now is 13 — he had shown absolutely no interest in learning to read or write. Laing said that school officials in London were distressed but willing to go the extra mile because Max, after all, had a famous father.

Laing asked Max what the problem was, and Max said that reading and writing were dumb and boring, and that he wanted no part of them. Laing said that he didn't think they were dumb and boring — or else he wouldn't spend so much of his time reading and writing. But he pledged that he never would force Max to learn to read or write. If push came to shove, Max could change schools, if he wanted to, and they even could move to another country. But nobody was going to insist that Max did anything that Max didn't want to do.

Six weeks later, said Laing, Max submitted to him an original poem — in which Max discussed the beauty of the world and the joy of being a boy and having fun.

Said Laing: "That's my boy!"

Moral of story: People do things when they're ready to — and there's not much anybody can do to change their timetable. A lot of therapists try, and a lot of therapists fail.

"Parents often lose the childhood that is within us all. We're adults all day long, and we don't remember the past . . . and we don't have easygoing connections with our children. . . . Children are tremendous teachers . . . because so much has not been cultured out of them. If communication is there, one is liable to have a much different picture of a child's mind than cognitive studies show."

ALTRUISM: WHAT A GRAND IDEA
July 24, 1988

It happened years ago, but the memory of it has remained fresh to Scottish gerontologist W. Ferguson Anderson. "I was talking to a group of retired shipyard workers, and this chap in front was shaking his head to everything I said. I'd talk about the value of regular health checkups, of proper diet, and he'd shake his head — in obvious disagreement.

"Then I said, 'One point I want to make is that maybe every one of you can help somebody else . . . for nothing. You know, as a volunteer.' The chap in front didn't shake his head about that. Afterwards he came to me and said, 'In my whole life, nobody ever asked me to do something for somebody else for nothing. What a grand idea.' "

The point of it all, said Anderson, is that many people — because they have been so wrapped up in themselves and their own struggles — have never realized what they have to offer to others and the joy that can come from the mere offering.

"When people realize the potential they have to help others when they're older, we'll have happier older people," said Anderson.

■

Anthropologist Ralph Blum, who wrote *The Book of Runes*, travels the country as what he calls a "self-help advocate" for a string of retail bookstores. "I'm kind of a Johnny Appleseed" who encourages people to talk about their lives.

What are people talking about these days?

"I don't find greed, a drive for power. I'm beginning to get a profile of people who are thinking about things beyond their venal self-interests."

In other words, Blum, like Anderson, is finding people who are caught in something bigger than themselves. That something is altruism.

■

al-tru-ism n. Concern for the welfare of others, as opposed to egoism.

■

When my father retired at age 67 after a lifetime of work, it was not in the beginning a time of any great joy.

In fact, there was little joy at all. For the most part — and it manifested itself in so many ways — there was a sense of being unproductive, and in Pop's mindset, being unproductive was akin to being nobody.

It was a mind-set that had carved itself into his psyche during those dreadful years of the Great Depression, when he was without work for so long, when he surrendered the house in which I was born because he was unable to keep up the payments, when he lost just about everything except his will to live. I often thought — and once he confirmed it for me — that his will to live was less for himself than for us, for Mom and me, who depended on him.

When he finally got back to work on a regular basis, Pop clutched his job as if it were a lifeboat in a typhoon — because that, in fact, was what it was to him. Much of his identity came from his work, much of the recognition that can be the fuel of self-esteem.

So when Pop retired, he gave up more than his job. What was he going to do? What was he good for? Was he good for anything? Was he — once again — a nobody?

In the first years after retirement he dabbled in any number of volunteer efforts, but, as he later shared with me, he received little inner reward from any of them. "It's like make-work," he said. "If I didn't do it, somebody else would — so what's the point of my doing it?" You may not agree with his philosophy, but if you loved the man, as I did, you had to accept that it was what he felt in his heart.

Once he told me that the days had become long and barren because he felt that he wasn't contributing anything to anybody. Mom tried — and I did, too — to help him brighten his outlook, but not much changed. The truth was that Mom was burdened, too, by the feeling that the two of them should be doing "something more" — whatever that meant.

Yes, eventually they did find something more. And, yes, it was altruism, and it changed everything in their lives.

They — and especially Pop — found value in helping others, and through that they helped themselves.

What they discovered was a universal truth that, if we are lucky, we all discover at some point: Always there is somebody who needs help. Always, Pop once told me, there is somebody who needs to go to the doctor's office but who doesn't have a way to get there. Always there is somebody who needs to go to the grocery, to the drugstore, to the barbershop, beauty shop, post office. Always there is somebody sick or otherwise housebound who could be cheered by a visit or a telephone call — or by a ride along country roads.

Pop once said you give of yourself to others not because it comes back to you but because it's the right thing to do. Yet when you give, you do find that the goodness is returned, not one for one but 50-fold. For Mom and Pop, it was returned in the form of satisfaction, purpose, joy, feelings of being productive.

Once they found their contentment through altruism, they became avid readers and in their final years they explored religion and philosophy to a degree to which they had never had time before. The beautiful irony was that the more they did for others, the more time they seemed to have for themselves. They really didn't have more time, of course, but the time they did have was free of remorse and conflict — and so it was happy time.

In one of our final conversations, Pop summed up what he said was everything he had learned: "Life is being of service to others. That's where the value of living comes from."

When they died, six years apart, they were happy people because they felt that they had done some of what had been meant for them to do.

There is a lesson in this for all of us.

al-tru-ism n. Concern for the welfare of others, as opposed to egoism.

It is more than a word. It can be a direction.

THE HAIRY MAN INSIDE
January 15, 1991

The year was 1982, and those of us who didn't read much poetry were being introduced to Robert Bly, a Minnesota-born poet who was beating the drums, figuratively and literally, for what would become something of a men's movement, a turning inward to get in touch with what it meant to be male.

It was an interview with Bly in New Age Journal, titled "On Being a Man," and in the years that followed, it would be so widely reproduced and distributed that it would come to be seen by many as a classic work on the subject.

In the interview, Bly decried the loss of true masculinity, not what he called "snowmobile masculinity" but the deep energy that "gives rise to forceful action undertaken not without compassion but with resolve."

The problem, said Bly, was not that men had gotten in touch with their softness — that they were "not interested in harming the Earth, or starting wars or working for corporations." The problem was that so many of these men were unhappy — because at some level they sensed that softness was not enough, that more was needed for them to be whole and complete. What was missing, said Bly, was their masculinity, "something wet, dark and low," their very souls.

It's an image, lifted from mythology, that Bly often calls into play in the countless speeches and workshops he conducts around the country — that the masculine is a hairy creature who lives at the bottom of a lake and who, if called on by men, can help them find what they're missing.

■

Bly has written half a dozen books of poetry, including the National Book Award-winning *Light Around the Body*, but his new book, *Iron John* (Addison-Wesley), is all prose — and so powerful that it made The New York Times best-seller list just two weeks after its publication date in November. In the book, Iron John, an ancient, hairy man who came from the water, becomes mentor to a young boy, and each event or adventure is regarded as a stage in male growth.

Writes Bly: "When a contemporary man looks down into his psyche, he may, if conditions are right, find under the water of his soul, lying in an area no one has visited for a long time, an ancient hairy man. . . . Making contact with this Wild Man is the step the (soft) Eighties male or the Nineties male has yet to take. . . . Contact with Iron John requires a willingness to descend into the male psyche and accept what's dark down there."

■

Bly lives in a log cabin at Moose Lake, Minn., and has an apartment in Minneapolis, where he was when I interviewed him.

I first met him in 1986, when I worked with him and Harvard psychologist Samuel Osherson at a father-son seminar outside Philadelphia. I was spellbound — as the audience seemed to be — as Bly lectured, chanted, sang, recited poetry, strummed a mandolinlike instrument, beat a drum.

His theme, then and now, was that the Industrial Revolution, by taking men out of the fields and putting them into factories, deprived boys of their fathers, left them without the male influence they needed to grow into men, and eventually caused them to compensate in ways that ranged from being sissies to being macho, from dropping out to overachieving.

■

I asked Bly if he had perceived much change in men since the 1982 New Age interview, and his answer was, no, not much. "A long, slow process of increasing isolation got men into trouble, and it'll take a long time to come out of it. It's not men's fault. It's just the way it is. . . . But there is one change I see. Men are so much more able now than even 10 years ago to understand the issue of wounding" — how they and their fathers before them had been shaped by the blows that life dealt them.

I asked if Bly felt responsible for this increased consciousness — since he talked a great deal about wounding in his acclaimed public television series, *A Gathering of Men* with Bill Moyers in 1989. He didn't know for sure, he said. "Probably it has to do with the gradual growth of awareness, of courage, as part of the whole movement toward psychology in our culture." As a society, we're changing from ethical thinking, where the emphasis is on what people should do, to psychological thinking, which raises questions like "Why?" and "What if?"

In his seminars, Bly talks at length about the importance of — and the demise of — tribal rites in which boys were initiated into manhood by older men. I asked him if present-day society has any equivalent to this.

"Men have been prepared for tribal initiation for 500,000 years — as prepared for that as women are for childbirth. In some ways, it's just as painful. Then it stops, the initiation, and there's nothing to take its place. . . . No longer are there older men around to love us, mentor us. . . . Men live in tension — between their need for initiation and the absence of it."

I asked Bly how men could get in touch with the hairy man in their souls.

"If you follow the metaphor, the hairy man at the bottom of the lake, you have to descend to get to him. It's not through higher consciousness. It's through feeling our pain and grieving."

Bly said the people most hostile to his hairy-man approach to masculinity were not women but 27-year-old male journalists. "They think, 'I'm OK, Jack, but what's going on with those wimpy guys who are crying?' They are extremely frightened of any kind of emotion. Maybe that's why they became journalists — so they could observe and not have to participate.' "

ALONE WITH OURSELVES ON A ROCK
July 6, 1982

Dare we risk the ultimate adventure, next to which white water pales, deserts fade, and the mountain becomes commonplace? Dare we face the challenges of ourselves, the roaring turbulence of our own fears, and the treacherous path of self-doubt as we struggle to understand and come together?

— Rod Napier

Well, all of that is mighty high-sounding, but what exactly does it mean? And does it have any relevance for those of us who don't frequent the white water, the deserts or the mountains but who toil in the tall buildings amid what has become known as the asphalt jungle?

That's what I asked Philadelphia psychologist Napier after I read his remarks in a brochure describing the Deep Water Outdoor Leadership School in the

Canadian wilderness 250 miles north of Toronto, where he is a staff member.

Is he suggesting that some us could benefit by fleeing the city for a while and coming face to face with nature?

Yes, he said in an interview, that is exactly what he is suggesting because in confronting nature we necessarily must confront ourselves too — in a way that's not possible in the cozy environment in which we customarily live. Napier twice has gone into the wilderness, and the first time, three years ago, was the beginning of what he calls his "journey of self-discovery." Listen as he talks about it:

"The Indian medicine men say that you need time to go off by yourself . . . and so they teach you the way of the vision quest, where you're alone in a climate in which you create deprivation without water and food. The belief is that if you have nothing to do and are deprived . . . this allows visions to come to you. Visions don't come if you are fat and wander through life, as most of us do.

"You come into an environment in which you are vulnerable. We are so protected in our society — protected by house, job, habit, routine. Then the protection is gone and you're thrown naked on a rock in the wilderness far from anybody." In the wilderness, Napier said, a person becomes "totally vulnerable. You sit on a rock, and you have just a blanket. The only person you're left with is yourself . . . and you quickly know what a sham you are."

In his two days on the rock, Napier "felt like an invader from Mars. I knew that I was an intruder. The animals and the insects knew of my presence and they made me aware that I didn't belong. They shouted, cackled, screamed at me to get the hell out of their territory."

He became sensitive to everything, he said. "My perception was very acute, and that alone is an incredible experience. Our senses are so dulled by the damned tube, by constant noise. We go from newspaper to television, and we're aware of nothing. Out there, I was aware of my body, heat, cold, mosquitoes, rain. I heard everything. I thought I heard wolves. They were circling in an 80-mile radius, and I thought that they'd end up on my rock. I was in their territory . . . It was a humbling process, and the beginning of self-understanding — and the realization of what a charade we live."

Napier was aware of the "natural cycles of the rock" on which he sat. "Before, I'd never sat for 10 minutes and done nothing. Now I was sitting for 48 hours, and the rock's cycles were apparent. In the morning, some insects took over the rock. Then it became hot and they left and other insects came . . . and animals and birds. At night, six-inch dragonflies took over the rock. I feared that they were going to get me. Later, bats came . . ."

He watched the setting sun, the arrival of the morning star and "got some understanding of the mythology of multiple gods. As I searched for the morning star, I saw what looked like a lantern through the woods. It was the morning star, but it looked a foot across. As an Indian, I'd have been scared to death. It seemed as big as the moon, but as it rose in the sky, it became smaller, like a star."

Being with nature, Napier said, gave him "a perspective of the city and what we've done."

During the two days, he had "a couple of visions," which were like daydreams, "minute squibs of visions. Others had come back from the wilderness with extreme visions and dreams, and I felt cheated and ashamed. I was competing with myself for a vision. I couldn't even get away from competition when I was sitting on a rock in the woods."

Napier shared one of his visions with a disciple of the late Swiss psychiatrist Carl Jung. The Jungian told him: "That's a classic." Napier was baffled because it made no sense to him, but when he shared it with a second Jungian, he again was told: "That's a classic."

In the vision, Napier "observed myself in a room with my back to me. In front of me was a dark-haired woman, beautiful, but nobody I knew. To my right side was a crib, which held a 5-year-old girl, who watched us. The woman raised her arm and with a pistol shot me five times down the body. As an observer, I was shocked. There was no reason for the shooting. I staggered to the crib and fell over."

Why was this vision a classic?

As the Jungians helped Napier unravel it, here is what developed:

"I was dealing with issues of sexuality . . . and my struggle with the male and female parts of me, the dominance and control of the male and my trying to bury the female parts. In men, the male parts are predominant and the female parts are felt to relate to being effeminate or to homosexual behavior.

"With the work I was in, I needed the female parts, the intuitiveness, and I was in a constant struggle to eliminate the macho, controlling aspect of my maleness and to let in the sensitive, caring female parts.

"The struggle came to a head five years ago, which was symbolized by the five bullets. The Jungians asked if anything had happened to me about five years ago, and, of course, that was when I was separated from my wife. This probably is what allowed me to become the person I am now, because I had to incorporate into my life some strong feminine aspects. . . . The picture of what I had been, in the vision, gave me permission to explore further."

It was, Napier said, "damned profound . . . and worth a few days on a rock."

The next year, he went out for four days on a rock and had more visions. "The greatest therapy is the facing of your own reality. We never take time to do it otherwise because we're too busy facing our own environment. . . . We need the courage to jump off the train and face ourselves.

"We spend our time with reading, listening to music, writing, cooking, planning, and we have no time for anything else. Two or four days with yourself is an extraordinary gift to yourself. You sit quietly . . . and the trees, birds, clouds all seem to talk. It's a gift of space and time without impingement of the environment.

"You talk to yourself or to your god. Whatever you are comes out. You have the answers. You meditate or whatever, and it evokes responses that you have within yourself. The vision is truth coming up."

The lure of the ocean
October 22, 1989

The man is a big-time executive recruiter, commonly dealing with positions that carry compensation far into six figures. I asked him if the people he seeks out to fill these positions have room for anything in their lives besides work. He smiled and said that, yes, he was encountering more and more people who, in middle age, were considering things besides position and income.

"It's not at all uncommon for me to be describing a big job to a guy, and before I even get into the big stuff, he stops me and says, 'If it's not within 100 miles of salt water, I'm not interested.' This happens so often. . . . People are thinking more about the quality of their lives apart from work. . . . Being close enough to the ocean seems very important to a lot of these people."

He said that he didn't fully understand the fascination with salt water, and he wondered if I could explain it to him. I asked him how much time he had.

■

I grew up in the Midwest and, as a kid, I never saw the ocean. When you're in Missouri, as I was, the ocean seems as far away as China — and just as out of reach. To me it was a place where rich people went on vacation. My uncle once brought me a little jar of sand from the Florida seashore, and I kept it on my bookshelves, along with my other treasured possessions, until I went away to college.

I never saw the ocean until I was 22, when I drove through Biloxi, Miss., on my way to New Orleans. I stopped the car, took off my shoes and ran through the sand. I watched the waves crash in. I listened to the roar. I saw the sun light up a sailboat. I got goosebumps. "My God, I never knew there was anything like this."

Little did I realize that thirty-something years later I'd still have the goosebumps.

What is it about the ocean that fascinates so many of us? What is the magic of salt water?

To me the ocean represents life — awesome power, beauty, tranquillity that can turn into rage literally in the blinking of an eye. Yet there is amazing consistency and predictability. At my beach place, I have a tide clock that is a never-ending reminder of how predictable the ocean is. Every once in a while I call the Coast Guard station and ask for the time of the next tide change — just to check on the clock — and you know what? The clock's always right on the mark, not because it's a special clock but because the ocean has a special consistency.

The ocean is a relaxing place for me to be — even at those times when the world seems to be caving in around my ears. It's no accident that so many therapists, when they're coaxing a patient into relaxation, ask the patient to imagine a peaceful scene "like the seashore." It's no accident that so many relaxation tapes carry the sounds of rushing surf and floating seagulls, that so many so-called sleep machines use the ocean's roar to block out the noisy environment.

There is something about the ocean that brings out the best in me — and I'm beginning to understand what it is. I never feel closer to nature than when I'm at the seashore, and when I'm closer to nature, I'm better able to put things into perspective, deal with the hard questions, roll with the frustrations. I'm like a little kid again. Only now it's better — because the scar tissue of life enhances my ability to appreciate where I am and what I'm doing.

Psychologist Dan Kiley, who has been a friend for many years, was telling me a while back that he left his practice in the Chicago suburbs and moved to Tucson, Ariz., because he wanted to get closer to nature. He takes long, solitary walks into the desert, sits and communes with nature. It's almost a religious experience, he said, and suddenly the pieces begin to fall into place — just as they do for me when I'm at the ocean, or as they do for some people when they're in the mountains.

Undeniably, there is, for many of us, a benefit to getting back to nature that transcends our ability to fully explain it. But we can appreciate it, and we do.

Some of my best right-brain time comes when I'm walking on the sand. It's when I'm most creative, best able to focus. Hassles seem so far away, so remote, so unimportant. At times I'm tempted to bring along a notebook — to record my thoughts and feelings. But I never have, because I don't want to interfere with the magic.

People tend to be relaxed and friendly. We smile and speak to one another as we pass on the sand. Sometimes we stop and talk — people who, back in the city, wouldn't give each other the time of day, not necessarily because they don't want to but because they're in too much of a hurry. There's too much to be done, too little time. But at the seashore, there's plenty of time. Nobody runs, except for reasons that have more to do with aerobics than with the clock. A lot of people smile.

Late in the afternoon I sit on my terrace, sip my favorite drink, look and listen. A wave breaks in from the northeast, curls along the top, crashes down hard, sends white foam bubbling up onto the sand. Then it's quiet — until the next wave.

The shape of the beach changes, often overnight. Sand washes in, almost to the point of overload. Then it washes out. Beaches may change, but in the long run the balance is preserved.

I climb aboard the catamaran. Boy, that's a good wind out of the south. I'll really fly today. Rudders down. Sails cleated. I am flying. The wind whistles. Donald Trump never had it better than this.

■

I asked the big-time executive recruiter if he better understood the magic of salt water. He didn't answer — but I had the sense that it wasn't because he wasn't attentive. Rather, I like to think, it was because he was hearing the roar of the surf and the whistle of the wind.

CHAPTER 2

PARENTS AND CHILDREN: THE TIES THAT BIND

As we grow and develop, our relationships and experiences with our parents come into clearer focus and we begin to discover their impact in shaping us into the people and parents we become. They may have conveyed love, wisdom, affirmation, support and encouragement or aloofness, indifference, benign neglect or outright abuse — or a combination of all those. These experiences become imprinted on our core and help nurture or drain our self-esteem.

Part of the "growing-up" work of taking responsibility for ourselves is learning how to keep and cherish the gifts of our parents, appreciate their humanity, forgive them their imperfections and work to heal the wounds so that we don't pass them on to our children. Darrell often spoke of being a "good enough" parent, acknowledging the complexity, the rewards and the hard work involved.

What is the right balance of meeting the expectations and needs of our parents, our children and ourselves? What do children need most from their parents? As an adult child, how can we bring closure to old hurts in our relationships with our parents?

The columns in this chapter explore a few of the many complexities of parent-child relationships and share some poignant stories about people who chose to actively work on creating the relationships they needed — with heartwarming results.

What is your unfinished work?

— M.S.

WHAT DO PARENTS 'OWE' THEIR ADULT CHILDREN?
December 23, 1986

The letter to me was from a man who asked a jackpot question: What do parents owe their adult children? Here is some of what he wrote:

"I'm only 46 years old, but I feel like 120 in terms of what my children expect from me or think I owe them. . . . I have a few bucks, but I'm far from rich. Three of my four children have finished college. I contributed to their college education by paying about half the tuition cost of a state school. However, they decided to go to non-state schools and, as a result, they owe a lot in loans . . .

"I also have a daughter, 23 and out of college, who works. She tells me that

79

she'll never speak to me again because I will not co-sign a $1,700 loan for her. . . . It's not just me. My friends tell me how they've taken out loans for their kids' college education, paid for their cars and insurance. . . . And I'm not talking about rich people. . . . I think there may be a lot of parents who feel as I do, but they're hesitant to say so because they feel that they would sound like bad parents. . . . What do you think?"

■

The question is one that I've thought about over the years because I have two grown sons. We're good friends, for the most part, and I give them plenty of space because that's what they have indicated they want and need. It's certainly what I want and need. We live many miles apart — Jay is in North Carolina and Grant is in Southern California — and the only thing they ever have asked for is advice, which I have given with the reminder that it was "only" advice and that I couldn't get out of joint if they ignored it totally.

But how would I react if they leaned on me for other things, like co-signing a note? How would I feel if one of them threatened never to speak to me again if I didn't do what he wanted me to do?

I think I might get angry. And then I think I might feel guilty.

What about you?

■

Psychiatrist Richard Moscotti has two grown daughters, 25 and 21, and I took to him the question: What do parents owe their adult children?

He answered with a question of his own: What do we owe ourselves? Let's listen:

"I had in therapy a man who so identified with his son, who so gave of himself, that he almost became anemic from overfeeding the son. One day in therapy, I asked him: 'Do you love your son enough to take good care of his father?'

"I really believe that we have to take care of ourselves. . . . Parenting is one of the most difficult jobs in the world, draining, and we need time away from it, for ourselves, for our marriage. . . . But sometimes we get lost in trying to be such wonderful parents. We want to transcend our own parents' parenting . . . and sometimes we overgive. . . . If you overwater plants, you do a disservice. It's the same with children. . . .

"The love of a parent is a love that leads toward separation. Our job as parents is to try to get our children off to as good a start in life as possible to the point that they can leave the nest at 17 or 20 or 22 or whenever and cope on their own. . . . I see the parenting role as standing on the sidelines of life and pretty much staying out of the game — but being available if our adult children should fall, bleed and desperately need help."

But what do parents owe their children?

"You try your best to get them a reasonable education, provide a reasonable home, give them reasonable goodies — so they can cope on their own with the world as it really is. . . .

"You have to be reasonably available, and everybody must define what that means. Today we have 25-year-old adults who get divorced and return home to cope economically. What should parents do? I think lines should be drawn, and it should be made clear that it's a temporary arrangement. 'Sally, I love you, but you can live here only for six to 12 months, and that's it.'

"But the trouble is that we overrespond to our guilt. We try to overcome the mistakes we made in child-rearing" by doing too much for our children after they are grown. This amounts to overwatering them.

"We need to ask ourselves, 'What would happen to my children if I no longer were available to them, if I died?' We need to help them to become competent adults — equal to us or better — by the time we feel our parenting is pretty much finished. When is this? It varies. Some are in school until they're 30 and need emotional and financial support. Others marry at 18 and are on their own."

What if a grown child pulls the parent's guilt chain by saying something like, "If you really loved me, you would co-sign my loan"?

Moscotti had a ready answer. "I would say, 'Look, don't try to manipulate me by playing into my guilt gland. "If you really loved me. . . ." I don't understand that. If you don't know by now that I love you, I feel you've missed the boat. I disappoint you? Well, you disappoint me by asking for too much.' If you have millions and your child owes $8,000, you might pay it off, but you should say, 'That's it. Don't ever expect it again.' " Children aren't helped to grow up, he said, by parents who continually bail them out of trouble.

In his office at the Institute of Pennsylvania Hospital, Moscotti has a sign that reads "How about that?" It's an important message for parents to consider, he said.

"Your child says he's disappointed in you as a father. Well, how about that? Sometimes to force children to grow up, we are required to take a hard line, with drill-sergeantlike rigidity. Eventually, the little bird must learn to fly on its own."

SEEKING FORGIVENESS FROM ONE'S CHILDREN
July 30, 1991

The letter was from a woman who lives in San Francisco and who said that . . . "My father is probably your most loyal reader. Every time I come home to New Jersey from California, he's cut out several of your columns and placed them strategically all over the house. You articulate what he thinks and feels but cannot say. . . .

"Enclosed is a letter he wrote and slipped into my suitcase during my last visit. The envelope said, 'Read this on the plane.' "

■

"I'm sitting at my desk having coffee with another foreman. I just finished telling him how much of a success I feel I am by being a part of raising the most beautiful person I have ever come across in my life. Just being near you and seeing how thoughtful and sensitive you are to your fellow human beings makes me feel so good. . . . I never made much of my life, but you make it all worthwhile. . . .

You make me a happy and worthwhile person. . . . I am very proud that you are my daughter."

■

"My father never gives any outward indication that he feels this way. When I was a child, during what he calls his 'crazy' years — he was stressed out, angry, repressed and often abusive — I was starving for even one-tenth of the feeling expressed in this letter. It never came. Through prayer, therapy and the model of a loving mother and grandmother, I continue to find my way to compassion and forgiveness. I believe that my father, on the other hand, lives with tremendous guilt that he will not let go of. . . . He lives with a block between himself and any chance of vulnerability, healthy dependence or relationship to his family. . . .

"Why am I writing to you? Because I know from reading your column myself that you believe in growth and life at any age. . . . Perhaps publishing this letter and some special thoughts that I have for my father could move him to some small action that would lead to an insight into how vast God's grace really is. Perhaps he'd find the courage to do or say something to the others he has around him that could lead to healing.

"What follows is a letter that I would like to write to my father."

■

Thank you, Dad, for "seeing" me. I guess that's really all any child or adult wants from their parents — to be seen for who we are, to be celebrated for the unprecedented miracle of creation that every human being is. . . .

You say that I make you a happy and worthwhile person. But I am not so powerful as that. The truth is that you see in me a reflection of your true self, a glimmer of your own heart, of how God sees you. You attribute too much to me because you couldn't imagine — because of your guilt — that you are a worthwhile person.

Yes, you made mistakes. But consider yourself forgiven by me. Let go of the anger and guilt that separates you from your wife, your children, your family and, most importantly, from yourself. Embrace courage and tell them that you love them. . . .

"Thanks, Darrell, and I wish you the very best."

■

I know a lot of fathers, myself included, who have felt guilty about what they did or didn't do when their children were growing up — about how they worked too much and played too little, criticized too many times and praised not enough times.

The hardest task that any father who recognizes himself here ever will face is confronting his children, looking them squarely in the face, and asking for forgiveness. It is the hardest task not only because it is humbling, which it surely is, but also because it involves great risk.

Your children may nod, agree that you were a poor substitute for a real father, condemn you for depriving them of something that they were entitled to and that they always will feel shortchanged about.

That's the risk that must be taken — before the words can thaw in the heart and work their way up through the throat. Yes, it's terrifying, but any father who wants to be a real father in his children's eyes doesn't have a choice.

I've written before about my confrontations with my sons.

With my younger son, Grant, it happened in the Blue Bar of the Algonquin Hotel in New York, when he was 19. I told him I was sorry. I asked for his forgiveness. He looked surprised. No, I hadn't been a perfect father, but I was a lot better than those fathers who never did anything with their kids. Those kids thought Grant was lucky to have me for a father, he said — and so did he. It was a time of great joy for me.

With my older son, Jay, it happened in the kitchen of my condominium, when he was 20 and visiting. I told him I was sorry. I asked for his forgiveness. He did not look surprised. I had a lot to be sorry for, he said. He wasn't certain he could forget what I had done and hadn't done, but he would try to forgive. He had within him a lot of stuff buried "in the well" and he would bring up pieces when he was ready. This was not a time of great joy for me, but I did feel relieved. At last it was out in the open. I wasn't carrying it on my back anymore. Jay knew how I felt, and it was up to him to decide what to do with the feelings.

■

Over the years I've talked to lots of fathers about their relationships — or lack of relationships — with their children. Many of them were hurting, as I was for many years. Every one of them who got back to me said his decision to ask the children for forgiveness had been a turning point in self-concept and, in fact, in all of life.

I would say to the man in New Jersey who is the father of the woman in California: "Do it! Do it now!"

A UNITED FRONT FOR THE KIDS
July 26, 1983

It wasn't all that many years ago when parents, based on what they had read and what they had heard, concluded that one of the most important things they could do was to always present a united front to their children.

Disagreement in the children's presence was bad. Period. The reason: It left the children with feelings of bewilderment because of the mixed signals they were receiving.

And that's the way it went. In household after household across the land, mothers and fathers became performers, acting not necessarily as they wanted to act but playing their united-we-stand roles to the hilt.

But, ah, yes, in the long run it would be worth it — because their children would grow up to be happy and well-adjusted.

Selma Kramer is a professor and head of the section of child psychiatry at the Medical College of Pennsylvania, and she knows better now, she said. But a long time ago, before she did know better, she and her husband "felt quite strongly that we shouldn't disagree and argue in front of our kids."

So that was a cornerstone of their parenting — no disagreements, no mixed signals that might confuse the children. But then, years later, an unusual thing happened, Kramer recalled in an interview.

"After my daughter was married, she and her husband began to have some problems, and I said to her: 'Well, that's par for the course, but it looks as if the two of you are working things out.' And she said: 'But, Mother, I never saw you and Daddy argue. I was devastated to think that John and I might argue.' "

The honest-to-goodness truth, said Kramer, was that she and her husband had argued — more than a few times — but never in front of the children. Because, after all . . .

Her personal philosophy had come back to haunt her in the sense that her behavior as a mother had caused her daughter to adopt an unrealistic view of marriage as a haven in which nobody argued or disagreed. And it's amazing, Kramer said, how many parents feel that they always must have "unanimity of opinion — the way their parents seemed to."

She's now certain, she said, that it's "healthy if kids know that parents can disagree and make up," and this knowledge can put them on the road toward:

¶ Understanding that disagreement is not such a sin.

¶ Accepting that people are different, that they can love each other and a child and still not agree on everything under the sun.

¶ Creating later in life the possibility of more autonomy in their own thinking.

All three points add up to good mental health, Kramer said.

"I have to tell you that I have a real prejudice in favor of the kid who asks 'Hey, what's this all about?' and who says 'I don't like that explanation.' But a child can't ever do that unless he has permission to challenge authority," and he is given tacit permission by parents who openly disagree at times.

A problem that arises when parents always agree is that the child has to agree, too, and "has to swallow everything whole hog. He can't express anger openly, and I like to see honest anger expressed" — not anger that comes out in devious, sugar-coated ways.

Kramer, who is now a grandmother, said her professional experience has been that children who come from no-disagreement homes often tend to feel lonely, left out and without anybody to stand up for them or give them an ear.

"If the parents are rigid, there's no recourse for the kid. The parents take the position, 'There's nothing you can do to change our minds because we're in agreement,' and the kid often feels so bereft and forlorn," she said.

She is not advocating knock-down, drag-out battling, she said, and it's a good idea for parents to try to work out major differences in advance. But when on-the-spot decisions must be made, it is perfectly all right for one parent to say in front of the children that he feels that the other parent is off base.

Doesn't open disagreement encourage a child to try to play one parent against the other for the child's benefit?

That's possible, said Kramer, because "kids are smart . . . and if they sense a weakness in the marriage, they'll play one against the other. But I suspect this will happen to a great extent only when there are real problems within the marriage. Average parents, if they think that the kid shouldn't do something, will get together and say 'no.' But where there is weakness and basic uncertainty about how to raise a kid, well, this is where the problem potentially is greatest."

The parent who sides with the child against the other parent may temporarily gain favored-parent status — yes, that's true — but usually the worm turns, and rather quickly, too, Kramer said.

Favored-parent status tends to shift at the next disagreement as parents' differences of opinion swing "out of balance and back into balance." With reasonable people in reasonably sound relationships this almost always happens, and the result is that first it's one parent aligned with the child and then the other parent.

A child in this kind of relationship has the inside track on being a winner because he'll have a basically realistic view of the world and he'll see his parents and flesh-and-blood people who don't play silly games with him or with each other.

How does it all look to you?

WE ALL HAVE OUR LIVES TO LIVE
August 5, 1990

We stood off to the right of the gate at the far end of the concourse, and Grant fingered the tattered envelope that held his airplane ticket back to San Diego.

"I had a good time," he said. "Thanks for everything. . . . You really put yourself out for me."

"No, I didn't put myself out at all," I said. "I had as much fun as you did. . . . I'm glad we had this much time together — 10 whole days. Thanks for coming."

I was starting to get a lump in my throat, and I turned away for an instant, then changed the subject.

"Let me know what happens in Los Angeles," I said. "I really want to know."

Grant smiled, then frowned, mirroring his concern. "Yeah, I wonder how it will go, but don't worry about my keeping you up to date on what's happening. I'll let you know."

The loudspeaker announced that it was almost time for the 8 a.m. flight to be on its way: "Now boarding Rows 20 to 28. Please have your boarding pass out for the agent."

We shuffled closer to the gate. "We still got a few minutes," Grant said, looking again at his seat assignment. "I hope your book proposal flies. Be sure to let me know about it, will you?"

"I will." The lump was returning, but this time I didn't turn away. "I wish I could see you more often. The letters and phone calls are nice, but they're not the same. I miss seeing you."

"Yeah, it's a long way from Philadelphia to California. Maybe someday I'll get a place back East, like in North Carolina. Wouldn't that be something — one home in the West and one in the East?"

"That would be something, all right."

It was the loudspeaker again: "Now boarding Rows 10 to 20. Please have your . . . "

"That's me," said Grant. "Thanks again for everything."

I grabbed his forearm. "I'll stand in line with you. That way we'll have a few more minutes together."

"Great. . . . When are you going back to the beach?"

"Probably late Thursday, if the weather looks good."

"Do you think anybody else enjoys the beach any more than we do?"

"If he exists, I never met him," I said.

The line had dwindled down almost to the two of us.

"I may be getting out to Southern California in October — on a business trip," I said. "Maybe we can get down to Mexico, to Rosarito, and have some of that lobster you're always talking about."

"We'll make that happen. I promise. We'll go and stay for a few days, eat lobster and drink beer."

"I'd like that."

"So would I."

It was the moment of parting, and I found nothing at all sweet about it. I took Grant's right hand in my left hand and put my right arm around his neck and hugged him with all my might. At almost 6 feet, 4 inches, he's two inches taller than I am, and as I hugged him, I had the sensation of pulling him down to my level.

"Come back whenever you can," I said.

"You know I will. See you in October."

I stepped out of line and watched as he handed his ticket and boarding pass to the agent. He moved toward the gate, stopped and smiled and waved at me. Then he was gone — my son, the little blond kid who became the big blond man, who left the North Carolina mountains for the beaches of San Diego, who at 30 now is going with the flow of his career — to Los Angeles.

I walked slowly back up the concourse ramp, behind a woman who had just given a goodbye kiss on the cheek to a young man I assumed was her son, a few years younger than Grant, who was boarding another airplane for another destination. As I passed her, I glanced at her face, which was streaked with tears. She smiled grimly; then, when she apparently became aware that I was crying, too, she brightened — perhaps to try to cheer me up.

"It's sad," she said, "but that's the way life is. We all have our own lives to live. We wouldn't want it any other way, would we?"

"No, I guess not . . . but sometimes I think there's something wrong with a system that keeps so many people so far away from the people they love."

"I try not to think about that," she said. "Goodbye — and good luck." Then she hurried off down a passageway to the left.

I walked to my car and drove back into the city, mentally preparing myself for my day at the office — a box full of 10 days of mail and telephone-call slips, an interview, the final touches on a speech, calls to my book agent and a former editor. I would be busy, and that would be good. It would take my mind off the lump, which had made it perfectly clear that it was going to remain lodged in my throat for some time.

It had been a remarkable 10 days for me and Grant at the seashore — sailing, golfing, sunning, walking, playing basketball, lifting weights, watching baseball on television, boiling shrimp, drinking beer, savoring sunsets. But mostly we talked — about who we are, what we want, about peace and tranquillity, about challenges, about risking, about what's important, about setting goals and paying the price to reach them, about being afraid, about love, about joy, relationships, disappointment, pain, sex, success, good health and hard times.

Because Grant and I have had a long-distance relationship for almost 15 years, we both try to pack too much into the brief time that we have together. At the end, we're always tired, stuffed with too much food and drink, sore from the games we play.

But we're also rejuvenated, as if we've each had massive injections of adrenaline, and figuratively that's what we've had — the adrenaline that comes from the kind of meaningful time that it's possible to have only with somebody with whom you have a long history of shared experiences.

There's also sadness — especially for me, because I mourn the time that will have to pass before he and I can be together again. Yet, it is, as the woman at the airport said, the way life is. We all have our own lives to live — busy lives that help shape us into the people we are becoming. And so, despite the sadness, I wouldn't want either one of us to change the script — solely for the benefit of the other.

I remember what a wise psychiatrist, now retired, once told me about conversations that he had had with his two sons, both physicians, who live many, many miles away from him. He said to them: "I hate that you live so far away, but if you moved back just for my sake, I'd hate that even more."

Anybody who can say that — and mean it — is, for my money, a good-enough parent.

FINALLY, LOVE PURGES ANGER
February 5, 1984

In what would be the final months of his marriage of 23 years, Kenneth Prusso sought professional help, and, as he sat in the paneled office, he was stunned when the counselor asked: "How long have you been angry?"

"Angry? What makes you think I'm angry?"

"I can see it in your eyes."

■

Kenneth Prusso's parents divorced when he was 5, and for most of the 40 years that followed he was angry — angry at the father who had left him and who never had attempted to contact him.

"He abandoned me. He never fought my mother to keep in touch with me. He never cared enough about me to have a hand in raising me. He never loved me. Oh, God, he never loved me."

The outrage turned to bitterness and eventually, as the years passed, to self-doubt. "I must be unlovable."

In his boyhood, he frequently sought reassurance from his mother, with whom he lived.

"Mom, you do love me, don't you?"

"Of course."

"A lot?"

"Really, Ken, what's the matter with you?"

"A lot, Mom? Please . . ."

Kenneth Prusso graduated from college and then, driven by the ghosts of insecurity, got one master's degree and then another — and quickly plunged toward a doctoral degree. "I have to work hard to prove I'm not a failure. I have to. I don't have a choice." Work on the dissertation almost drove him mad. "I can't possibly produce anything that will be acceptable. I'm not good enough." But he was good enough, and it was more than acceptable. The doctoral degree was his.

Along the way he married and fathered four children. "I can't fail — and, by God, they'd better not fail either." Especially were his screaming demands for perfection directed toward his two sons, one of whom, as a teenager, once told him: "Look, Dad, you can talk to me, but please don't yell at me. I don't deserve that from my father."

But even as he yelled, Prusso sought reassurances from his children — and from his wife. In muted ways he cried from the basement of his soul: "Please love me."

■

Kenneth Prusso, who is 45 and divorced, lives in suburban Willow Grove and works in special-education research and evaluation for the Philadelphia public school system. In an interview, he recalled the day last winter when he struggled to the Board of Education offices but went not to his desk but to the 10th-floor lounge, where he sat and cried.

The next day he cried, too. And the next and the next.

"Ken, what you have to do is go back and tell people what they do that upsets you. If they make you feel angry, tell them. Right now, your anger is internalized, and that's what causes depression. Tell them. Tell them."

It was the counselor again, the same counselor who had recognized the rage in Prusso's eyes at their first meeting.

"Who am I angry at?" Even as Prusso asked himself the question, he knew the answer. "I'm angry at my father. Dad, why'd you leave me? Why didn't you love me?"

He vented his anger in a letter to his father, a pain-seared letter of hate: "Why should I care anything about you now that you're old — when you didn't care anything about me when I was young? You can't be much of a man."

He mailed the letter to his sister, who had their father's address and who over the years had visited him and, on occasion, had invited Prusso to accompany her.

"I don't want to see him. I hate him."

The bones rattled in the closets of boyhood. "Any time I did anything that was the least bit inappropriate my mother would say: 'Oh, you act just like your father.' The image I had of him was as an irresponsible person, a drifter, somebody who was not much good. It probably was just as well that he'd left."

But sometimes in the quiet of the night, Prusso, first as the boy and then as the man, would lie awake and sob: "He doesn't love me."

Prusso's sister received the letter, read it and mailed it right back to him. "Are you sure this is what you want to say? If it is, mail it to him yourself. Here's the address."

Prusso rewrote the letter and mailed it to his father in Redding, Calif. "I'm hurting, Dad, and maybe you're hurting, too. I want to know more about you." Then he held his breath.

Finally, a reply came: "Dear Son: If I had a heart, I would have had a heart attack. What in the hell took you so long? Enclosed is a picture of me."

Prusso cried. Then he felt exhilaration. Then sadness. "He was an old man, an old, bald-headed man. I suddenly realized that I couldn't fight him. There was nothing to fight, no reason to fight."

Prusso wrote his father again, sent along a picture of himself. Ten days letter a letter arrived. "I love you. When will you come and visit?"

Prusso described what he felt. "It was wave after wave of relief and dissipation of anger. I realized that I would never treat my 14-year-old son in the same way again, feeling that he had to toe the line, had to be perfect, had to do what I said. All of a sudden I was not angry with my father. I was not angry with my son. I was not angry with myself. The anger had slipped off like layers and layers of veils, and I had felt it go."

The visit to California was the stuff of which storybooks are made. "Every day we talked and talked. After breakfast, about 10 or 11 o'clock, he'd get out a bottle of port and pour himself a glass and ask me what I wanted. 'Whiskey,' I'd say, and he'd pour whiskey. We'd talk and drink glass after glass during the day. To everybody he saw, he said: 'This is my son. He drinks whiskey.' And once to me he said: 'You know, Ken, I'm so glad you drink whiskey. I was afraid you wouldn't drink anything.'

"We drove around the country together; we shot pool; we played chess. He told me about himself. He told me about my mother. He presented his view about the divorce, about the outrage he felt in not being able to visit us, about the hurt he felt when, after I was grown, I never contacted him. His guilt, fears of rejection kept him away.

"Over the years, when people had asked about his family, he had told them: 'I have no son; my son is dead.' He was as hurt as I was. He was as angry as I was. He made it clear that he'd been no angel, but neither had my mother. She had struggled to grow up, too, and out of all of this my mother became human and my father became real. It allowed me to say: 'Hey, we all deal with this stuff in the process of growing up.' "

Prusso's mother had died the year before, and, as he looked back, he felt passionately that it had been wrong for her to "protect" him from his father. "I never was able to form my opinion of him based on my experience with him. I never had the chance to overlook his weaknesses or admire his strengths."

Much of what the father told the son confirmed what the mother had said, but "these things didn't make him less lovable to me. Instead, they made him real.

Most of all, I learned that he has a tremendous capacity to love me. He does love me."

Kenneth Prusso will remarry in June. His father, 71, will fly to Philadelphia for the wedding.

PARENTS' SUCCESS: A CHILD'S BURDEN
May 13, 1982

Sometimes it seems that from the dawn of creation, this debate has raged: Which child has the greater burden to bear — the one whose parents are super-successful or the one whose parents are absolute failures?

If parents succeed gloriously, we've been told, the child feels that he can't ever equal what they've accomplished — and he may not even try. He also may feel that he'll always be identified not as himself but as his parents' child. Most of us have read stories about famous people's children who turned their backs on wealth because they didn't want to pay the price of sharing it.

At the same time, we've heard that parents who fail set a pattern that their children follow because it's the only model in sight. The welfare rolls, we've been told, are clogged with people whose parents were on welfare, too, and who accept this as the way life was meant to be for them. We've also heard that children who could break out of the failure mold sometimes unconsciously choose not to because they don't want to "hurt" their parents by surpassing them.

What do you think?

Well, not long ago I asked psychiatrist G. Pirooz Sholevar what he thought — and he told me, without pulling any punches.

Sholevar, who is director of Jefferson Medical College's division of child, adolescent and family psychiatry, said that it could be tough to come from a history of failure, but that "one of the most difficult things is to be the child of a very successful person. From early on, the child concludes that the parent is treated like God. The achievement of the parent is so extreme that the child feels he has no chance to match it — so why should he try? And he gives up the possibility of trying at an early age."

Just imagine, said Sholevar, what it must be like to have a father who has become not merely successful, but wealthy too. "The father is in a position to develop a $5 million trust for the son — a trust that generates $700,000 a year. Now, how can a son go out and feel successful on his own" — no matter what he does?

It happens not infrequently, Sholevar said, that some parents succeed to a great extent even though they have underlying feelings of failure. "This has been a major factor in their path to success — this sense that they are failing. And they never rest; they always keep pushing. They succeed on the surface but underneath they think that they're failing. So they tend to set themselves up as competitors with everybody else, including their own children."

What happens, Sholevar said, is that the children are hurt not by the parents' success but by "parental competition, by parents who exaggerate their own achievements."

OK, doctor, but you're not saying that all parents who succeed damage their children, are you?

No, said Sholevar, not if parents really feel good about themselves, their work and their achievements. "If parents are invested in the process of what they're doing — rather than just in the end result — then their success is not such a hurdle for their children. You take super-successful baseball players like Mike Schmidt and Pete Rose. If they enjoy playing baseball and just happen to have the ability and determination to be great, if they invest in the process of success, then they're usually able to convey this to the children." The result is that the children can savor their parents' success and not be so intimidated by it.

But, said Sholevar, who has a 9-year-old son, "if parents look only at the end result, and use their success as a way to prove that they're not failures," they have quite a different impact on their children — and it's mostly bad.

The difference, he said, is that the parents whose success doesn't harm their children really enjoy what they do, and their achievements are secondary. The parents whose success burns their children tend not to find enjoyment in anything except succeeding.

Most of us, Sholevar said, should be able to identify with what he's talking about.

"In social situations, we've met people who told us what they did and what they achieved, who talked about their successes. When they left, we felt good about it . . . and enriched. It was almost as if we'd done it ourselves. We were glad we'd met them and we wanted to meet them again.

"But then we've also met other people who told us what they did and what they achieved, and when we walked away, we never wanted to talk to them again. The difference was that they didn't really enjoy what they were doing, and we sensed that. When they talked about their successes, we sensed that they were trying to make us feel bad. They were trying to say that they are better than we are."

Exactly the same thing happens between parents and children, Sholevar said, and children, too, pick up quickly that their parents are trying to hold them down and remain one-up. But unlike those of us at a social gathering, the children can't just walk away. They have to remain — and this is why the damage can go to the very core of their being.

It can explain, Sholevar said, why some super-successful people have such miserable relationships with their children and why the children often don't follow in their parents' footsteps.

WHEN A CAREER WOMAN BECOMES A MOTHER
February 4, 1985

Last July 26, psychologist Carol A. Gantman, at age 35, joined the army of career women who have waited until later in life to have their first child.

That's when her son, Benjamin, was born, and it was the beginning, she said, of a whole new experience — not only motherhood, but also the way in which she viewed herself and the world.

Being a parent "requires a major shift in focus and attention away from things that have been your mainstay. People used to meet me and ask, 'How's your day? How's your work going?' Now they only ask: 'How's your baby?' That's a major change.

"Before, I could focus my attention on caring for myself, my body, my husband. Now the baby comes first. . . . In my career, I felt powerful, competent, in control. I felt that I could handle anything. This changed when I became a mother and found myself confronted with a lot of unexpected things. . . . I'm no longer treading on solid ground. I'm in areas in which I have no experience," and if there's one thing that motherhood has taught her, it's that expertise and confidence aren't necessarily transferable from career to parenting.

"The baby needs you totally, and there's no adequate preparation for this. I've held crying babies before, but it's different when it's your own baby. . . . It's helpful to read books and talk to other mothers. This gives you some cognitive awareness, but we're dealing with two levels — cognitive and emotional" — and the emotional struggles are what tend to turn people inside-out.

Gantman said that feelings of confusion may be compounded if a woman delays motherhood until the middle 30s or later — after she has savored the sweetness of professional success for years. "When you're at home with the baby, you lose the arena in which you've achieved a major part of your gratification. The arena of work no longer is available" as it once was, and "in a sense it's history. Motherhood has priority . . . and remembering that you were successful in a career before motherhood is not always adequate" to keep the good feelings rolling.

The "disorientation and confusion" she felt as a new mother were profound, she said. "Here I was, a successful career person, and I was feeling overwhelmed by changing diapers. You wouldn't believe that this could happen, but it does."

Gantman worked until 10 days before Benjamin was born, and she returned to her office half-time three months after the birth — a schedule that she still follows. "The decision to work again was fraught with ambivalence and guilt . . . although I was returning to a primary source of gratification.

"At home, when I'd be feeding Benjamin, I'd think: 'Oh, I've got to get going on my career again and build it back to where it was before. But at work, in the beginning, I'd sit and think about what the baby was doing. . . . It was as if I wasn't at home in either place, yet I was at home in both places. Where did I really belong? The longer I'm back at work, the more my sense of mastery increases, but it is a tough transition."

Waiting until 35 to become a mother has pluses and minuses, Gantman said.

On the plus side, "it's important to have achieved a sense of success and accomplishment and to feel solid about it. I had a life of my own that I created and could come back to — a sense of values and priorities, a sense of myself and myself within the world. At 35, I don't get so ruffled as I might have at 20. . . . I think that the sense of what's important is more firmly in place at a later age."

On the minus side, "I have a feeling at times that my lifestyle has been changed more than it would have been at 20. The lifestyle is not so firmly entrenched at 20. . . . Change may be harder to take at 35 . . . and the energy level may be different. Last night, Benjamin didn't go to sleep until after 12:30. I had to get up at 6 this morning, and I thought, 'Gee, maybe this would be easier if I were 10 years younger.' "

For many career women in their 30s, motherhood means "a redefinition of success," said Gantman. "It's not just promotions or more money. These things are important, but they're no longer the only goals.

Is it possible for a new mother to return to her career with the same fervor as before?

"Motherhood doesn't necessarily inhibit a woman from pursuing her career actively, but it's more difficult — because it requires the same energy as before plus the extra energy for motherhood. It's very demanding . . . and women who return to work with a lot of energy deserve credit."

It's important for new mothers to reserve the right to change their minds about work — and about motherhood, too, said Gantman.

"A woman who wanted to be a vice president by 40 needs to consider that she may not feel the same way after she's a mother. This doesn't mean that she's less powerful, less feminist. It means that her values have changed. . . . She should pursue her career if she wants to — but not feel guilty if she doesn't want to."

On the other hand, said Gantman, a woman who doesn't find motherhood as satisfying as she expected should feel all right about plunging back into her career "as an important means of satisfying herself. A woman has choices about where she can derive gratification. She needs to work out the formula for herself."

Gantman said something with which she has struggled has been that "at times people seem to pay more attention to me as a mother than to me in my other roles. . . . I'm struck by how [motherhood] seems to attract people's attention and energy. This is not always supportive for the woman who wants to return to work" and to invest in other areas of her life besides motherhood.

Something that she has learned — in spades — is that "a new mother needs time for herself. An hour of my paying attention to me works wonders and is extremely reinforcing. It renews my resources. . . . At first I felt that this was a luxury, and I felt guilty about it. Now I feel that it's a necessity. I need the extra energy that this gives me."

THE 'NERVOUS BREAKDOWN' WHISPERS
March 24, 1981

As I prepared for a routine physical examination not long ago, I found that a flood of memories was released by this question on the back page of a four-page medical questionnaire that I had been asked to complete:

"Did anyone in your family ever have a nervous breakdown?"

The memories came from bits and pieces of some of the long, long talks in which Dad and I so often engaged during our visits in the last years of his life.

He, like many of his generation, had been trapped in the awful paralysis of the Great Depression and had lost just about everything that money could buy, including the house in which I was born. He also had brushed against the reality of losing something so important that it could not be measured by money: his health.

We had lived in the early 1930s in a little railroad town in north-central Missouri, and when hard times struck, the railroads tottered. Dad held onto his job far longer than many, but then the dreadful day came for him, too. He was out of work.

For four years, he struggled mightily to keep our heads above water. He worked a few days here and a few days there, but he never had a regular job, and he watched in dismay as his bank account dwindled and finally disappeared.

And then, when he no longer could keep up the mortgage payments, the bank foreclosed on the house, and we moved into a dreary one-room apartment.

Every morning, he would get up, dress in his only suit and, with forced optimism, tell Mom that this would be the day when he would find a job, a real honest-to-goodness job. But every night he would trudge back to us, his head down and his soul bent, and Mom never had to ask if he had found anything.

A few times, the railroad called him back to work. Was this the break that he was hoping for? Was this the lifeline to the future? Inevitably the work lasted only a few days or a few weeks, and then the despair settled in like fog in the early morning. Once, he told me, he found himself lying face down on the bed, flailing his arms, crying and asking, "What's going to happen to us?"

He found it difficult to relax at night. When sleep finally came, it often was accompanied not by dreams but by nightmares. His stomach turned cartwheels, and he could not keep down the meager amounts of food that he tried to eat. He lost weight, and he also lost some of his determination. He began to anticipate the rejections that always came when he knocked on a door and asked for a job.

He checked into a tiny hospital in a tiny town, and there a physician with a cold and tiny heart told him:

"Your nerves are shot. You're a wreck. You'll never be able to do a full day's work again."

Dad, they decided, had suffered a nervous breakdown. He could not handle the storm. His system had cracked under the strain.

In those days, it was more socially acceptable to jump out a window than to suffer a nervous breakdown when things got too bad. If a man lost a fortune on the stock market and in hopelessness leaped to his death, people talked about it:

"It's a shame what happened to Bill, isn't it?"

But if a man broke apart at the seams, people didn't talk about it. They whispered:

"Poor Charlie. It was too much for him. They say he'll never be the same."

Well, Charlie Sifford surprised them. He was down, all right, but he was not out. He found a job and moved us to the city in which I would grow up, where Mom still lives. He had no money in the bank, but he had steady work, and that was all he needed. His stomach no longer flipped and flopped. He ate well and slept well. He felt as Charlie Sifford used to feel — back in the good old days.

But the good times did not last long. His boss, like that physician, also had a cold and tiny heart. He used the scar tissue of the Great Depression the way some men used whips. As the work load increased, he did not add more people. He simply piled more work on Dad, and as the overload took its toll, as Dad fell farther and farther behind, he told him:

"If you can't handle the job, I'll get somebody who can."

The fear of losing yet another job filled Dad with a frenzy that caused him to work 10 or 12 or 14 hours a day, six and sometimes seven days a week. Often he would come home for dinner and then return to the office in the evening, and I'd go with him. I'd take a book, and he would get out his pencil and calculator and tackle the mounds of paperwork that rose before him.

Sometimes, when I'd look up from my book, I'd see Dad with his head down and sometimes he would mumble what sounded like: "It's too much . . . too much."

His stomach began acting up again. His weight dropped, and the nightmares returned. It was as if he could hear the voices from yesteryear:

"Poor old Charlie . . . nervous breakdown . . . a wreck . . . ."

He took a leave of absence and checked into a big-city hospital, and there it was his good fortune to meet a physician with a big, warm heart. Dad was not in such bad shape, he told him. Everybody has his overload point; it's nature's way of telling us when it's time to back off and slow down. People can do only so much, and to expect them to do more is unrealistic of those who expect it, not of those who are unable to do it.

No, Charlie Sifford was not a wreck. He was just a normal guy who was having a normal reaction to abnormally hard times. He needed some rest and some understanding. If his boss could not accept that, then he needed a new boss. Not everybody out there had a cold and tiny heart. There would be other jobs. He needed to remember that nothing was worth everything. He would be all right; the doctor was confident of that, because, after all, Charlie Sifford was a survivor. The worst already was behind.

The physician had been quite correct. There were other jobs and other bosses for Dad — and the contentment that came with the knowledge that he had weathered the storm and had not cracked but had simply reacted as any normal person would react.

He had reached his limits, and his body had told him to back away. That was not something to be whispered about. That was something to shout from the rooftops. It was what had saved him — and his family.

I fingered the medical questionnaire and re-read the question:

"Did anyone in your family ever have a nervous breakdown?"

Boldly I blacked in the "yes" box. It wasn't a whisper; it was my way of shouting a message that perhaps, especially in 1981, each of us needs to remember.

THE PAIN OF TRYING TO OUTDO PARENTS
January 6, 1983

Back in the bleak, hungry days of the Great Depression, when Leo Madow was a little boy, he trudged to the grocery store one morning and, as payment for food, presented not money but a beloved possession, his clarinet.

"The grocer took it and gave us food for it . . . as barter." Madow accepted the groceries and, in a little boy's way, he cemented a bargain with himself: "If I ever have children, this never will happen to them. They'll have it better."

In his impressive new book, *Love: How to Understand and Enjoy It*, psychiatrist Leo Madow writes that sometimes when a little boy feels that he is in competition with his father and cannot possibly win, he doesn't even try — and goes through life as a failure.

Madow relates this story: "I once asked George Gardner, a famous Boston child psychiatrist, why so many students were dropping out of schools and colleges, making no effort to prepare themselves for their place in society. He answered that these were 'our' children, who were trying to compete with people like us, their very successful parents, and they felt that there was no way that they could win."

Said Gardner: "Remember how it was when you and I were young? We could compete with and be more successful than our fathers; but our sons have a much more difficult level of success to surpass. They simply feel it can't be done, and so they give up."

To use Madow's word, children typically are in a "bind" if they're unable to do more, earn more and live more than their parents. So many of us have been brought up with the notion that more is better, and when we find that more is not in the cards for us, we tend to go to pieces.

"You could see this in the 1960s," Madow was saying in an interview the other day. "Kids dropped out of college, went into cults, into drugs . . . and it looked as if many of them just gave up. There were some real tragedies. A brilliant young man I knew at Harvard simply quit. He's a carpenter now, into drugs . . . and he's just barely making it. When kids drop out of college, the percentage of those who ever return is not very high."

This problem of surpassing our parents is one that many of us in our middle years never had to confront.

Our parents were wiped out, financially and professionally devastated by the Great Depression, and it was no feat for us to do better than they had. In fact some of us might even have felt a little guilty about it, because in some ways it was as if we were stepping over the dead bodies of those who had been shot down in life's prime. But we did it, and often with the encouragement of our parents, who saw reflected in our successes and even in our excesses the good times that had been snatched away from them.

But what about our children — yours and mine and Madow's? What's happening to them?

Many of them are hurting terribly, said Madow, who retired last year at 65 as professor and chairman of the department of psychiatry and neurology at the Medical College of Pennsylvania and who is in private psychiatric practice.

The way out of the box for them and for us, he said, is to realize that "the nubbin of the thing is this: Who says they have to surpass us? An important issue in parenting today is getting to children the message that they don't have to do better, that it's more important for them to make their own lives in their own images."

Would today's young people buy this idea if it were presented to them?

Maybe they would, Madow said, but it wouldn't be easy because there exists so often a burning need for a son, let's say, to cross swords for supremacy with his father.

The roots for this probably are to be found in the Oedipus conflict, in which the son competes with the father "in the family constellation. The father is physically bigger and stronger and a lot more successful in work," and it amounts to a terrible battle for the son, but it's as if the son has no choice but to compete. "It's almost inherent in child development," said Madow, and to get off the merry-go-round a child would need direction, encouragement and loads of love from parents.

The futility that so many children find in life these days can be traced to family backgrounds of extremes, Madow said.

On the one hand, there are parents — like Madow, who, as a boy, traded his clarinet for food — who take the position: "I had it rough, and I'm going to make it better for my children." One result is that the children can grow up "overindulged and not develop their individuality. In a sense, parents who come from this position have deprived their children — because they've made it easy for them and left them with nothing to strive for. So the children start out feeling defeated."

On the other hand, are parents who have accumulated wealth and who either give their children too much or else don't give them enough — in the sense that they transmit to their children the feeling that nothing the children can do will make a difference since the family course already has been irreversibly charted by the parents.

But, said Madow, "because you're rich doesn't mean that this has to happen. You can look at the Kennedy family and see that. The children were made to strive and earn . . . and they turned out to be high achievers. They weren't just handed things. They had, I guess, a sense of their value and felt that they were special people."

Does the Kennedy family know something that the rest of us could learn from?

Yes, perhaps, Madow said, and it probably has to do with helping children acquire the proper amount of self-love or narcissism — the good feeling that is essential in tackling the world and coping with adversity. What is the proper amount? That's a difficult question to answer, he said, but a less difficult question is defining what is excessive or deficient narcissism.

"Too much or too little is what is nonfunctional. That's when it becomes pathological."

The thrust of therapy with confused, disappointed children, Madow said, is to "try to get them to develop a sense of their own value" and to give themselves permission to follow their own interests in constructive ways.

In other words, they have to be helped to learn how to get satisfaction from sources that may be different from their parents' sources.

What do you think?

THOUGHTS FROM AN ONLY CHILD
April 2, 1985

It was a column that I had written through tears — a few weeks after my mother died last year — and in it I had searched for an explanation of why her death had flattened me more than the death six years earlier of my father, to whom I was closer emotionally.

"When Dad died," I wrote, "I still had a parent and a family home, a place to come to at special times. I still had somebody to whom I could write special letters, mail my columns and send funny cards on birthdays and holidays. I still had somebody to whom I was a child and from whom radiated the kind of love that only a parent can offer.

"When Mom died, all of that died, too. The connection to childhood now is severed — except in memories — and, as an only child, I sometimes feel terribly alone. . . . For the first time in my life, I wish for brothers and sisters."

■

It was the morning's first telephone call — before 9 o'clock — and it came from a woman who had saved that column and who now wanted to know what I really thought about being an only child. She remembered some of the columns that I'd written over the years about the advantages of being an only child, but in the column about Mom's death, I had seemed to expose the other side of the coin. On balance, how did it look to me now?

She wanted to know because she and her husband were wrestling with a big-league question — whether to stop with the one child they had or to have one or two more children. They weren't going to base their decision on what I had to say, but they did want to hear something straight from an only child's mouth.

■

It was during what would be my final visit with Mom. She and I sat on the front porch on a sunny autumn afternoon, and I asked if she and Dad had decided that one child would be their limit.

Yes, she said, that judgment had been made — after my birth. The pregnancy had occurred during the bleak years of the Great Depression, a time that was far from ideal for beginning a family, especially since Dad's job was on the line and extended unemployment was a distinct possibility.

The pregnancy was unplanned, she said, but she stressed, just as Dad had years before: "Don't ever think that you weren't wanted. There's a big difference between being unplanned and being unwanted. Nobody ever loved a child more than we loved you."

Why had they decided against any more children? After all, she was one of three children and he was one of five.

She and Dad had come from poor families, families that had known near-poverty at times, and they had agreed that it would be folly to have more mouths to feed and more minds to educate than they could afford. "After you arrived, we knew that was it because we'd be strapped to take care of you the way we wanted to. So we stopped."

They never had any regrets about it, she said. She and Dad liked having an only child, and I never had displayed any of the negative qualities that commonly are pinned on only children — like being selfish and overly ego-centered.

They had loved me, she said, in a way that was wholehearted and without strings. But they had done as much as was humanly possible, she said, to discourage me from thinking that I could walk on water.

"How'd you do that?"

"By setting limits, by enforcing rules, by trying to create an environment that emphasized that other people have rights, too. . . . By telling you when we thought you were out of line. We always tried to praise more than we criticized, but we didn't shy away from being critical when we thought it was appropriate."

I asked if she'd been pleased with the way things had turned out. She kissed me on the forehead, refilled my glass with champagne and said, smiling: "What do you think?"

■

Some years ago, I interviewed a psychiatrist who is an only child — Frederic F. Flach of Cornell University — and to this day it sticks in my mind as an unusually solid exploration of what makes the only child tick. Here are some of the commonalities that Flach listed:

¶ Sky-high achievement. Why? It's because the only child "has no brothers and sisters to identify with, so he forms a strong identification with his parents. He has more ambition to grow up." The down side of this, said Flach, is that the only child may become insecure because he can't compete successfully with his parents. Yet this insecurity may be responsible for much achievement because the only child tends to work harder to compensate for his feelings of insecurity.

¶ Discomfort with being alone. The only child is more sensitive to loneliness. He "can't take for granted that there'll always be people around" — so he tends to form strong one-to-one relationships as a guard against being left alone. When these relationships are broken — by death or divorce — the only child tends to be more devastated than somebody with siblings.

¶ A posture of being self-centered. This doesn't mean that the only child is selfish. Somebody who is selfish is greedy and wants what others have. Somebody who is self-centered tends to "think of the world in terms of himself. He sees the world through his eyes and he is the center of his world. It's a perceptual thing," and it's not necessarily negative.

¶ Difficulty with learning how to be successful in interpersonal relationships. It's difficult for the only child to set limits for others because "you can't set limits for your parents."

Flach said his patients included a number of only children. "Because they form strong attachments to people and things, they're more vulnerable if the attachments don't work out. But, conversely, if things do work out, then they reap more benefits."

Flach said he was glad that he was an only child. He wouldn't have it any other way. Neither would I — even though I think that I, as an only child, was burdened with extraordinary feelings of loneliness after Mom's death. I explained all of this to the woman who had called, and she seemed satisfied.

What do you think?

SHAPING EMOTIONAL PATTERNS
August 11, 1981

As adults, we basically are the products of what happened to us, good and bad, between birth and age 6, says psychiatrist Leon J. Saul. It's a safe bet that if "enough injurious experiences" upset us when we're little, we'll continue to be upset when we're big — and not even the mightiest tools of psychiatry can fix every one of us.

Saul, 80, is the author of a dozen books, many of which deal with the effects in adulthood of emotional patterns that originate in childhood. His most recently published books are *The Childhood Emotional Pattern in Marriage* and *The Childhood Emotional Pattern and Human Hostility*.

The first six years are critical in shaping these emotional patterns, Saul says, and it's not uncommon for all of us to be bent somewhat out of shape because our parents flailed us with one or more of what he calls "the three D's." They are:

¶ Deprivation. "The child is not loved or not really wanted. You see a lot of this in relatively normal families . . . and you also see it in teenage mothers — not in all but in many. It's an ego thing for them to have a baby, but the day-to-day care becomes a big nuisance. It's a 24-hour job" and after a while they get tired of it — and the baby suffers.

¶ Domination. "Parents tell a child to do this or not to do that. They try to bring up a child to be perfect. They are well-intentioned, but their error is in doing what they do too quickly, too harshly and in beginning too early. "There are parents, he said, who criticize their 2-year-old child for acting like a 2-year-old. What they forget is that "it takes 19 years to get to age 19."

¶ Depreciation. "Parents treat the child as if he knows nothing, as if he's not as good as little Willie next door. This is common in the most socio-economically privileged families. The child is made to feel that nothing he does is really good."

In adulthood, what are the scars from exposure to the three D's in childhood?

The adult who was deprived of love as a child "never feels sufficiently loved," Saul says. "He may engage in a lot of affairs. His marriage may break up because he feels that he's not loved enough. But no matter how much the wife loves him, no matter how much she shows her love, he has the deep feeling that he's not getting it."

The adult who was dominated as a child tends to be too submissive or he may rebel against authority that is not unreasonable. "It comes out everywhere. He has a good job and a reasonable boss, but he feels that the boss is exerting too much authority over him. Because he hates authority, he may not be able to get along with the boss — even though the boss is a good guy. Eventually, he may lose his job."

The adult who felt depreciated in childhood may lack self-confidence and have the feeling that nothing he does is any good, Saul says. "The extreme of this is the person who does nothing because he feels: 'What's the use of trying? I'll just fail again.' "

To some extent, Saul says, "we all suffer from the D's. But I hope that the importance of this gradually will seep into the general population, and child-rearing will improve. That's the goal in writing my books. I hope that I can change the course of lives. But who knows? Maybe I'm overly optimistic."

The amount of help that psychiatry can offer hinges on "how early the trauma occurred and the severity and consistency of it. Was there a sibling or a grand-parent who gave support while the child was handling the trauma? It's that complicated," Saul says.

The person can be helped "if the condition is helpable. That depends on the interplay of emotional forces in the person . . . on the presence of compensating motivations."

Saul once had as a patient a man who was not able to travel outside the United States. "He dreaded it. His phobia was based on going through Customs. He didn't like for anybody to open his bags. He didn't like authority.

"We traced this directly to his relationship with his mother, who dominated him. But his father was subjected to the same treatment, and he had sympathy for the son and supported him emotionally. He said: 'It's OK; you don't have to take it so seriously.' There was enough counterbalance emotionally from the father so that the son could overcome it."

In the transference that took place during therapy, Saul became the father and asked the man: "Why do you take it so seriously? You were small then, but now you're a grown man and you can handle it." The therapy went well because "I had a nucleus primed by the father to build on. If there had been no father, it maybe would have taken a long time. It's hard to build something if you start with nothing."

There is nothing wrong with "a little domination," Saul says. "It can give you strength of character. To have strong parents who set limits can make life much easier. But if the parents go too far, then that's something else . . . The key is quantitative. Most normal and healthy people have in them some small part of the same things that trouble others. But [those who aren't normal and healthy] exaggerate them to neurotic or psychotic intensity."

Being traumatized as a child and scarred as an adult don't necessarily mean that we can't be reasonably successful and happy — if we're in luck. We can dis-cover that by reading a little history, Saul says.

"If Napoleon had grown up not at the time of the French Revolution, nobody ever would have heard of him . . . or maybe he would have been another neurot-ic. But his enormous ambition was sublimated into military genius at the right time in history. The two fit together — Napoleon and history.

"It's the same with marriage. If we waited until we found two healthy, non-neurotic people to get married, then we'd have no marriages. But if the neuroses fit, people can get along well." What that means is that if somebody who needs to be dominated marries somebody who needs to dominate, they likely will make it just fine. The trouble can arise if one of them changes.

How close do parents have to come to perfection to feel realistically confident that their children will grow into healthy adults?

"Let me answer that with an old saying, a cliche that really is an ancient truth: Love conquers all. I mean that. If a child feels really loved, feels that everything that the parents do is for his welfare, that the parents are on his side, then the parents can do a lot of pretty bad things, and the child still will come out all right.

"I've seen some miserable people, but if they never doubted their parents' love, then I always felt that they eventually would be all right. And most of them were."

Is it possible that parents can love a child but that the child won't perceive that he is loved?

"I don't think that you can fool young children one bit. They catch on. If you love them, they feel it and know it."

THE PAIN OF CARRYING A FUNNY NAME
July 30, 1984

In the song "A Boy Named Sue," Johnny Cash recounts a man's years-long quest to track down his father and claim retribution for saddling him with a name that made his life a miserable series of taunts and fistfights.

Eventually, son finds father and in the battle that follows the son comes to understand why he was named Sue. The reason: It's a tough world and only the toughest survive. So what better way to make a boy tough than to name him Sue? It was an act of love, and Sue understands that, but, as the song winds down, he vows that he'll name his son Bill or George — anything but Sue.

When the song is finished, the audience goes wild . . . and why not? After all, this is only make-believe. Or is it?

■

His name is Cyril, and more than anything else in his life, he told me, his name is responsible for his being the way he is today. And how is that? By Cyril's definition, he is confrontational, combative, aggressive, unwilling to be leaned on by anybody.

He talked to me one day about it: "With a name like Cyril, you have three choices: You can go to court and change it; you can become shy and try to hide; you can learn to fight. . . . I learned to fight," and, symbolically, he has been fighting ever since.

Parents really ought to be careful about what they name their children, he said, because a funny name can set up children for a lifetime of pain.

Is Cyril a funny name?

"How'd you like to have it?"

■

I was interviewing psychiatrist Leonardo Magran about adolescent suicide, and, as we wrapped it up, I remarked, "Hey, with a name like Leonardo, you might have had a fight every day when you were a kid."

"No, I didn't. Why would you think that?"

"Because Leonardo is a funny name."

"It's not funny in Argentina, where I grew up. In Argentina, Leonardo is as common as Leonard is here. If you were named Leonard, would you have a fight every day?"

"No, probably not."

"It makes a difference — whether or not the name fits into the culture." It's something, Magran said, that parents should keep in mind at child-naming time.

■

One of my close boyhood friends — when I was 8 or 9 — was a boy with the unlikely name of Shirley Joe. Even then, he was painfully aware of what his mother had done to him — a mother who obviously had wanted a girl and wasn't willing to concede totally that she'd given birth to a boy.

"I hate it," he said more than once.

When we played baseball against kids from other neighborhoods, as we often did, Shirley Joe was ragged out of his mind.

"Oh, Shirrrllleeeyyy," the opposition would shriek when he came to bat. "Oh, Shirrrllleeeyyy, can we get a ribbon for your hair?"

Not infrequently, Shirley Joe answered with his bat — not by hitting the ball against the fence but by chasing, with blood in his eye and the bat in his hand — those who baited him.

Afterward he often asked, "Why did it have to happen to me?"

■

What do parents do to their children when they bestow strange names on them? And why do they do it?

I put the questions to psychiatrist Gene (that's Gene, not Eugene) Corbman, who is assistant director of inpatient psychiatry at Albert Einstein Medical Center, Northern Division. He understood — all too well, he said — what I was talking about.

"With a name like Gene, I had to defend it as not being a girl's name" when he was a child, Corbman said. "I was named after somebody my parents were very proud of. . . . The name probably accounts for my sensitivity to names. It certainly made me more aware of this issue."

Children with what Corbman termed bizarre names are "faced with ridicule . .

which can affect self-image, respect and who they are. A name is not just a title; in a sense it's a whole identity," and parents need to consider this when they select names.

Sometimes, he said, parents pick bizarre names "out of total ignorance. They don't take into account" that the name will condemn the child to a lifetime of struggle. "Other parents pick a name that they think is cute for an infant — without thinking how it will be later. They don't consider the consequences for a grown person with that name."

It's not uncommon, he said, for ethnic groups to continue to use names that are "perfectly OK in their own tight subculture. If the child attends a parochial school where the subculture is continued, the child won't feel out of place," but the trauma may hit later when the name stands out as unusual — or worse.

Some people with unusual names do become belligerent, Corbman said. "They are defensive not only about the name but about everything. It becomes their posture in life — and it can come out in a lot of different ways."

What parents need to keep in mind in selecting a name, he said, is the importance of achieving a balance between a child's wanting "to fit in and be one of the crowd and, at the same time, also wanting to be recognized in his own right as an individual." What that means is that it's probably a good idea to pick a name somewhere between Joe/Mary and Cyril/Ardamissa.

"It's nice if a name has a certain amount of meaning — a name that can offer a sense of pride and elevate self-esteem without being so peculiar, so idiosyncratic as to make the child feel a lack of confidence."

What about naming a child "junior" or "3d" or "4th" or something like that?

That's a tough question, Corbman said, because "it's like asking somebody to discuss politics or religion. You can't win with it." Translated, that means that parents who name children after themselves are quite proud of it and not open, generally, to discussing the merits of it. But being named after a parent can "put a tremendous burden on that child, who will be measured for better or worse . . . because he follows in the footsteps" of the person for whom he is named.

There's another potential problem, too. Calling somebody "junior" after he's beyond the stage of being a kid in short pants can freeze him into being a child in long pants and retard his growing up.

What are some very popular names at this time?

Corbman's guess is that Jonathan and Jennifer probably would top the list — although neither was too common a decade ago. Like everything else, names come and go.

'DAD, I'M HERE TO GET TO KNOW YOU'
June 20, 1982

The man and his friend had ended their five-mile run, and now they were in the house, their chests heaving and demanding more air. "I was sitting on a couch," the man said, "and suddenly I had an overwhelming urge to cry. I couldn't restrain myself. My friend asked why I was crying, and I cried harder. It was almost primal sobbing, mixed with hysterical laughter."

Finally he was able to speak. "It's my father," he gasped. "He doesn't know me, and I never told him I love him."

The next day, the man canceled a full week of business appointments and left for England, where his father lived. There, outside Oxford, he walked up the country driveway and said to his father: "Dad, I'm here to get to know you."

From the very beginning, his relationship with his father was distant and formal, said the man, a Philadelphia psychologist who asked that his name not be printed because "this is a story that I've shared with only a few good friends."

The psychologist's father was from the South and, in the son's words, "his idea of what it meant to be a man was to care for women and be in control. His father died early, and he was raised by a mother who was spoiled. He took care of her. He always was very polite, always very much the gentleman . . . and a certain kind of formality in relationships was created around politeness."

The son's relationship with the father was at arm's length. "He was not often playful or affectionate with me. He was the authority, a model of righteousness and ethics. He was an Eagle scout, a Sunday school teacher, a Phi Beta Kappa. He had the highest grades in the history of Georgia Tech." And he also had a manner that set him apart from the Midwestern people with whom he lived after he moved away from the South.

"I remember four or five times when he got down on the floor to play 'bear' with me and my sister. It was so delightful . . . and so rare because of the customary formality. Clearly he was the boss, and you never, ever disagreed. We'd sit together for dinner on Sunday — that was the only time we ate together as a family because he traveled a lot. At dinner, my sister and I would practice our manners . . . and try to look nice, try to eat right. We never got to know our father, but I always respected him, honored and appreciated him."

The closest that the son ever felt to the father was "when we played table tennis . . . and I saw his joy when I finally beat him. . . . I knew there was a playful person underneath. My aunts regarded him as a boy who was so much fun when he was courting their sister. But I never saw that. Basically, I saw a respected, reserved executive."

His own mother, the man said, filled a traditional caring role. "She was a perfect complement for his formality. She was soft and more gentle . . . and was able to show her own fears and anxieties. It was much easier to relate to her than to my father, the stone."

The father, in various ways, put pressure on the son to excel. "I always struggled to be accepted. Would I be Phi Beta Kappa? An engineer? I always felt I was coming out of a hole just to get on even ground. It was a burden. I avoided academics in high school . . . and put my energies into sports and into being a student leader, areas where he was not so accomplished."

The father leaned hard on the son to become an engineer. "It was clear from my aptitude tests that I couldn't be an engineer, and so he thought that it would be fine for me to be a businessman. I became an economics major — and I detested it."

Finally, the son "broke out of expectations" and went into a graduate program that had nothing at all to do with business.

"My politics were more liberal; he saw me as a pink. I gave up formal religion, which he always pushed but never modeled . . . When he and my mother moved to England, we'd never had an argument. He was 6-feet, 4-inches tall and dominant, [he was] bigger and more intelligent than I was. Who could argue with God?"

The son was 26, married and a father when he first visited his parents in England.

"We'd rarely ever talked. I don't think we'd ever had more than a 15-minute total conversation. But after dinner we talked, and I mentioned something about Kennedy. My father burst out and listed all the great, horrendous disappointments that he'd found in me. I had voted for John Kennedy without talking to him. I had gone to Ghana, a black country, without seeking his counsel. I had married a Catholic. He had a laundry list of eight or 10 items he didn't appreciate.

"I said 'Hey, wait a minute!' — and mother took flight from the room. She knew what was going to happen, and he and I went at it for three hours. I told him of his hypocrisy . . . and from then on he saw me as a man . . . and later he even sought my counsel on certain things. But we couldn't relate — not really. We saw each other maybe once a year, and there always was this formality that separated us."

Then came the year of the father's retirement . . . which was when the son erupted into tears with his friend after their five-mile run. "It would have taken 10 years in therapy to understand the pain and anguish that I was carrying around," he said. But it all came out, washed into the open by torrents of tears.

What, the man wondered, had made the father a proud, ethical, yet distant authority? He had to find out, and so he went to England, where his father had undergone surgery to remove a cancerous growth on his lung.

"I never thought he would die," the man said. "Gods don't die. I walked up the driveway and there he was, hoeing in his garden. He was very, very frail. I said 'Dad, I'm here to get to know you,' and he said 'Well, ho, ho, I know you, big boy.' I told him that he was going to know me even more. We spent six days together, talking, reminiscing, exploring, searching. Who were we? Who had influenced my life? His life? Why was he distant? I asked him all my questions, and he answered them all. It was remarkable because I'd never asked him a personal question before."

On all counts, it was a week-long high for the two of them, as they discovered each other. The son found out that the father was "not really so private. If anybody had knocked on his door and asked to be let in, he would have let them in." But nobody ever had knocked.

The son visited the father's physician and asked for a report on the cancer. It was only a matter of time, the physician said.

"When are you going to tell him?"

The physician seemed ruffled. "You don't tell people they're dying unless they ask. If they don't ask, they don't want to know."

The son returned to the United States, saddened by the medical report but buoyed beyond words by the realization that his father, after all, was a warm, feeling person who returned love with love. Then, at Christmas, the son and his family went back to England for what would be a final visit. The father picked them up at the airport. "He looked like a skeleton. Six-feet, 4-inches and 115 pounds . . . but he was a perfect host."

Late one afternoon, after a nap, the son came downstairs, and there was his father. "Can I fix you a drink, big boy?" the father asked. Then the father looked the son in the eye and told him: "Don't worry; everything's taken care of."

The father walked into the kitchen and collapsed. "It was the last time we talked," the son said. "I gave him mouth-to-mouth resuscitation. He had turned blue, but I brought him back to life. To do something life-giving to somebody who had been God was unbelievable, to put my mouth on his."

At the hospital, the son saw his father "laid out on a table with all the things stuck into him." The doctor asked how the father would like living in an artificial lung. "He can't maintain breathing without it," the doctor said.

"He'd be mortified," the son said. "He couldn't stand it."

The choice, said the physician, was limited, but the son stood his ground. "There's no question that he wouldn't want the lung."

In a way, the son said, "I sealed my father's death, but it's the only thing he would have wanted. I knew him enough to know that."

Without the artificial lung, the father died within an hour. "To this day," the son said, "I have had not an instant of remorse" about the decision.

Also to his day, the son said, he has cherished the discovery of his real father — a discovery that proved anew that it's never too late to get to know the important people in our lives.

CHAPTER 3

BECOMING MASTERS
OF OUR WORK

Work can be a stage on which we grow, prosper, make a unique contribution and gain both personal and professional fulfillment, but it can also enslave us, taking over our lives, draining our spirits and undermining our self-confidence and ability or opportunity to make a difference.

How much satisfaction we derive from our work is determined by a combination of what we do, why we do it, who we do it with and how much of ourselves we bring to it.

The question begins with each of us. If we understand and appreciate our skills and unique talents, our values, our own definition of success and our life goals, we are in a much stronger position to exercise control over our work and how it fits in with the rest of our lives. Some circumstances are beyond our control. However, instead of becoming victims of those circumstances, we can choose to take the responsibility of discovering options or creating opportunities where we can make a unique contribution.

And there is much more to life than work. For many, if not most of us, the most meaningful, rewarding and joyful experiences of our lives come from time we spend with our families and friends, work we do in our communities and time alone to renew ourselves and recharge our batteries. If we allow ourselves to become prisoners of work, these parts of our lives get shortchanged and ultimately we become depleted and have less to give.

Whatever we do, each of us makes a difference in the world and the lives of the people around us. We may be positive or negative role models for our children. We may help others to learn and grow. We may simply make the environment a better place to be because of who we are with our colleagues and how we go about our work.

Darrell was fortunate to have discovered his calling as a writer at a young age. He loved his work, he touched people's lives, he savored his successes, he struggled to find the right balance of work and play, and he shared his experience with all this. The columns in this section provide insight and guidance that each of us can use to enrich our lives.

— M.S.

'I HOPE HE HAD ENOUGH FUN'
May 5, 1986

Before I ever met Arnold Lazarus, I was positive that I was going to like him. How could I be so sure? Because it seemed to me that he and I viewed the world through the same porthole, at least in one important area: the value of fun.

I was interviewing Julian Slowinski, a Philadelphia psychologist who has collaborated with Lazarus on a number of professional papers, and he told me that Lazarus, on hearing of the death a friend, always says: "I hope he had enough fun."

Think about that for a moment, as I did.

Lazarus doesn't say "I hope he made enough money." He doesn't say "I hope he had enough success." Or a big-enough title. Or enough windows in his corner office. Lazarus says, "I hope he had enough fun."

Can anything be more important — or more difficult — than having fun?

■

Lazarus, who is a professor of psychology at Rutgers University and has one of the best-known names worldwide in the therapy field, told me in an interview that having fun is "a difficult philosophy to articulate. . . . It's because of the work ethic. In some circles, fun is viewed as the least preferred mode, and fun and sin are almost synonymous. . . .

"The emphasis on achievement . . . So many people are trying to prove something to themselves — that they're adequate, worthwhile, good.   It's pernicious as all hell. They're driven, and they see fun as a waste of time. . . . Leisure interferes" with their head-first plunge into work, and they tend to regard fun as the enemy.

You can look in just about any direction, Lazarus said, and find people — lots of people — who would rather "work hard to get ahead than have fun. . . . The Japanese culture seems to put little emphasis on fun. What they teach their little kids is produce, produce, produce. . . .

"When I look at some athletes, read their histories, I feel sorry for them. They start at age 3 or 4, and they're driven. This doesn't sound like fun to me. . . . We're so socked into the work ethic, the orientation that accomplishment is all that matters, that we don't know how to have fun. We go on vacations loaded down with books and journals. . . .

"I'm not saying that work can't be fun" for many people much of the time or even for some few people all of the time. "But we need the added dimension of genuine pleasure, with a tinge of hedonism, with the things that spice up life."

Lazarus said he often asks people if they're having fun. Many say no, not right now, but they're planning to have fun in the future — after their list of achievements is high enough to represent a crowning glory. "But the catch is that they never live to see it — or else they're so conditioned to work that they can't handle fun. . . . Some people feel guilty about having fun."

As a therapist, what does Lazarus do about this?

"I try to assuage their guilt, any way I can. . . . But it's a psychological fact that if you do something steadily for eight or 10 hours — what we call 'massed practice' — you don't do it as well as if you rest and pause — what we call 'distributed practice.' It's a fact that distributed practice always wins over massed practice. . . .

"So if people can begin to see leisure as a way of recharging their batteries, maybe they'll be able to give themselves permission to have fun so they can be more effective at work. I would hope that this then would become contagious in a positive way and catch on, that people would begin to get into having fun for its own sake, not just to be productive."

Ah, yes, having fun for its own sake.

"Two people die. About one we say, 'Well, Charles dropped dead at 36. [He] never seemed to have any fun. His trip through life was so arid.' But then there's William, who also died at 36. 'It's sad that he died, but, boy, he packed a lot of fun into his life.' What a difference. What an incredible difference."

It's so important, Lazarus said, for people to "get joy from this, warm fuzzies from that. Some confuse this with a drop-out philosophy — don't work; just have fun. That's not what I advocate. I'm talking about balance, about distributed practice, which is a philosophy that goes a long way. . . . Total fun without any counter would have to be very dull. We have to have night to appreciate day," and we have to have work to appreciate fun. But not all work and no fun.

Lazarus said his own "fun prescription" was born in 1970 when he was at Yale University. "Fun always had been incidental to me before, but this was a turning point. At Yale, I was around eminent professors. I saw these people not having fun. Many of them had reached the top of the hierarchy — but their marriages were on the rocks, their kids strung out on drugs, their personal lives a mess.

"I could come out of a movie at 11 or midnight, and the lights always would be on in their offices. They always were working. . . . They could say that they were having fun. Well, maybe so, but I have difficulty believing it. . . . Some said they had fun playing chess, but then all they'd do was play chess, which became obsessional. . . . Fun is easy, without the driven quality. . . .

"I asked myself: Do I want to be one of them? To be like them, I'd have to serve on more committees, play more political games, give many more talks and write many more papers — instead of doing fun things. . . . I wanted to write and do things for fun — not because I had to."

The result of his decision back then is evident today. "I publish less than my more ambitious colleagues," but he has more fun.

"Our early conditioning tells us to compete, to achieve, to do better. It's malignant. It has to be put in perspective" if we are in any way to savor life.

WHEN IT'S TIME TO QUIT YOUR JOB
May 9, 1988

How do you know when it's time to quit your job? It's a simple question, and psychologist Peter Wylie had a relatively simple answer:

"The number-one thing to pay attention to is your day-to-day level of happiness, contentment and satisfaction on the job. If you walk in and you're bright-eyed and bushy-tailed, raring to go, that's one thing. But if getting out of bed with the prospect of going to work is a major effort, then you need to pay attention to that. . . . I talk to so many people for whom the very thought of work is miserable."

Wylie is co-author with psychologist Mardy Grothe of the book *Problem*

Bosses: Who They Are and How to Deal With Them. He and Grothe are best friends and partners in Performance Improvement Associates, a management-consulting firm based in Boston and Washington. In an interview, Wylie said there were at least two other benchmark reasons for thinking seriously about quitting a job:

"If you're ambitious and you work in a family-owned business — somebody else's family — you will find that the way to the top is pretty much blocked off. No matter how good you are, you'll not be able to get around the son-in-law or brother who is heir-apparent to the throne. If you want to be a chief executive officer, you'll have to go somewhere else."

"If you're in a situation where the boss is doing something illegal, unethical or so contrary to your basic values and beliefs that you can't tolerate it. You wake up one morning and say, 'I can't abide this any more. I've got to get out.' You've got to be able to look at yourself in the mirror," and if compromises you're asked to make at work cause you to turn away, then it's time to take a walk.

■

Why are so many people apparently so unhappy in their work? I told Wylie that I, too, hear from people who are enormously distressed, who have lost the passion, fire and enthusiasm for what they do — if, indeed, they ever had passion, fire and enthusiasm. What's the problem?

"I work for myself, and I'm happy," said Wylie, "so you're going to get a biased answer from me. What I think is that most people you talk to who are unhappy are working in an organization for somebody else. They're salaried. They've traded off their sense of independence, enthusiasm, freedom and excitement about work for the security that a job in a stable organization offers. . . .

"They have a good salary; their job is not going to dry up tomorrow; they have excellent benefits. . . . They also have a couple of kids ready for college. They think they need the job, the security . . . and the tradeoff is to work for somebody who may be a problem boss, who doesn't pay attention to their needs, to work in an organization that has specific roles and slots for people" and doesn't deal individually with people.

"It's a form of modern enslavement," said Wylie. "You get paid, but what you do doesn't make your life exciting. It's what leads people to the lives of quiet desperation that you read about."

■

Is it possible to reshape a job so that a person gets more of what he or she likes and does best and less of what he or she doesn't like and does poorly?

Yes and no, said Wylie, but it's a good thing to think about.

"Jobs vary tremendously in the amount you can tinker with. But regardless, the important thing to remember is that we all have got the capacity to ask ourselves, 'How would I like to change my job to make it better?' If you had your druthers, how would you redefine your job? Even if you don't have the freedom to do it, it's a good question to ask. It's a first step — and then you can work back. If you don't ask the question in the first place," you never have the opportunity to initiate change, and you continue to slog along in a job that grinds you down.

■

114

Darrell Sifford's high school life revolved around sports and he won a football scholarship at the University of Missouri. But he dropped out of the football program after a year.

Darrell knew in his 20s . . .   . . . that he wanted to write.

Marilyn and Darrell in their Philadelphia condominium in 1981.

Hazel Sifford, Darrell's mother, during a 1978 visit to Darrell and Marilyn.

Charlie Sifford, Darrell's father.

Hazel and Charlie were married 53 years.

Darrell and his sons, Jay and Grant, in 1982.

At a health fair at the Hospital of the University of Pennsylvania. Marilyn Sifford was Director of Human Resources Development there.

Darrell devoted great effort to mending his relationships with his sons, Jay and Grant. His 1982 book, *Father and Son*, told that story.

Darrell and Marilyn in Guatemala, two days before his sudden death.

A river trip into the mainland of Belize was part of the fantasy trip he wrote about before his final vacation. He died three days later.

A 1982 portrait photographed for his book, *Father and Son*.

Is it possible, in a healthy way, for boss and employee to have a personal relationship that transcends the professional relationship in the office? I told Wylie that, as a boss, I had decided against any personal relationships after I had to fire a friend who broke an unbreakable rule. It was agony for me, and I vowed after that always to keep friendship out of the office.

Wylie had an interesting response.

"There's been an old injunction in the business world against being too personal . . . but the fact is if you look at the work world, you see all kinds of very strong friendships between bosses and employees. . . . It's evident to me that social relationships that go far beyond normal business relationships can and often do work to everybody's benefit. . . .

"So one day you have to fire a friend — it happens — and this is a reason why people say if you get too close, when the time comes to make a hard decision, it's much harder. That's a sound argument . . . except that when you're talking about two people who work together, it's hard to put the brakes on things that are so natural and basic as good chemistry between people. It's hard to hold back feelings that automatically bond people together. . . .

"You get close. Yes, it makes it hard when the relationship ends, but is that a reason not to have a relationship? It's a little bit like asking kids not to get attached to their parents or for neighbors not to get attached to neighbors. When parents die or neighbors move away, there's tremendous pain," but there's also the tremendous joy that remains from the relationship.

Who can say that the one is not worth the other?

THE DEMAND FOR WORKAHOLICS
July 30, 1981

It's not uncommon these days to read stories proclaiming that a new enlightenment has flooded into the dark corners of corporate life. Big business, we're told, now grasps the concept that an employee who leads a balanced life — who doesn't think that the job means everything — is a healthy and valuable employee. No longer must an employee put everything — and then some — into the job to succeed.

Sounds great, doesn't it?

Well, hold on. A businessman is getting ready to tell us that if we believe those stories, we probably believe in Santa Claus and red-nosed reindeer, too. The truth is that big business, for the most part, still demands that last drop of blood.

Edward H. Kuljian, who is president of his own management consulting firm, Edward H. Kuljian Associates, says that pressure still abounds in corporate life to be a workaholic. "If you do the job well and lead a balanced life, but if a peer is a workaholic, then I'm afraid that the sentiment in the executive suite often goes with the guy who is there until 8:30 every night — even if your work is as good as his."

The people who are talking about how corporations have changed really haven't spent much time in executive suites, Kuljian said.

"When it gets to the top, a lot of those people make unreasonable demands on employees," he said, and this is going to continue until corporations, from top to bottom, make a decision "not to penalize people for wanting balanced lives."

Kuljian formerly was chief executive officer of Kuljian Corp., a family-owned business that designed and built power plants and industrial projects around the world. He left not long after it merged with a foreign company in 1978 and two years later founded his consulting business.

In the wonderful world of big business, he said, it's not uncommon for a chief executive officer "to call a Sunday afternoon meeting, to tell you to forget your weekend and come on in. If you analyze what caused the urgency, you can't find anything. But if you say that, no, you can't come to the meeting because it's your daughter's birthday, then your loyalty is judged to be misplaced."

Why don't people simply quit rather than work under unreasonable conditions? Well, said Kuljian, some do — usually "self-confident people who find that the [work] environment is not tolerable, who say that this is absurd and not suited to their lifestyles. But if you've been with a company for 15 years and established a track record, if you're in a senior position, maybe you're afraid to say 'no' to unreasonable demands.

"In many ways, it's a bondage that pays extremely well. A boss tells you that he'll pay you twice what you're now making if you come to work for him. You say: 'Good Lord, that's great!' But the caveat is: 'Now that I own you body and soul, I don't want any nonsense when I call you at 2 in the morning; I don't want to hear about your going on vacation or planning a free weekend.' It sounds crazy, but you look at some of the big Fortune 500 companies, and you find that they have CEOs who act that way."

Selling your body and soul to the corporation is fine if that's what you really want, Kuljian said, but be aware of what can happen." The consequences [usually] are horribly damaging to any family relationship. You sort of become a monster . . . and it's hard to get out of it — especially if your peers are doing it, too."

Before you're trapped, it's a good idea to back off and make a conscious decision to keep your options open, Kuljian said. That way you can abandon ship if a goofy boss constantly tries to pull you away from the family and into the office on weekends.

Here are some ways to keep options open:

¶ Become active outside the corporation so that people will know you. "Get involved in trade or professional associations; author papers; get into leadership roles; serve on a reasonable number of institutional boards." Pretty soon the word will get around that you're a solid character — and you'll have job opportunities thrown at your feet.

¶ Discuss with the family whether you — all of you — are suited to run a small business on your own. If you are, you can give it a try sometime.

¶ Be aware that universities increasingly are looking to business people for leadership." If you have scholarly credentials, you even could be a visiting professor."

¶ Don't automatically turn your back on government jobs. "Suppose there's a job for a year or two in a state that's looking for a director of energy resources. It's something that fits your skills, and you could gain great visibility" that would permit you to move on to something else.

What it all adds up to, Kuljian said, is that "you should be trying to flirt with your thoughts and do something to give you visibility in other markets." People can do things other than stay in the same industry — despite what is commonly believed — if they develop broad interests.

Kuljian, 48, said that he never was trapped in the dismal world of workaholism because "I had a couple of ulcers by the time I was 30. I made a judgment that when I recovered, the job would not be everything to me. I had a goal — to do my best. But if I didn't succeed, the world wouldn't come to an end. I was not indispensable to the company or the world. I decided that I could get enjoyment from other things — from hobbies, from friendships.

"As my epitaph, I hope they'll write: 'He wasn't expert in everything, but he sure . . . was a well-rounded guy who did a lot of things.' That helped support me when I had to face up to leaving the company. My outside interests and friendships gave me support."

If he had been an 18-hour workaholic, would he have survived his company's merger? No . . . and he probably wouldn't have kept his health either.

Is there anything left to say?

REDEFINING SUCCESS
July 10, 1986

Not long ago, Rabbi Harold Kushner was speaking to physicians at Johns Hopkins Hospital in Baltimore on a timely topic: how to avoid burnout.

His message was that burnout stems not from working hard but from feeling that the work is futile. Doctors who define success as saving the lives of patients are going to be buried in feelings of futility, he said, because it's not possible to save everybody. What doctors need to do is redefine success as keeping as high as possible the quality of life that remains. If they do that, he said, there will be less futility — and less burnout.

It was a message, he would say, that he learned the hard way, from personal experience.

"There was a phase when I considered leaving the rabbinate — as did all of my classmates, less than half of whom are still congregational rabbis. What happened was that we saw adults in our congregations living lives and holding value systems that were against what we preached. . . . And we felt like failures. . . . I had to redefine success. I asked myself, 'How many have I helped through terrible crises? How many have I taught to find transcendental meaning of life?' Then I felt good," because then he felt successful.

■

Rabbi Kushner, 50, is rabbi of Temple Israel in Natick, Mass., near Boston, and he became known around the world five years ago with his international best seller *When Bad Things Happen to Good People.* His new book is *When All You've Ever Wanted Isn't Enough*, which lays out a roadmap for people who are searching for a life that matters.

In an interview, I asked Rabbi Kushner what he considers the cornerstone of success, and he said that it unquestionably centered on touching other people in positive ways.

"I'm gratified by my last book not because it brought me some measure of fame and fortune, but because five years later I still get letters from people who tell me how it changed their lives. If my airplane crashes on the way to Chicago today, I will leave behind people whose lives I touched."

I asked him how people who are not highly visible can help other people. After all, it's one thing for him, as a popular writer, to say that the greatest success possible is to touch others. But it may be quite another thing for a harried homemaker in Mitchell, Ind., or a plumber's helper in Jefferson City, Mo. What about that?

It was a good question, said Rabbi Kushner, but "I would insist that virtually everybody can do on a less conspicuous scale what you and I do in the public eye. If we measure success in human terms, we have a lot more successes that people might think.

"There was a woman, 55, who called on a radio talk show to tell me that she felt like a failure. Her children hadn't turned out as well as she had hoped; she was in a dead-end job; she didn't want to get up in the morning. . . . What did I say to her? I said that if we could spend an hour together, I was confident that we could find ways in which she had succeeded. . . .

"We have to stop defining success as money, as the thickness of the carpet, as the power to shape others, as how many people salute when we walk in the office in the morning. . . . We have to define the degree to which we have become authentically human. Only then is it possible to define ourselves as successful. . . .

"Are you a responsible, reliable person, a good wife and mother — even if your kids didn't turn out the way you wanted? You can't take all the blame. The kids have got to assume some of the blame. . . . If you're not completely satisfied with that, then start over now on that part of yourself. If the job is dead-end, if the career as mother is mostly over, then try to isolate success in areas you can still change. Work on your image of wholeness . . . so that at 60 the world will look different to you."

■

Rabbi Kushner said that he was visited in his office a while back by a woman from the congregation who told him that she felt as if her life added up to zero.

"She was unhappy with her kids. . . . Her marriage was very dull and she was in a job she hated. What did she have to look forward to? She seemed to think that most of the nice things that were going to happen to her already had happened.

"She had two kids, and she said, 'If they marry people I approve of, I'll have two weddings to look forward to. If they marry people I don't approve of, even those won't be happy days. At best, I'll have two happy days out of the next 30 years.'

"Now this is a nice, pleasant, attractive woman. . . . What did I say to her? First of all, I didn't try to help by giving her an answer. . . . I help most by taking her seriously as a person. She knows how busy I am, but I find time to see her one day after she calls. I tell my secretary to hold everything except emergency calls during the hour that I spend with her. The message I'm trying to give is, 'You are an important person.'

"I tried to point out the successes in her life . . . and her need to redefine success. It's spring, the baseball season is here, and flowers are blooming. Exciting things are going on in the world. . . . The meaning of life is not found in great successes and in great events. No one gets an answer to what life is about from a single success. That's like trying to find the answer to hunger with one great meal. You've got to eat a pretty good meal every day. . . . The meaning of life is found in the ability to do human things every single day. . . . To be a human being is something you do a little bit of every day."

The answer is to do what Ecclesiastes recommended: "Go, eat your bread in gladness and drink your wine in joy."

Said Rabbi Kushner: "If logic tells you that, in the long run, nothing makes a difference because we all die and disappear, then don't live in the long run. . . . Learn to savor the moment, even if it does not last forever."

GRINDING IT OUT, 9 TO 5
unpublished

It was a column about unhappy people in the workforce, people who, if they had it all to do over again, wouldn't. They work because they must, and they work without joy and reward. For them, it's a grind every day.

Here is one letter that in some ways speaks for many that I have received from all around the country. Work-related unhappiness, you see, knows no geographical bounds. The letter:

■

"I work for a large bank that seems to have uncaring management on too many levels. When our department went through a change, I thought the morale was as low as it could get. It didn't take a lot for morale to rise because the new crew said and did all the right things. The problem is that it was short-lived, and now we are treated worse than before, if that's possible. . . .

"A few of us whose positions always have paid overtime have suddenly been made exempt from overtime pay. Our jobs demand overtime and in addition to not getting paid for it, we now have to take work home from other areas, too. We get frequent last-minute demands to do extra work after hours. One person who explained that she had a prior commitment was told either to get it done before she went out that night or to do it when she got back. It's as if we aren't expected to have a life after work . . . . These demands come from managers who work strictly 9 to 5 and hardly ever work a full five-day week. . . .

"Recently we were called to a meeting and given new times for lunch and breaks. Anyone who had a buddy for these times quickly learned they were given separate schedules. My supervisor told me later that these relationships were broken up to prevent gossiping. . . .

"Most of the positions in our department are low-paying and have repetitive tasks. We work on constant deadlines and this produces a great deal of stress. Everything we do is a priority and, therefore, we have no non-essential items we can eliminate or delay. . . . All the bad things that happen to us are on top of the bank's cutting our benefits to the bone. . . .

"To add insult to injury we are expected to recognize our managers and supervisors on special occasions with gifts and to buy whatever their children's private schools are selling during their fund-raising drives. . . .

"I am my sole support, and I'm too old to make a change, so I'll have to tough this out. The way I get through it is some positive reinforcement with a brief reading from my Bible every morning. I work hard at not allowing negative thoughts to hang around too long. . . .

"Short of quitting, what ideas can you offer those of us who are in this trap?"

■

I rebel at the thought that anybody is "too old to make a change," but I hear it so often that I have to assume that many people believe it. So for today, let's assume it's true and the woman who wrote the letter and her friends have to make the best of the situation.

What can they do?

My first thought ordinarily would be that they need to get together with their friends at work for some old-fashioned schmoozing, diversion that brings them together emotionally and keeps their minds off their troubles, as much as possible. But schmoozing is out — because of the bank's commitment to minimize gossiping. What then?

If there's any virtue in low-paying, repetitive jobs, it is that they can be done by rote, without much conscious thought. This means that it's possible to some extent to daydream, to fantasize, to transport the mind to new ideas and exciting places while the body stays behind and grinds out the work. This is a possibility — and for some people it may be the option of choice, the only option.

But there's something about this that bothers the idealist in me. I don't like it when people merely go through the motions, maybe because I had a few people like that, for a while, when I was a newspaper editor. What I like is for people to speak up if they're unhappy, to tell me that they want some pride of ownership in their jobs, that they want to get involved in changing the way things are done.

Can people in by-the-number jobs ever really get involved?

Yes, they can — sometimes. Jim Smith, the psychologist who directs Temple University's vocational counseling clinic, was telling me the classic story of the commercial building that was going to the dogs because it was dirty and dingy and nobody seemed to care. Then employees of the cleaning company got together, promised to produce results if they had a hand in running things. An enlightened boss recognized opportunity when he saw it, and he let workers set their schedules and standards for cleanliness and select and buy their supplies. The result: a building that gleamed.

So it can happen, and I think it's worth a try. After all, management can do no worse than say no, in which case by-the-numbers workers haven't lost anything, except their expectations.

What if management wants no part of it? What then?

The word that comes to mind is compartmentalize. Workers need to do what they can, as best they can, on the job, and then at day's end they need to leave it all behind, intellectually and emotionally, and try not to let their frustrations dampen the rest of life. They can try to get their fun, identity, and reward from what they do after 5 or 6 or 9 o'clock.

It's not the way I'd want to live, but for too many people it's the way they must do it. We have to play life's game with the cards we're dealt, and sometimes the cards are not good enough.

It's not fair, but life is not necessarily fair. That's a fact that needs to be recognized sooner rather than later.

NAVIGATING A JOB INTERVIEW
August 10, 1986

If you were a fly on the wall in the corporate offices in which job interviews are conducted, you'd probably hear a lot of the same questions asked time after time.

This is because the good interviewers know which questions to ask to find out not only about the applicant's skills but also about how the applicant thinks, how he or she views the world, how committed he or she is to getting the job done and still preserving some sense of balance in life.

These are the questions, said psychologist Raymond P. Harrison, that job-seekers need to study and for which they should prepare answers that are honest and, if possible, tell the interviewers what they want to hear.

Harrison, who is a vice president in the Philadelphia office of Drake Beam Morin Inc., an international consulting firm, said that he often works with displaced executives to help them get relocated, and that a key part of the help consists of their rehearsing responses to questions that surely will be asked during their interviews.

Drake Beam Morin gives these displaced executives a list of 59 of the most-often-asked and difficult questions — and some possible responses for them to consider. Anybody who is preparing for an interview should expect to field many of the questions, said Harrison. Here are some of the questions and comments:

¶ Tell me about you. "Keep your answer to one or two minutes; don't ramble. Cover four segments — early years, education, work experience, recent times — with an accent on the latter."

¶ What do you know about our company? "Know products, size, income, reputation, image, goals, problems, management talent, management style, people, skills, history and philosophy. Don't say you don't know much. . . . You should state that you would like to know more."

¶ Why do you want to work for us? "You wish to be part of a company project; you would like to solve a company problem; you can make a definite contribution to specific company goals."

¶ What can you do for us that someone else can't? "Relate past experience that represents success in solving previous employer problems that may be similar to those of the prospective employer."

¶ What do you look for in a job? "Keep your answer opportunity-oriented. Talk about the opportunity to perform and be recognized."

¶ How long would it take you to make a meaningful contribution to our firm? "Be realistic and say six months to one year."

¶ How long would you stay with us? "As long as we both feel achievement-oriented."

¶ You may be overqualified or too experienced for the position we have to offer. "Strong companies need strong people; experienced executives are at a premium today; the employer will get a faster return on investment because you have more experience than required; a growing, energetic company rarely is unable to use its people talents. Emphasize your interest in a long-term association."

¶ Why are you leaving your present job? "Stick to one response. Don't change answers during the interview. Give a 'group' answer if possible — 'Our office is closing.' Another possible answer: 'We agreed to disagree.' "

¶ How do you feel about leaving all of your benefits? "Concerned but not panicked."

¶ Describe what you feel to be an ideal working environment. "Where people are treated as fairly as possible."

¶ How would you evaluate your present firm? "An excellent company that afforded me many fine experiences." It's important, said Harrison, not to bad-mouth past employers or bosses. Bad-mouthing tends to reveal more about you than about those who are the objects of your comments.

¶ Why haven't you found a new position before now? "Finding a job is easy but finding the right job is more difficult."

¶ Had you thought of leaving your present position before? If so, what do you think held you there? "Challenge. But it's gone now."

¶ If I spoke to your previous boss, what would he say are your greatest strengths and weaknesses? This, said Harrison, is one of the so-called TORC questions — Threat of Reference Check — that are popular today. They almost always produce not only honesty but also perspiration. It's important, in your response, to "be honest but not too negative."

¶ What are your strong points? "Present at least three. Relate them to the interviewing company and job opening."

¶ What are your weak points? "Don't say you have none. Turn a negative into a positive answer: 'I am sometimes impatient and I get too deeply involved when we are late.' "

¶ How much do you expect if we offer this position to you? "Be careful; the market value of the job may be the key answer — 'My understanding is that a job like the one you're describing may be in the range of . . . .'"

¶ What was the last book you read? Movie you saw? Sporting event you attended? "Talk about leisure books to represent balance in your life."

¶ Will you be out to take your boss' job? "Not until I get the current job done."

¶ How would you describe the essence of success? According to your definition, how successful have you been so far? "A sense of well-being . . . Pretty successful with the usual ups and downs."

■

At some point in every interview, said Harrison, the interviewer will say something like, "Well, I've done most of the talking; now do you have any questions for me?" It's important that the applicant have some questions — and some good ones — because questions can reveal as much about the applicant as answers. Here are some good questions to ask the interviewer when the time comes:

¶ Why is this position open?

¶ How often has it been filled in the last five to 10 years?

¶ What have been the primary reasons for individuals leaving?

¶ What would you like done differently by the next person who fills this job?

¶ What is most pressing? What would you like to see done in the next two or three months?

¶ What are some of the longer-term objectives that you would like completed?

¶ What freedom would I have in determining my work objectives, deadlines and methods of measurement?

¶ Where could a person go who is successful in this position and within what time frame?

¶ How is one judged? What accounts for success?

■

Well, there you have it. Any more questions — or answers?

A FARAWAY LOOK IN HIS EYES
February 21, 1984

The Man was 39 and correspondent in a state capital bureau for the Associated Press. The Boy was 20 and a third-year journalism student.

They didn't talk much — not because the Boy didn't want to talk but because the Boy thought that the Man was too busy to be bothered. After all, whenever their paths crossed, the Man seemed always to be on the run, a cigarette glued to his lower lip, his eyes focused on something that the Boy never was able to see.

The Man had two offices — one in a corner of the Capitol press room, the other, six blocks away, on the second floor of the building that housed the local newspaper for which the Boy worked afternoons and nights while he went to college. The Man had one full-time writer who worked with him and, when the state legislature was in session, he often had three or four helpers. But when the chips were down, when it was a big story that rode deadline, it seemed that the Man always was the one on the firing line.

123

Sometimes the Boy wandered over to the press room to watch the Man as he battled — and inevitably defeated — the clock that hung from the wall above the cumbersome machine into which he punched stories that would be relayed to newspaper offices around the country and, sometimes, around the world.

There was no magic computer in this era — just a pale green machine that spat out perforated tape, a machine that couldn't accept words as rapidly as the Man dispensed them. Often, as the clock ticked off the minutes, the Man quietly cursed the machine's slowness and, sometimes, if the story was big and the hour was late, he cursed loudly.

The Boy marveled not so much at the Man's flying fingers as at the Man's mind. How was it possible to tie words together so quickly? Often, it seemed to the Boy, that the Man hardly consulted the scribbling in his notebook. It was almost as if the contents had been committed to memory, and now the Man simply was repeating what some little voice was whispering to him.

Sometimes, the ashes at the end of the dangling cigarette accumulated until, jarred by the pounding fingers, they tumbled onto the keyboard and lay there in little gray mounds until the Man swept them away, which he did without missing a keystroke.

Once the Boy summoned courage to ask the Man, when deadline temporarily was defeated, how he did it, how he wrote with such speed.

"You do it because you have to do it," the Man said. "I can't give you a better answer than that."

The Boy wanted more, but the telephone rang, and the Man, after a conversation of no more than half a dozen words, grabbed his notebook and ran from the room. The deadline race had begun again.

Sometimes, the Boy covered the same story as the Man, and the Boy always thought that watching the Man close up at work was the most meaningful part of his education — something that no journalism school ever could re-create. Occasionally, the most meaningful part came after the story was written — when the Man allowed himself the luxury of a few minutes over a cup of coffee.

The Boy never forgot the day that a racial demonstration erupted at the local university and produced not only big news, but also considerable property damage. They wrote their stories, the Boy and the Man, and then, quite by accident, they met over coffee at a neighborhood cafe.

"You know what just happened?" asked the Man.

"What?"

"I talked to the president at the university and he said: 'We don't need this kind of publicity.' He asked me to go easy on the story."

"What'd you do?"

"I told him that I don't deal in publicity; I deal in news."

It was something else that the Boy never forgot and, over the years, he used that line himself — when somebody asked him to back away from a story. "I don't deal in publicity; I deal in news." It was truly a great line — not just because the Man had uttered it, but because nobody could counter it. Inevitably, it ended the conversation.

There were other memories — like the time when a convict escaped from the state prison, and again the Boy and the Man worked on the same story. The people with the sawed-off shotguns and the hounds caught the convict just after midnight, and the Boy and the Man raced back to the newsroom and sat next to each other and wrote.

No, that's not exactly the way it was. It's more precise to say that the Man wrote and the Boy watched — watched the flying fingers in awe.

"How do you do it? How can you be so fast?" the Boy asked when the Man was finished.

"You have to write the story in your head while you're on the way back to the office. That's the trick. Write it in your head. Then, when you sit at the typewriter, all you have to do is transcribe what's in your head. Anybody can learn to do it. All it takes is practice."

Now the Boy understood what it was that the Man had focused on all those times when he had that faraway look in his eyes. The Man was writing his story in his mind. That's why there was no time for small talk. The Man was at work — even as he drove his car and ran up and down steps.

It was a lesson that the boy never forgot and, over the years, he practiced what he came to call "mind writing" — practiced until he was very fast. Not as fast as the Man — nobody ever could be that fast. But very fast.

The Man never realized the impact that he had on the Boy because the Boy grew up and moved far away. But the Boy always remembered the Man, and someday, when the time was right, he would tell the Man how indebted he felt to him.

Larry Hall is 71 years old now, retired from the Associated Press and from the Missouri State Senate job that he held after that. He looks to me much the same as he always did — except that he wears a gray beard. "When I went to work for the Senate, I thought I needed to look scholarly," he said, "and I liked the beard enough to keep it."

Not long ago, he and I met for lunch at the State House restaurant in the Governor Hotel, a few blocks from the Missouri state capitol in Jefferson City, and I told him:

"Larry, you influenced me professionally more than anybody in my life. You taught me how to write fast."

He looked surprised. "Gee, that's such a nice thing for you to say. I never knew that. Thank you."

I thanked him. And then we munched our sandwiches. It was like the old days because for a few minutes I was the Boy again and he was the Man. And it was sentimental and glorious.

Do you understand what I mean?

THE ESSENTIAL BALANCE IN LIFE
August 24, 1986

In the current issue of the Shingle, the magazine of the Philadelphia Bar Association, Chancellor-elect Seymour "Sy" Kurland writes about the magic of Mount Kilimanjaro.

"Its gentle, inviting slope and snow-covered dome rise suddenly and majestically out of the open plains of Tanzania. It is Hemingway's mountain, filled with mystical connotations of courage, manliness and self-discovery in the course of physical adventure."

He writes about climbing the mountain last winter and what he thought about as he scrambled for its 19,340-foot-high summit.

"My mind feels especially clear and is filled with thoughts of life's meaning. I think about what people constantly tell each other when a common friend becomes seriously ill: 'Be thankful you have your health; that's all that matters.' In our everyday world, that is a momentary truth. Out here, I believe it even more because it seems to me you have to use your body hard, feel its parts working smoothly, open your lungs fully, and sweat in the presence of trees, open sky, rocks and dirt for that truth to sink in at all with any permanence.

"I think, too, about staying in shape. To exercise just for the sake of staying healthy is boring and soon becomes work. I, at least, need a goal, like getting ready for a hike such as this. And as much fun as it is to be here in the outdoors feeling fit and alive, I couldn't simply spend my life doing that either. I have to earn it first with productive work and feel the contrast for it to be fun. Yet, to just work without the perspective that comes from physical exposure to nature is also stupid. It is a matter of balance in life."

■

Ah, yes, balance. It's what I talk about most when I get on my soapbox, and so right after I read Kurland's story, I made an appointment to interview him at his office in Center City, where he is a senior partner in the law firm of Wolf, Block, Schorr & Solis-Cohen.

Kurland, 56, who will become chancellor of the 10,000-member bar association in 1987, said that he didn't climb Kilimanjaro because he had anything to prove. "I was here in the office, feeling tense and anxious with all . . . that was going on, and I decided to take the trip. . . . Now I'm looking at a brochure on Nepal."

He started his love affair with the great outdoors 10 years ago — when he went on an Outward Bound program in North Carolina. That experience hooked him and opened up a process that eventually reshaped his philosophical approach to life. "The older I get, the more involved I am, the more I love nature," said Kurland, who has climbed mountains in Italy and Switzerland and hiked along Peru's Inca Trail.

When he's not working or traveling, Kurland often can be found "walking in the woods and reading Emerson. He's like my guru," since it was Emerson, through his writing, who introduced Kurland to the concept of balance.

"I come from the Jewish-European ethic, where you believe that life has to be productive and useful, that you must do something to advance civilization, to make the world work. . . . I feel it strongly. . . . I'm also 100-percent American Yankee, and from that perspective it's important that I do some things that are useful and productive. . . .

"I handle a good case, see a child grow up, run a dance for charity . . . and it feels wonderful. But I know that I can't just do that. If I did, I'd lose perspective and the enjoyment of it. It would become too all-encompassing . . . and I wouldn't be good at it anymore, and it wouldn't be fun."

Happiness, said Kurland, is "being able to enjoy a lot of things — not just work. It's listening to music, riding a bike, enjoying the outdoors. It was not just work but eight-hour walks that refreshed Emerson."

The problem with working too long and too hard, to the exclusion of other important things, is that your view of the world gets skewed, said Kurland.

"I work and I work, and I begin to feel that the whole world depends on whether this guy comes in and we can work things out. I think if this doesn't happen right, it's the end of the world. A momentary thing becomes total truth. . . . My whole life becomes the case," and this is when Kurland knows that it's time to bail out — and tackle Kilimanjaro or root around in nature closer to home.

For some people, he said, moving outdoors doesn't help because they simply take their neuroses along with them. "They wonder, 'Am I the best? Does the climbing instructor like me the most? Will I be first?' . . . They might as well stay at work. . . . You have to rise above that and enjoy where you are and what you're doing."

He's able to do this, he said, and it "takes me away from the narrow approach I have. It broadens my perspective and makes me feel good," and when he gets back to work, he feels fresh and ready to go again. At least for a while. "Sometimes for a full 28 minutes I have a sense of balance" before the rat race takes its toll. But at least he's aware that there is another side, that his whole life won't be a failure if he doesn't win the next case.

"I got to the top of [Kilimanjaro]. But some didn't. Are they failures? Am I a success? It's so foolish, but people do feel that way. . . . In Peru, I didn't make it all the way. I turned back, and for years I felt that I'd copped out. . . .

"A lawyer can win 28 cases in a row, and he has a good feeling for a day or two. But he loses one, and it hurts forever. The one you lose always says that you weren't good enough. And you feel like an impostor."

What is important to remember — and it's what Kurland preaches to young lawyers — is that in the long run, nothing is so serious that it commands a mind-set of gloom and doom. Even if you can't climb a mountain to escape, you can "go to a baseball game, eat a hot dog and play with the kids" to help bring home the reality that other things matter, too. "If you just bother with one thing, it gets too much significance. You lose your sense of balance . . . and you lose fun."

During his Emerson-like walks in the woods, Kurland encourages his mind to fly like an eagle. "I ask questions like, 'What makes water run? What is the original theory of the universe?' It's fun. My mind soars, and I end up re-evaluating life, and I have a new perspective. . . .

"I spent my life worrying if I'd be a senior partner, get a corner office, win the big case. . . . We get locked into a value system that protects us. I have a corner office, a private secretary, a senior partnership, and I'm locked into a system where I feel safe, where I can't be hurt. It's almost like I'll never die. . . .

"In a way we're all like this. We lock in, most of us, at a level that's too low.

We compromise and live in a house that's too little, work at a 'safe' job we don't like, marry somebody we may not love. We get locked in — and stop living. . . . We have to fight our lock-in, take everything we have and re-examine it. . . . What does it all mean? I go on my Sunday walks and argue with myself about my lock-in. That's how to free yourself from the lock-in," by challenging it.

"It's a way to step back and get out of the rut, to enjoy life more with a larger perspective. . . . I work at feeling good and being happy."

Sometimes that can be hard work.

"I go to Europe, and at first I'm unhappy. It's because I'm scared. I'm in a little hotel room. I'm carrying strange-looking money. My defenses are gone. . . . Nobody knows me. What I do in Philadelphia doesn't matter to anybody. I ask myself, 'Why am I here?' I could be in my home, with my furniture, with my car in my parking space. 'Why am I here?'

"So I'm unhappy for a day or two, then I notice that the people there have a way of life that's different. They sit and drink wine in the afternoon, and the world doesn't end. I start asking myself, 'Why do I take my stuff so seriously?' I think most of us are too serious, too frightened. What if I don't climb the mountain and they laugh at me? So what?"

If he feels that he is losing perspective, Kurland may "go over to the Y, get into my running clothes, talk to the guys I play handball with, run in a circle for three-fourths of an hour. . . . And I come out with my closing speech," which had eluded him back at the office. "Physical activity restores my mental balance. I use up energy and come out refreshed, with a clear head."

IN A FATHER'S PROFESSIONAL FOOTSTEPS
June 6, 1988

When he was growing up, Joel Fish perceived his father as "an emotional man who was passionate, curious and open to new ideas. He communicated to me the importance of feelings, of being sensitive, of how helping people could be a personally rewarding thing to do. He seemed happy and fulfilled at what he was doing, and he was able to make a living."

When the son added up all of that, he decided that, professionally, he was going to follow in his father's footsteps. "It felt right," and he became Dr. Joel H. Fish, a psychologist, like his father, Dr. Edward B. Fish. Now 33 and in practice for eight years, Joel said that he never has regretted his decision.

His older brother, Neal, 36, has a doctoral degree in social work and a master's degree in psychology. Obviously, the message that it was important and worthwhile to help people was received by him, too.

"Our grandfather was a rabbi," said Joel, "and we watched him and our father and identified positively with them. The expectation we felt was not so much that we go for graduate degrees as it was that we should be helpers. But it was very subtle. Nobody said, 'Business is not the direction in which you should go; you've got to be helpers.' Their actions spoke quite loudly to us . . . and we internalized the family's values."

Joel said that his father "never once told me that being a helper was the only way to be fulfilled. I can be stubborn, and if he had turned the screws on me to do it, I would have rebelled. I have a strong independent streak. But having freedom to choose, without any pressure, gave me the option of following him, and I believe I made a free choice."

■

What's it like when the child follows the father's career? Do they sit together and sip brandy and talk shop? It's something that I've overly romanticized, probably, because my sons long ago said that writing held about as much appeal for them as bullfighting. Is this additional parent-child bond really as great as I think it is?

It depends, said Joel Fish, on whether you're asking father or child. "I think the father's feelings about this are probably greater. My father is proud that I'm a psychologist. He was my model. From my end, I'm proud of him, but I probably don't have the same sentimentality about it that he has. It's the difference between being my father's son and being my own person."

What about shop talk?

"Our relationship fills a variety of needs. We talk about our work in a general sense, and we learn from each other, but I don't believe we talk about psychology any more than people talk about their work in unrelated fields. The core of our relationship is not talking shop. We talk about ideas, about life in general. Our curiosity about people permeates our conversation."

■

How does Ed Fish, the father, feel about things?

"We all like to think our kid is a chip off the old block. I'm proud . . . that he picked it for the right reasons. It was something he wanted to do. . . . I'm glad he adopted some of my value systems but, at the same time, retained his own individuality. The tricky part is for him to be Joel Fish, not Ed Fish's son, but to have a relationship with me that enables us to communicate on so many levels about so many subjects."

■

Joel Fish set up his private practice two blocks away from his father's office in Center City. "I wouldn't share an office with him . . . and I try to minimize getting referrals from him. I don't want to ride his coattails. I want to make it on my own. I want people to see me not as Ed Fish's son but as Joel Fish. This is important to me. If I ever was seen primarily as his son, it would be easy for me to fall back into a different role and be his son instead of an independent professional. . . .

"I would not want a partnership with my father. I understand some of the potential problems in family business, whether you're selling shoes or practicing psychology. It's important that he be my father, not my father/business associate. I need him to be my father, period. I don't want the role diluted, confused or contaminated. I want my relationship with him to be pure father and son."

He is able to take this stance and articulate his feelings in public, he said, because his father is "secure in his own competency, and he communicates this to me. I don't feel it's threatening to him for me to make more money, to carve

129

out my own spot. But if I sensed insecurity there, it would be difficult for me to be more visible, more successful."

■

I always wished that my two boys had gone into newspaper work — or at least given it a try. For a while, I thought that they were pointed in that direction. They succeeded each other as editor of their school newspaper, and we had some great times, I always thought, talking about how to develop stories, how to communicate concepts, how to lay out pages that would draw in readers. But their interest faded rather quickly, and, to their credit and my dismay, they didn't beat around the bush in explaining why.

I was at the peak — or maybe rock bottom — of my workaholic phase as an editor, frequently tired and almost always cranky and short-tempered. They logically assumed that this was what the newspaper business did to people, and they wanted no part of it. Grant once told me, "If this is what it's like to be a success, count me out." Actions do speak much louder than words, and by the time I repented, it was too late.

■

Joel Fish said that the reason for a good deal of father-child estrangement is that the father "feels rejected if the child doesn't follow his career. . . . What the father needs to articulate is that 'my child can love me and respect what I do and make a different career choice.' The trick is not to connect choice to love."

THE IMPOSTOR SYNDROME
September 28, 1986

Moss Jackson was talking about what has widely come to be called the "Impostor Syndrome" — feeling that you don't deserve the good things that have happened to you — and he asked these questions:

"Who are the impostors? What is the terror that must be avoided? Is anyone immune? How does one deal with failure?"

And then he responded:

"Shame depends on one's orientation to learning versus performance standards. In learning, for example, mistakes are a necessary source of information and intrinsic to the learning process. In performance, the emphasis is only on accuracy. Impostors appear to worry too much about performance and not enough about learning."

■

Jackson is a family therapist and executive director of the Center for Creative Development in Ardmore, Pa. In an interview, he talked about a friend, a man in midlife, "with the basic position: 'Don't be afraid. Be independent and brave.' He's like Gary Cooper. . . . He doesn't learn from his fears because, to him, fears are to be ignored, handled or squashed. . . .

"Anything that touches on fear makes him feel vulnerable — so he avoids it, and a big part of his feelings is inaccessible to him. He has polio of the emotions. . . . With such inflexibility, he can't really be present. He's a non-learner. He's a performer. He's more interested in performance than in learning about himself."

He's an impostor.

■

Jackson said that impostors have an "extreme need to be successful. Yet it's hard for them to know what success is. . . . In therapy they often don't define success, but they talk instead about 'making a mark.' They put tremendous emphasis on the outside — instead of looking into the self and asking if what they're doing fits with their value system."

The emphasis, said Jackson, is on looking good at all costs, including the bending of integrity. "They say things like 'What does it matter — as long as you look good?' They've living up to external standards, instead of asking, 'Does it serve me and my goals?' "

The primary fear of many impostors, said Jackson, is that "in the background is the little kid who may come out and say that the emperor wears no clothes, who may say, 'Hey, you don't know what . . . you're talking about.' "

Impostors invest a lot of energy in muffling the little kid, that inner voice that is the true self. In doing so, they deceive themselves — and in some ways they kill a little bit of themselves.

■

Impostors, said Jackson, tend to come from two types of parents:

¶ Those who are perfectionist. "Nothing the kid does is ever quite good enough, and the kid decides that he has to prove that he is good enough. The kid equates feeling good about himself with high performance . . . and he forever tries to make up for the lack of support at home. He's always striving for approval," which, sadly, always eludes him because an impostor can't get enough approval to wipe out the self-doubts.

¶ Those who wildly cheer their children on. "The message is, 'As a family, we are No. 1.' I once saw a family of five impostors. All were successful but scared stiff. They were afraid that they would embarrass or shame the family by not being good enough" — no matter how good they were.

■

Impostors tend to be victims of what Jackson called the "law of the three P's" — perfectionism, procrastination, paralysis.

"You have to give a speech, and you feel the excitement and you say, 'This has to be the best.' So you work hard, but you're not satisfied, and then you begin to procrastinate. You feel paralyzed because of the possibility of rejection and, worst of all, ridicule. The danger is in looking foolish.

"As you get close to the time of the speech, you panic, but you get it done. It's true that impostors break through. Despite everything, they do get the work done, and usually it's pretty good. They get objective evidence of their success, but they don't believe it. They say, 'I was just lucky. Next time they'll see through me.'

"Impostors give themselves no credit for a good job. They leave the competency piece out."

■

Historically, said Jackson, people worked their way up the ladder of success, one step at a time. "There was a long apprenticeship with a mentor . . . and clear guidelines to follow for success. Now it's relatively easy to be a quick success and make a lot of money. It's the 'Silicon Valley Syndrome.' You're good at data processing, say, and at 26 you're put into middle management — although you're not worldly enough to supervise people, make decisions and engage in developmental thinking. . . .

"What follows is rapid burnout — and often drug or alcohol abuse and conspicuous consumption. . . . Our society is rewarding performance so quickly that the person doesn't know on the inside that he can do it," and so the person becomes an impostor who gives himself no credit for competency.

"If you ask people, 'Why are you successful?' would most say, 'Because I'm capable,' or 'Because I'm lucky'?"

There's a little bit of the impostor in all of us at times, said Jackson, but in some people it's the dominant force in their lives, the skeleton that must be wrestled with every single day.

"The impostor has three symptoms: misery, anxiety, depression. The acronym is MAD. . . . They feel it'll be a catastrophe if they're not good enough," and the Catch-22 is that they can't ever be good enough. "They operate with a kind of logic that imprisons them in nonsatisfaction."

■

What can the impostor do to free himself or herself?

Jackson offered these suggestions:

¶ Become aware of the pattern. "Do you see yourself as an impostor? Are you scared of other people's evaluations? Do you believe their compliments?"

¶ Come out of the closet. "Tell people that you're an impostor. Say, 'I want you to know that about me.' You can be authentic about being an impostor — and this may get you more open to praise."

¶ Try some mental imagery. "Envision yourself as being responsible for your successes. . . . In your mind, go back to childhood and, as an adult, say to your father what you really experienced as a child. Deal with the toxicity of no praise or too much praise. Reconceptualize your past."

¶ Make little changes, one at a time. "Don't bite off too much. Ask a friend for a little feedback, a little praise — and then stop the friend before you begin to think, '. . . he thinks I'm better than I am.' "

¶ Drop the perfectionism. "Hit the underlying assumption: 'I have to be perfect to be loved.' Challenge it with a new assumption: 'I will fail sometimes, but I'm still OK . . . and what I do or don't do has nothing to do with who I am.' "

CHILD'S PLAY TO LIFE'S WORK
October 4, 1983

The penmanship is unmistakably boyish — loose, looping letters forming words that ride precariously atop the blue lines of the two-ring notebook paper. The paper is terribly smudged with fingerprints, and some of the holes along the margin are ripped out, so that the pages sometimes slide out of the

orange-and-black notebook, the back cover of which is hanging on by a few fragile strands of thread.

One of the short stories in the notebook is titled "Itching Fingers," and it
begins this way:

Slim Dalton, ace gambler of Dodge City, was seated at a gambling table at a
saloon. He and three other rough-looking men were gambling. Slim was dealing
the cards, and quickly he dealt a couple of cards from the bottom of the deck.
One of the ruffians saw Slim do it, and said, "OK, Slim, I wouldn't do that."
Slim's face was getting red. At last he shouted, "What are you going to do about
it?"

The ruffian answered, "This!" — and quickly drew for his gun. But Slim, the
fastest gun-drawer in Dodge City, was too fast. His gun rang out, and smoke
filled the room. The ruffian dropped his gun and heavily fell to the floor.

Quickly the two other men drew for their guns, but Dalton, seeing that the
odds were against him, fled for the steps. The other men followed after him.
Turning and firing, Slim let another one of his slugs enter one of the men, who
immediately fell backward. By that time, the other men from the saloon were
now after Dalton. They had him cornered in a lone room at the dark end of the
hall.

Just then, a tall stranger entered the saloon. He was all dressed in black. His
name was Ken Maynard.

As you turn cautiously through the notebook, you find other stories that
reflect the interests of a 10-year-old Midwestern boy — stories about cowboys
and baseball and about military pilots and soldiers, who were heroic-beyond-
belief figures of the times. This, you see, was 1942, and it was at the beginning
of the war to save democracy and make the world safe for everybody's children
and grandchildren.

The 10-year-old boy who wrote the stories knew beyond question what he
wanted to do with his life. He would be a writer, and he never would consider
anything else. The sounds of words fascinated him, and stringing together
words to create a thought or paint a picture was as much fun — or almost as
much fun — as listening to the radio broadcasts of his beloved Cardinals or taking that prized once-a-year trip with his father to St. Louis to watch the
Cardinals play baseball.

Once or twice a month, the boy would drag out his father's old Underwood
typewriter and slowly, one finger at a time, peck out on carbon-paper-thickened
sheaves of paper the stories that made up his neighborhood newspaper. Then he
would stick one sheet under the screen door of every house along his street.
Once he even went to the neighborhood grocery store and asked, with great
reluctance, if the grocer would like to buy an ad in the newspaper.

"How much would it cost?"

"Does a nickel sound like too much?"

"I think I can afford that. Go ahead and put in my ad — and here's a nickel."

It was a day the boy never forgot. His mother never forgot, either — not just
that day but all of the days, when the boy sat and wrote in the tiny room with
the shelves that were piled high with his collection of Big-Little Books and

Little-Big Books, each of which was numbered and catalogued on a master sheet that he had taped to the wall.

Over the years, the mother and father moved from house to house, but always the mother made it a point to find a safe place for the orange-and-black notebook that protected the boy's short stories. She never was sure why — except that the stories represented a piece of the boy, a piece that the passing of ever so many years never could diminish.

One day, the boy, now a man, went into the mother's attic and began to dig tenderly through boxes that housed the yesteryears of his life — a Lonnie Frey baseball glove, an autographed picture of Marty Marion, an electric football game, a 37-mm shell casing that an uncle had brought back from the war — and an orange-and-black notebook.

I, of course, was the 10-year-old boy who wrote the stories, and I'm now the 51-year-old man who has the orange-and-black notebook. It's a vignette that I often tell, after a speech, when, during the question period, somebody inevitably asks how I became a writer.

Knowing forever what I wanted to do was, I suppose, something of a mixed blessing. The plus was that I could pursue my writing with single-mindedness and avoid the pangs of confusion, bewilderment and indecision that so many face as their career decisions painfully evolve. The minus was that I might have been better suited for something else — but because I never considered anything else, I shut all other doors, without even realizing that other doors existed.

Why do some decide so early and with such decisiveness what they will make their life's work?

I put that question to Gilles E. Richard, who is vice president of Hay Career Consultants, a division of Hay Associates, an international company that has its headquarters in Philadelphia.

It's highly probable, Richard said, that if 80 percent of the nation's work force is unhappy, as is widely reported, then the other 20 percent is made up largely of people who always knew what they wanted to do and, in doing it, found genuine satisfaction.

These are the lucky people, Richard said, because, for the most part, they have been spared the occupational fires that have scorched so many. Why some people from Day One have pointed themselves toward certain careers is not fully understood, he said, but these are common denominators that he has observed:

"As kids, they had a lot of nurturing from their parents, and, as a result, they always had a lot of self-confidence. Even when they were 4 or 5, you could see that these kids were different . . . because they felt loved to an extraordinary degree. They were made to feel special. . . ."

"As these kids grew and did whatever it was, they were praised and rewarded — not only by their parents, but also by their teachers, friends and peers. People recognized and supported their talents, and from a very early age they were surrounded by expressions of success. . . . These things gave them affirmations that what they were doing was right for them" — and they plowed ahead with vigor.

It's a combination of factors that rarely occurs, Richard said, but, when it does, it creates people "whose work is an expression of themselves." In other words, he said, for these people work isn't really work. It's almost like play, and it's as natural — and necessary — as breathing, sleeping and eating.

Well, I had to admit to Richard, I'd never thought about it quite that way, but I like the sound of it.

I'm sure Mom will like it, too. And Dad — if he only could know. Somehow, I think he does know.

HOW TO SUCCEED IN RELAXING
March 24, 1985

Psychologist Julian Slowinski opened the letter from his longtime friend Arnold Lazarus, a behavior therapist at Rutgers University. The two of them had collaborated on a recently published article in the Journal of Sex Education and Therapy, and they were planning more work together. But now Lazarus seemed to be posing a universal question: How much is enough?

He wrote that he had once been told by another behavior therapist, Andrew Salter: "I do not know anyone who on his deathbed said he wished he had put in more time at work."

So, asked Lazarus, what does it all mean?

■

Yes, indeed, what does it all mean?

Slowinski thought about the time that the dreaded telephone call had come: "Julian, your father is dying. Please get here as quickly as you can."

In the car, grieving as he drove, Slowinski found that a verse from Psalms kept running through his mind: "Fear of the Lord is the beginning of wisdom."

The application of that verse to everyday life was obvious to him. "You need a reference for things," he said. "You need to learn to slow down and put things in proper perspective. . . . Over the long haul, what's really important — to sign that big deal or to experience life more fully?"

What is really important, he would conclude, is balance, that often difficult to achieve blend of work and play. With all his heart he believed it, and with all his might he would continue to work toward realizing it.

■

It is a house with a view that must be seen to be believed — in France, near the Spanish border. Snow-topped mountains rise behind the icy-blue Mediterranean Sea, which washes almost up to the front yard, with waves so gentle that the dazzling colors of the sailboats docked there seem to be painted into place.

It's a house that Slowinski bought for himself, his French-born wife and their son, who is 9.

"I could rent a place in France much cheaper than I can own," he said. "But I wanted my own place, where I could go when I wanted, a place that I could pass on to my son. . . . We go there every August — for the whole month. . . . There's a difference between buying a place for an investment and buying a place for fun. People say, 'It's a lousy investment.' I say, 'So what? It's fun.' What makes sense isn't always what's best for us. In America, what makes sense is to make a profit."

In a lot of ways, said Slowinski, that's part of what ails America — and Americans.

∎

Julian W. Slowinski, 43, is director of outpatient service, child and family mental health, at the Hall-Mercer Center of Pennsylvania Hospital and a research associate in the University of Pennsylvania's psychiatry department. Before he became a psychologist, he was for eight years a Benedictine monk. So, in his words, "I was Father Slowinski before I was Dr. Slowinski."

As a practicing therapist, Slowinski said that he almost daily witnessed the residue of lives that are out of control, without balance and, as a result, without much hope.

"People get into the achievement-oriented rat race, and they can't get out. . . . In two-career marriages — I have one myself — the stress often is incredible because people have no time for anything but work. . . . I see college kids who are neurotic about getting straight A's so they can be admitted to medical school. They forgo all pleasures in life to try to get straight A's. . . . I see kids come out of the Wharton School and get onto Wall Street and in a couple of years they're chewed up and spit out . . . and burned out.

"The cover of Esquire not long ago showed a young executive clutching a briefcase. 'Success! It is the religion of the '80s; everyone pursues it' was what it said. People fall for that hook, line and sinker, and they often put success in the business world over personal happiness, because they equate success with happiness."

It's an equation that doesn't work, said Slowinski, but tragically many people don't discover that until later in life, when it's perhaps too late to do anything about it, too late to go back and sip the champagne.

"My rule of thumb," Slowinski said, "is: Because you can do something, it doesn't mean you have to do it. Translation: Learn to say no. The keys to making life work are emphasis, priorities and being able to let go.

"If something happened to you, you'd be replaced in your job tomorrow. Your family and friends would miss you, but you'd be replaced at work. The job would survive even if you weren't there" — and this is something that needs to be understood by people for whom work is everything, people who can't let go because they . . .

Who knows why? There are almost as many reasons as there are people who are slaves to their work.

"Every time a friend dies, Arnold Lazarus always says the same thing: 'I hope he had enough fun in life.' This is not to suggest hedonism, but balance. The problem is that materialism and consumerism get in the way. And we, ourselves, get in the way . . . because we put our whole ego into the job.

"This business of 'I am a psychologist, you are a journalist' bothers me," Slowinski said. "There's a lot more to a person than that, but it takes some reflection often for us to realize it." And it often takes some commitment for us to act on it.

"We need to take time to have a concept of ourselves and to understand what we see as really important. On the deathbed, we always wish we had done this or that. The trick is to do it while we're alive.

"In France," he said, "the factories close in August — by law. Everybody must be paid for a month's vacation. There's no such thing as a poor blue-collar guy who doesn't get a vacation. He may not have a lot of money to spend, but he's required to take a vacation. I think that's wonderful, but I can't imagine that it could happen in America, where we think so much about profit. . . .

"I like to celebrate. I'm always looking for opportunities to celebrate. Years ago, before it became popular, I discovered cheap Spanish champagne — it was about $3 a bottle then — and I kept the refrigerator full of it and celebrated with it. . . . The thing to remember is that the more we do things we enjoy, the more we increase the chances of doing them again."

How can people learn to turn loose?

"We're obsessed with the need to be active and productive, and a sudden change can be a shock to the system. When you work hard all year, you shouldn't go cold turkey" and suddenly begin having fun and relaxing. "Periodically, you need to learn to relax. It's like dieting. You do it, and eventually it becomes part of your lifestyle.

"How do you learn to relax? By setting some rules: Bring no work home at night; don't work on weekends. Who says you have to bring home the briefcase every night and work until midnight? Why not watch TV with the kids? I'm not talking about going to Bermuda to spend the weekend. I'm talking about doing the little things."

What kinds of little things?

"Buy season tickets to the symphony, to the ballpark; join a health club. Money often is an incentive. 'Gee, I've already paid for the tickets, so I got to go.' Prepaid activities are very important because they force you to go. . . . Make a contract with your baby sitter: 'For the next six months, I have you every Saturday night.' Then you've got to think of something to do with your spouse every Saturday night for the next six months. . . .

"I bought two weeks of time-sharing at Christmas," Slowinski said. "I'll have two weeks at Christmas for the next 25 years. I have to go on vacation — because I've paid for it — and so I do it. I find that you don't miss an awful lot by not being in the office. It's not the end of the world if you don't get everything done today; you can get some of it done tomorrow. . . .

"I take at least six weeks away every year, and I'd like to expand that. Yes, I lose income when I go away, but I'm able to pay my bills and send my son to school. So what's important? If I don't do it, nobody will do it for me." And that's a regret — not having had enough fun — that Slowinski does not intend to have to wrestle with on his deathbed.

YOU DON'T BORROW TOOLS, EITHER
May 20, 1986

For the first 18 years of his life Donald D. Bilyew lived in Rochester, Ind., a town of 6,000 near South Bend. During the day, he worked in a cheese factory, and at night, to make ends meet, he pulled a shift at a gas station. One evening, as he sat there with no customers in sight and time on his hands, he asked himself a pivotal question:

"What will I be like when I'm 50 years old?"

The next day he ventured down to the Army recruiter's office, and in a little while he was off on what he would call "the best learning experience of my life. It was my first time really away from home. There were some hard lessons, and in a lot of ways I grew up at 18."

Because he carried a strong Midwestern work ethic, Bilyew tried to be a conscientious soldier. One time early in basic training, when the others in his barracks had gone out for a night on the town, Bilyew stayed behind because he wanted to learn to make a bed, Army-style.

"I got somebody to show me how, and then I practiced. I made everybody's bed, and then I went to sleep. Some time later, they came back, woke me up, and they were furious. They thought I'd short-sheeted their beds, and they dragged me down and threatened to beat me until somebody checked his bed and said, 'Hey, it's OK.' Then they let me up and said, 'What the hell's the matter with you?' I said, 'All I did was make your bed,' and they said, 'Yeah, what the hell's the matter with you?' "

It was one of Bilyew's hard lessons: Not everybody grew up in a little town in northern Indiana where people didn't need a reason to do nice things for other people.

■

Bilyew is a therapist who for more than 20 years worked with emotionally disturbed and mentally retarded children and their parents. He now operates Clinical Hypnosis Associates in Paoli, outside Philadelphia. I first met him a couple of years ago when he and I were involved in the filming of a made-for-television movie in which I played a middle-aged writer and he played a middle-aged therapist. How's that for fail-safe casting?

During the time between shootings, we tended to share a lot about our Midwestern backgrounds — I'm from Missouri — and we found ourselves more than once tabulating the gains and losses that we experienced in our moves around the country and, ultimately, to the metropolitan Northeast.

Over lunch the other day, we picked up on that discussion, and he said that when he first came to the Philadelphia area, people "made fun of me because I said hello to everybody. They'd say, 'You don't even know them — so stop speaking or they'll think something's wrong with you.'

"One day I stopped to help somebody fix a flat tire, and he really seemed to appreciate it, but when I told a friend, I was told, 'We don't do that around here. You're taking a chance, and you'd be smart not to do it again.'

"A neighbor moved in, and I went over to help. He's from New Jersey, and he couldn't believe it. He asked, 'Why are you doing this?' and I said, 'It's just the way we did things where I grew up. Somebody needs something done, and so you do it.' "

Bilyew learned the hard way that you don't drop in unannounced on neighbors. That is Rude. Anybody who doesn't know that is Strange.

Bilyew also found out that you don't just borrow tools, either.

"I went over to borrow a saw, and the man said, 'I don't lend any tools.' In Indiana, that would be unthinkable. In Indiana, at least where I came from, if you got it, anybody can use it."

■

Bilyew has been in the Philadelphia area for more than 20 years, and, despite what you might think, he likes it in the big city. "Would I ever go back to a small town?" he said. "I don't know if I ever could. It would mean narrowing my life choices, and I don't believe I would want to do that."

But every day in the big city is a reminder of how far he is — geographically and philosophically — from that little town in Indiana.

"My grandma used to say, 'A clean shirt, clean jeans and hard work — and you'll be fine — no matter where you go.' But it's just not so. It's how good a deal you can cut. . . . When you're really honest with some people, they don't believe you. They wonder what you're really saying, what you're trying to get out of them. . . .

"It used to be, a long time ago, that when I entered a business deal, it was a handshake, and that was it. I went on my gut. Now I call my lawyer and my accountant and act on their advice — not on my gut feeling. People may say that's good business, and maybe it is, but if you can't trust people and accept them on their word," you've got bigger problems than the business deal you're trying to close.

From time to time, Bilyew gets clients who have moved to the area from tiny towns and are struggling because they feel naive and vulnerable.

Bilyew's advice to people who are new to the big city: "You'll need to be more independent and self-reliant, and you'll have more associates but fewer close friends. . . . People in the city are friendly, but it takes longer for it to show. . . . What will surprise you is that much of the time people won't bother to respond to you. Why not? Because they're busy — and wary."

THE FIVE STANDOUT INTERVIEWS
December 30, 1984

My job amounts to interviewing people and, over the years, I've interviewed — let's see now, how many? Thousands? Yes, surely, thousands, and the other day somebody asked me a question that, surprisingly, rarely ever is asked. The question: Of all the interviews, which ones really stand out?

That's a tough one, and I had to think about it for a while. But eventually five emerged, some of them with their nostalgic shadows in lockstep, because the interviews took place many years ago. Was there a common denominator, something that these interviews taught me or reinforced in my mind?

Yes, indeed, and it was this: Successful people tend to be nice people — because they no longer have to prove anything to anybody.

The five interviews:

Stan Musial. The year: 1948. I grew up in Missouri in the early 1940s, and, like many boys, I tended to regard some of the St. Louis Cardinal baseball players as bigger than life, as godlike figures who never failed to whip the hated Dodgers in the September games that decided pennants.

One of my heroes — and everybody else's, too — was Stan the Man. I always wondered what it would be like to talk to him, and then that summer, I had my chance, incredible as it was.

I was a high school senior, working on my hometown newspaper in Jefferson City, the state capital, and Musial, who was friendly with many politicians, was in town to visit some of them. The city editor whistled me over to his desk and told me to interview The Man for that afternoon's edition.

With folded copy paper in hand and mushy lump in throat, I scurried off, and, without hesitation, a secretary said that Mr. Musial would be happy to see me. We could talk in a private office so we wouldn't be disturbed.

I tiptoed into the private office — and there he was: God, in a navy blue suit, white shirt and navy and white polka-dot tie. I had some questions in mind, but when I tried to speak, nothing came out. My throat was so dry from fright that I was mute.

"Uhhhhh."

Musial looked at me, smiled, asked me to sit down. "Son, are you a baseball fan?"

I nodded.

"I've always been a baseball fan, too, and. . . ." For the next 10 minutes Musial preached a litany about what baseball had meant to him and how, without baseball, he might have ended up pumping gas somewhere. I took notes frantically. Finally, he asked: "Son, do you have enough now for your story?"

Again, I nodded.

"It's been nice talking to you," he said.

Musial had recognized me for what I was — a scared kid who needed a story — and he had responded to my need.

I got back to the office and wrote my story. The city editor was pleased. "Hey, what an unusual approach to take — about how much baseball means to him."

He used the story on the front page, and somewhere, after all these years, I still have it.

Louie Armstrong. The year: 1958. He was in my Missouri town to play a concert, and his manager gave me Armstrong's motel room number and a time at which Armstrong would talk to me.

I knocked on the door about 6 o'clock, and he appeared — with a white towel wrapped around his head, wearing a white silk monogrammed shirt and white boxer shorts with big blue dots on them.

He invited me inside, and in his gravelly voice told me how nice it was of me to drive all the way out to the motel. It was, again, an interview in which I didn't say much — not because I couldn't speak but because Armstrong was going so well that I didn't want to interrupt.

He and his wife were sharing a plate of chicken, and between bites, he explained his secret to longevity, how he'd been able to blow the trumpet so well for so many years.

Actually, there were two secrets. Every night he rubbed witch hazel on his lips. And every day he took a laxative. After all, a man is only as good as his regularity. The laxative he used was made from herbs and packaged in foil by his wife. Wouldn't I like to take a package or two home with me? And maybe I should try witch hazel, too. When I nodded, he gave me a bottle.

What a story. What a guy.

Duke Ellington. The year: 1959. How lucky can you get? Even in those days I walked around humming "Satin Doll," and now here was my chance to meet Ellington, who was playing a concert at Lincoln University in Missouri.

I couldn't set up anything in advance, but I bought a ticket to the concert and, at intermission, I wandered toward the dressing room — the concert was being held in the gymnasium — on the assumption that Ellington might be there.

As it turned out, he was there, all by himself, in a little room that the coaches used. He looked tired, and the circles under his eyes were pronounced. He was wearing a pink oxford shirt, open at the collar, and his necktie was pulled so far down that it folded in his lap. He was eating shrimp out of a cardboard box.

I knocked on the jamb of the open door, introduced myself and asked if we could talk for a few minutes. I half expected him to say "not tonight," but he smiled wearily, stood up, shook my hand. Without my asking, he talked about life on the road, living out of a suitcase, his love affair with his music and with those who enjoyed his music.

When it was time for the concert to resume, somebody came to the door and Ellington, as he left, apologized because he couldn't spend any more time with me.

Sam J. Ervin Jr. The year: 1975. Ervin had retired as a U.S. senator from North Carolina in January, and in the heat of summer I drove 70 miles from Charlotte, where I was working, to his office in Morganton, a town of 10,000 in the foothills of the Blue Ridge Mountains.

He sat there in a gray-and-blue herringbone sportcoat, gray-and-white checked pants and reddish-brown patterned necktie and told me that one of the great problems in the world is that there are no real characters left. Everybody's pretty much the same.

"Back in the old days," he said, "The differences between lawyers were very great. One lawyer would depend on his study of the law to win his cases, while another could depend on his natural talents as an orator. . . . One time, one of these orators stood up in court to object to something another lawyer had said: 'I deny the allegation and I defy the alligator.' Well, I'll tell you, that just broke up everybody."

But it couldn't happen today, said Ervin, because everybody is cut from the same mold. We all come from more similar backgrounds, go to the same schools, read the same books.

"We're never going back to those old times — and I'm not saying we should. But, you know, it was kind of nice, wasn't it?"

Arnold Palmer. The year: 1975. What made this interview memorable was not so much what it enabled me to put in the newspaper, but that it helped me to get on television.

141

Palmer owned a Cadillac agency across the street from The Charlotte News, of which I was executive editor, and he spent quite a lot of time in Charlotte. In the interview, he told me something that I don't think he'd ever shared with a writer before — that he knew that his career was winding down and that he was concentrating more on life after golf. He used the phrase "nothing lasts forever," and the headline writer picked it up. It was a story that got good play around the country.

But the fun began after the interview. I asked Palmer if he'd do a television commercial for my newspaper. No, I couldn't pay him anything — because the budget was bare and the controller was stern. But I'd let him plug his Cadillac agency in the commercial — if he'd do it for free.

"Gee, I don't know," he said. "Nobody's ever asked me to do something like this for nothing. Even if I wanted to, I'm not sure I could" — because of his contract with agent Mark McCormack. "But I'll tell you what. If I can do it, I will. I'll call you in a few days."

True to his word, he called in a few days, and we set up filming of the commercial, which pictured Palmer scissoring from my newspaper an ad about his agency. It was absolutely a dynamite 30 seconds, and nobody could believe that Palmer had done it for nothing. When I took it on the road, to show at editors' meetings, I became known as the guy who "conned" Arnold Palmer.

But I'm pretty sure I didn't con him. The day he finished the filming, which took about an hour, I shook his hand and said, "I want you to know how much I appreciate this."

Palmer stared at me and, without any hint of a smile, answered: "You should."

That's the part that I never told the other editors.

MAKING IT ON YOUR OWN
June 23, 1987

The tourist felt hopelessly lost, but then he spotted a man carrying a violin. "Can you please tell me how to get to Carnegie Hall?" he asked.

The man with the violin had a three-word answer: "Practice, practice, practice."

It's a story that Jerry Greer often uses as a lead-in when somebody asks him how to become a successful entrepreneur. He has a three-word answer, too: "Plan, plan, plan."

■

Jerome W. Greer is a vice president in the Philadelphia office of Drake Beam Morin Inc., an international firm that deals in the management of human resources. Much of the business involves outplacement — working with people who were turned loose when their companies streamlined — and more and more of these people are looking not to return to corporate life but to start their own businesses, to become entrepreneurs.

Greer estimated that 20 percent of the clients "have some degree of interest in discussing entrepreneurship, although not all end up doing it." There are at least four reasons for this increased interest:

¶ With more two-income families, people are better able financially to take the inevitable risks.

¶ Many people who are being displaced today have 30 or 35 years of service, and they leave with "relatively sophisticated packages," which means that their companies have given them substantial insurance and cash benefits. So they have money to invest in a business.

¶ These people are aware that corporations offer less security today than 10 years ago, and they're not eager to return to the chopping block. The feeling of many, said Greer, is this: "If I'm going to be insecure, I want to be insecure on my own terms."

¶ People are retiring earlier these days and "they're retiring not to a rocking chair but to something else. The entrepreneurial field is part of this."

■

In working with prospective entrepreneurs, Greer sets up "a series of hurdles. If they pass over these hurdles, they probably have a reasonable chance of success" — even though the failure rate of new businesses in the first three years is 70 to 80 percent.

The hurdles:

¶ Health. "Bad health is a primary reason why businesses fail. People think about money and planning — and these are important — but without good health a person can't withstand the workload that is required to start and sustain a new business."

¶ Money. "We ask people to draw a personal financial plan. How much do they need to live comfortably for six to 18 months with no income? Then we ask them to draw a business plan. How much do they need to finance the business until it becomes profitable? Then we ask them to multiply this figure by two because everybody always underestimates what it will take. We add the two figures together — personal and business — and ask if they have this much. If they do, they pass this hurdle. . . . If somebody is going into consulting, where what you offer is your service, not so much money is required. But if you're buying a business, you're talking about megabucks."

¶ Planning. "You have to plan and answer all the right questions before you invest one dollar. You need a marketing analysis, a plan for marketing, a cash-flow analysis. What outside help is needed? You have to approach a new business in — guess what? — a businesslike fashion. If you let emotions get in the way, it's a recipe for disaster."

¶ A gimmick. "If you want to be successful, you've got to find a niche and fill it," and a gimmick is needed, usually, to draw attention. "A hundred years ago, a physician found that a lot of pills were passing right through patients and had no therapeutic value because they didn't dissolve. He invented a new coating for pills and merchandised it by a demonstration in which he took a soft pine board, put old pills on it and whacked them with a hammer. The pills didn't break up. But his new pill splattered. This was the friable pill, and a $2.3 billion business was born out of the idea." The physician's name was Upjohn, and he started the pharmaceutical company that bears his name. It's the company for which Greer worked before he joined Drake Beam Morin.

■

How many would-be entrepreneurs pass all four hurdles? Not too many, said Greer. "About three-fourths of the people who think they want their own business decide ultimately not to do it."

The successful entrepreneurs, said Greer, are "not high risk-takers. They do their planning and assess the risks carefully. They eliminate the risks that can be eliminated, and they devise a plan for dealing with the other risks. Then they're not afraid to make decisions that involve moderate risks. . . . They have good ego strengths. They want control. Money is important, but it's not a high motivator. They want to see the things they have created."

People who have "the right idea always can find people to lend them money" — the venture capitalists who, on average, accept fewer than 5 percent of the ideas that are presented to them. They expect one-third of these ideas "to succeed dramatically," said Greer. "Another one-third will do OK but will not hit home runs. . . . One-third will fail."

Greer's final word of advice to entrepreneurs: "Don't ever be content with the size of the business. You must keep growing. You must have some growth goal — in quality, diversification, or revenue. If you stop growing, you start dying. You can't stand still."

WHAT WE CAN LEARN FROM GEESE
March 8, 1992

This column had been pre-printed by The Inquirer, and was published two days after Darrell Sifford's death. It was the last Sifford column to appear in The Inquirer.

The next time somebody says, "Hey, you have the sense of a goose," you should take it as a compliment.

How's that?

Well, that's what this column is all about.

Not long ago, I received in the mail a copy of Dialogue, which is described as "an occasional newsletter" from Haskell Associates, a Philadelphia human-resources consulting firm that specializes in team building and employee productivity. The head of the firm is Jean Haskell, whom I've known for many years, and I called her for permission to use her page-one story, titled "Wisdom From Nature." No problem with permission, she said. As a matter of fact, she'd found the material in a talk given by anthropologist Angeles Arrien. I started to ask if Arrien had gotten the material from somebody else, but I didn't.

The story is about — geese. Join me now, won't you? It's fascinating.

■

Fact No. 1. As each bird flaps its wings, it creates an uplift for the bird following. By flying in a V formation, the whole flock adds 71 percent greater flying range than if one bird flew alone.

Lesson No. 1. People who share a common direction and sense of community can get where they're going quicker and easier because they're traveling on the strength of one another.

Fact No. 2. Whenever a goose falls out of formation, it suddenly feels the drag and resistance of trying to fly alone and quickly gets back into formation to take advantage of the lifting power of the bird immediately in front.

Lesson No. 2. If we have as much sense as geese, we will stay in formation with those who are ahead of where we want to go and be willing to accept their help as well as give ours to others.

Fact No. 3. When the lead goose gets tired, it rotates back into the formation and another goose flies at the point position.

Lesson No. 3. It pays to take turns doing the hard tasks and sharing leadership.

Fact No. 4. The geese in formation honk from behind to encourage those up front to keep up their speed.

Lesson No. 4. We need to make sure our honking from behind is encouraging, and not something else.

Fact No. 5. When a goose gets sick or wounded or shot down, two geese drop out of formation and follow it down to help and protect it. They stay with it until it is able to fly again — or dies. Then they launch out on their own, with another formation, or they catch up with their flock.

Lesson No. 5. If we have as much sense as geese, we, too, will stand by each other in difficult times as well as when we are strong.

■

Haskell expanded on the lessons to be learned from nature — especially about the advantages of working together.

Let's listen:

"While there is a lot we can do by ourselves and a lot we can do with a partner, the power of what we can get done when we travel on the thrust of one another is a quantum leap. Have you considered involving work group members in your major projects and decisions? Is your team really a team?"

Haskell said that "with people, as with geese, we are interdependent on each other's skills, capabilities, and unique arrangements of gifts, talents and resources. As the workforce becomes more and more diverse, there's a real dividend to be had by getting acquainted with all of its members and taking advantage of the resources that they bring. . . ."

"Shared directions and common goals help build a sense of community and enable the group to get to where it is going quicker and easier because members travel together and energize each other. Are your team's goals and objectives clear and understood by everyone in the group?"

Haskell said it's no secret that "the power of encouragement is mighty and that production increases many times over when there is support and praise. Have you told members of your workforce lately that they're terrific?"

"We learn, too, that it's a good idea to stand by each other when times are difficult. In these days of economic hardship . . . we must find ways to reach out and help those in need, rather than just worrying about our own paycheck or profit margin. Perhaps we can be creative about cutting costs instead of cutting people. Perhaps everyone could live on a little bit less, rather than forcing some to cut way back."

■

I think Haskell has hit the center of the target. Listening to her, I began to think about what happens to many people as they climb the career ladder, as the payoff increasingly is tied to what they can do as individuals, not as members of a team.

That so many of us become solo players is unfortunate — but almost inevitable.

Remember when we were little kids? We played games as part of a group. That was much of the fun, working with others to achieve the best possible result.

Remember when we were somewhat bigger kids? We played sports, where the emphasis was on what the team did. Individuals sacrificed themselves, if they were told to, for the good of the team.

But when the time arrived that we no longer were kids of any size, we found that the rules of the game were different. During interviews, employers never asked about team-building skills or the ability to work with others to complete tasks. Instead, they asked questions that essentially amounted to "How much work can you do?" and "How fast can you do it?"

Identity and reward no longer came from being part of a team, and we quickly forgot what we had learned as kids.

■

There are lots of geese on the lakes around the golf course where I live, and I often talk to them when I'm taking a walk. Usually I say, "Hi, geese, how're you doing?" I think that now I'll say, "Thanks, geese. We needed that."

146

CHAPTER 4

FEELINGS:
VALUING OUR OWN
AND OTHERS'

When I was 10 years old, my 17-year-old brother, Wendell, was killed in a car accident. Later, while riding down the highway in the back seat of our navy blue 1951 Ford, I remember wondering about the life stories of the people in the other cars we passed. What pains and tragedies did they endure — largely unnoticed by the world around them?

When I was 20, my sister, Dianne, to whom I was very close, died of a cerebral hemorrhage. Thirteen years later, the unfinished business of mourning her loss surfaced to be completed.

Darrell's death was my most horrible nightmare come true — my biggest fear realized. Each day, I experience a combination of feelings evoked by precious memories of good times and tender moments as well as painful images related to his death.

A reader, whom I have never met, offered this advice in a letter: "Put your pain to work." If each of us could learn to apply this simple but profound idea — "Put our feelings to work" — we would truly honor our feelings, help heal ourselves and our relationships and be fully present to those around us.

Those in the helping professions have a special contribution to make. They can augment the effectiveness of the healing process by recognizing and treating the Whole Person — thus helping patients tap their own inner resources.

Our feelings can be a powerful positive force in our lives when we are in touch with them and find constructive and authentic ways to express them. When we deny their expression, they may emerge in disguises that even we do not recognize — sometimes in destructive ways.

— M.S.

LOOKING BACK AT LIFE'S END
July 4, 1991

I am seldom at a loss for words, but the other day somebody presented me with a question that absolutely stopped me. I didn't have even a vague sense of what a reasonable answer might be. The question:

How do you console, on the deathbed, somebody who has not lived a life of accomplishment and who feels sad — and even bitter — about it?

My reaction was that it's probably the most desolate, icy situation that can be conceived. Imagine, if you will, looking back at life's end and thinking: "I didn't do anything. . . . I didn't touch anybody. . . . I'm leaving nothing behind." What makes this so terrifying, in my mind, is that it raises another question: "Did I ever really live?" It's a question that can reduce the most hardy of us to ashes.

What do you think? If the question about a life without accomplishment were handed to you, how would you respond?

■

I was having lunch with an old friend, psychologist Julian Slowinski, 48, who was a Benedictine monk and who likes to tell people that "I was Father Slowinski before I was Dr. Slowinski."

I asked him what he would say to a person who asked that question, and guess what? He'd dealt with it that very morning — in a conversation with the son of a 70-year-old woman, a widow, who was bitter because . . .

Let's listen as Slowinski talks about life in the slow lane:

"I preached my mother's eulogy when she died a year and a half ago. . . . I was with her on her last day. Her son, the priest, was there. . . . In some ways I was ambivalent about, and angry with, my mother. She was a lot of the reason why I became a priest and a sex therapist — because of the way she felt" about women and sex, and the ways in which she paved the road for Slowinski, as a young man, to avoid intimacy.

"In the eulogy — my brother and his six adult children and their spouses were there — I talked about Mother, who was unschooled, from an immigrant family, who preserved family tradition, who passed on Christianity, faith, ethics. She taught us. . . . She was neurotic, angry and depressed, but she gave us something that helped us live our lives" although she wasn't fully aware of it or able to acknowledge it.

All of us can leave behind something of value, Slowinski told me, "whether we recognize it or not. . . . The most disappointed people usually are those who tried hard, without the payoff that they expected, or who felt misunderstood. They are disappointed because they raised their kids one way and the kids behaved another way . . . or because they loved their spouse and their spouse left them. . . .

"People in this situation, bitter about life, can't be consoled if they don't want to be. It's a mistake to debate it with them. At the moment, they're invested in being the way they are — feeling that they made no contribution. . . . But, although they may be disappointed now, they may be able to see later that they did leave behind legacy and tradition."

This doesn't happen only to people at life's end, said Slowinski. "I went to the 50th anniversary of Brother Aloysius. I said, 'Congratulations, Al,' and he said, 'Ah, that's 50 years shot to hell.' He was a grouchy man, but in his way he touched people, many people."

Slowinski said he sometimes encounters people, high achievers, who feel that they have accomplished nothing, who feel that they are impostors. "They've done a lot, but they feel that they've done nothing. How people feel doesn't necessarily have to balance with reality."

In our own ways, we touch people, all of us, said Slowinski, and contribute to the personal happiness of others and maybe even to the culture — even if we don't know it at the time.

Why don't people know it?

They could be depressed, he said. "You can't see it if you're depressed. People could be suffering from anhedonia [the inability to experience pleasure]. . . . Often they're feeling sorry for themselves. Often they're covering up a lot of anger. Anger usually comes up where there's a lot of unrequited love."

I asked Slowinski what he would say to somebody who felt that his or her life had amounted to zero.

"I would acknowledge what they're feeling, but I would tell them that they have left behind a legacy that they may not be aware of — the values they passed on to their children, the traditions they carried on."

■

I thought back 20 years, to when Charles Starling, a prominent psychiatrist in Charlotte, N.C., told me, during an interview, that he was quitting psychiatry forever because he felt like a fake. He never helped anybody, he said. All he ever did was "peddle them my neurosis, and because I was so enthusiastic about my neurosis, they bought it."

I wrote a column about Starling, and I was not prepared for what followed. For weeks, I got telephone calls and letters from around the country from former Starling patients who essentially said the same thing: "Starling may think that he never helped anybody, but he certainly helped me." They wanted to know how they could get their message to Starling, and I told them that I would deliver it.

When I shared with Starling, a longtime friend, what they had told me, he was absolutely amazed. He didn't believe it, he said, but it was nice that they believed it.

I raised the possibility that perhaps he wasn't a fake at all, that perhaps he was a good psychiatrist who had done a good job.

He smiled. He didn't say anything. He just smiled.

Brother Aloysius, are you listening?

GRIEF, A LITTLE AT A TIME
December 31, 1978

My mother talks about what it was like the night my father died unexpectedly, back in the spring, ending their 53 years of marriage and, she says, forever changing her life:

"At the hospital, I just sat there like a mummy, without any feeling, so shocked I couldn't even cry. It was unreal, like a dream. The doctor came out and held my hand and told me: 'He's not responding, I'm doing all I can.'

"And then a Catholic priest came up to me and said: 'Would you like for me to give him the prayers?' We're not Catholic, of course, but I told him: 'Yes, thank you, I most certainly would.'

"Then in about five minutes, the doctor came back and he got down on his knees with me, held both my hands and said: 'I just did all I could, but he's gone.' He didn't say Pop was dead. He said he was gone. Then the priest came out and told me he had given Pop all the prayers. I thanked him.

"By that time, the others [her nephew, niece and Methodist minister] were there and the doctor asked if we wanted to see Pop before the funeral home came to get his body. We went in — the four of us — and Pop was lying on a table, a high table, higher than my waist.

"I looked at him and his face was so blue, not at all like his face. I put my hand on his head and he was warm. I still couldn't cry. I stood and looked at Pop. I don't know for how long.

"Then I walked out. I didn't realize what had happened — or I would have been hysterical. Gene [the minister] put his arm on my shoulder and said: 'Hazel, you're the bravest person I've ever seen.' And all I would think was: 'Oh God, you don't know what I'm feeling inside.' "

That happened more than eight months ago. My wife and I immediately flew from Philadelphia to Jefferson City, Mo., where Mom and Pop had lived since right after the Depression and where I had grown up, gone to high school and worked for the newspaper after college.

When we arrived, my greatest fear was that Mom wouldn't survive the stunning suddenness of Pop's death and the loneliness that would follow. I sat in the backyard, crying, the evening before the funeral and asked my wife: "My God, what must it be like — after you've curled up against somebody in bed every night for 53 years, not to have that person anymore?"

When we left nine days later, I still had that fear — although Mom had surprised me with what seemed to be a reservoir of strength into which she was able to dip during moments of choking despair. In her weekly letters to me since then, she at times reflected on her loneliness ("Sometimes I miss Pop so much I don't know what to do"), but for the most part her letters were cheerful, inquisitive and filled with details of how she was learning to do for herself the things that Pop always had done — paying the bills, trimming the hedge, hiring a contractor to paint the house, confronting the assessor when the new property assessment seemed out of line.

But how was she doing, *really*?

Well, Mom and I and Marilyn, my wife, have spent many hours talking since Mom came the other day to spend the holidays with us. I want to share with you some of what she said because I think it offers hope for all of us at those times when we feel the sky has fallen on us and we are overwhelmed by the odds that seem to be against us.

Mom is 71 now, and she had been married to Pop since she was 17. They had done everything together, two lives fused into one. She talks about what happens after separation by death:

"At first I felt I couldn't continue, that it was not possible. Every morning Pop and I would eat breakfast at our little table in the kitchen. After he died, I just couldn't eat at that table. I just couldn't do it. I'd sit on a stool and eat off the countertop.

"One day a friend — a woman who also is a widow — saw what I was doing and told me that it was not the thing to do, that I had to face the reality of what had happened and try to continue life the way it always had been. So I started sitting at the table to break myself from feeling that things never could be the same again. And every day it gets easier. Life goes on — and that's something we can't forget, no matter how much we hurt.

"Sometimes, at first, it was like Pop still was with me. I'd be fixing lunch in the kitchen, and I'd imagine Pop was in the basement, in his workshop, like he always was, and I could hear him asking: 'When are we going to eat? What are we going to have?' That's what he always asked. At first that made me very sad, and I'd stop what I was doing, sit down and cry. I couldn't help it.

"But now it's different. Sometimes — a lot of times — I still think I hear his voice — 'When are we going to eat?' — but it doesn't make me sad. It makes me glad because it's like we're still together. Some people might think that sounds crazy, like I'm holding onto a dream, but I don't feel that way."

The first two months were the toughest, Mom says, and "I did a lot of praying. I'd go to the basement to do things I'd never done before, and I'd pray: 'Oh, God, you've got to help me. I can't do this by myself.' I'd go to hoe the tomatoes, and I wouldn't know how to use the file to sharpen the hoe. Or I wouldn't know how to use the electric hedge clippers or the grass shears, because I'd never done it before.

"A lot of times I have to make decisions I've never made before. I used to always ask Pop and I'd tell him: 'What would I do if I didn't have you to ask?' But now I think about it and sometimes I pray: 'What am I supposed to do?' And usually I figure out a way. I have a feeling it's the Lord's way of answering my prayer.

"That day at the funeral, when we stood at the casket the last time, I prayed: 'Oh, God, give me the strength to go through this' — and a peace came over me. You can't tell me that God doesn't hear prayers. I know He does.

"If I didn't have my faith, I don't know what would have happened. If I thought death were final, that I'd never be with Pop again, how could I go through with it? Without faith that this is not the end, what is there to hold on to?

"When you die, if you've led a good life, if you've believed, then I think the spirit goes to the Lord at the instant the last breath leaves. That's the victory in death that people talk about. It's tougher for those left behind to see that victory because we miss so much the one who's gone and we feel sorry for ourselves."

When she goes to the cemetery to put flowers on Pop's grave — she's done this six times — Mom says she "can be happy because I know he's happy. His spirit is gone. What's left behind are the remains, nothing else. It's like clay. I want to keep flowers on the grave in memory of him. But I don't go to the cemetery to be with him. I don't talk to him when I'm there — because he's not there."

Mom says she has "turned loose of my grief" a little at a time and "each month I can tell that it becomes easier to do the things I have to do." It helps, she says, to become involved with other people, to help those who need help, those "whose burdens are heavier than mine."

The grieving, she says, is a painful, heart-tearing process that must be completed before life can have any real meaning again. "Nobody can do it for you. You have to let out all the tears. I've let out mine. I still have days when [the grief] comes back over me and I felt like I did when it happened. But it passes. Thank God, it passes, and I can go on with life."

Life can't ever be the same again — "it's forever changed," she says — but that doesn't mean that life can't be good again. "It's a matter of how you approach each day, of being thankful for what you have."

Mom says she perhaps has had an easier time in her grief work than some people because "Pop and I never had any bad feelings about each other. We always said what was on our minds, never went to bed mad. I don't have any regrets, and maybe this is why I've done as well as I have."

I think she has done well. When we finished the 90-minute conversation on which this story is based, she was dry-eyed and composed. I was tearful and sad, although at the time I didn't know exactly why.

Upon reflection I think I now know why. I think Mom is further along in her grief work than I am in mine.

'IF I DON'T DESERVE IT, WHO DOES?'
December 27, 1983

It was a few years ago, and an old friend, psychiatrist Charles Starling, had driven me to Los Angeles International Airport for my flight back to Philadelphia. We sat in the bar, sipping our bourbons, and I shared something with him:

My life was going so well, and everything had fallen into place. There was nothing more for which I could ask, except . . .

Except what?

"The little voice that talks to me sometimes, the little voice that I wish I could muzzle. It says things like 'You don't deserve to have it this good.' "

"It really bothers you?"

"Yes."

"Well, the next time the little voice appears, ask it this question: 'If I don't deserve it, who does?' Nobody gave you what you've got; you worked hard for it."

Although I knew intellectually the truth of what Starling said, I needed to hear him say it. That gave me permission to challenge the little voice and, when I did, the little voice became strangely silent.

Whatever happened to the little voice?

■

His name is J. Kent McCrimmon, and he is a psychologist who is on the staff at Psychological Sciences Institute in Baltimore. Earlier this year, he copyrighted the term "prosperity psychology" — a form of therapy to enable people to accept without guilt or reservation the good things that have happened to them.

Reading about prosperity psychology bought back memories of my little voice and convinced me that McCrimmon was somebody with whom I should talk to try to get some handle on the scope of the problem. Are there really lots and lots of people who can't handle success and good fortune without being plagued by their little voices — or the equivalent?

Yes, said McCrimmon in an interview, and it hit him squarely in the face a few years ago when he found that many of his clients fell into two distinct groups:

Those who solved the problems that brought them into therapy and who then went on to get much more from life and feel good about it. "They were willing to have prosperity come to them."

Those who also solved their problems but who, as their personal and professional dividends piled up, felt hounded by unworthiness. They were not willing to accept prosperity.

McCrimmon wondered what made the difference in the two groups and, when he investigated, he found that "clearly those who accepted prosperity were higher on self-esteem and 'deservability.' Those who weren't able to get past thinking that they weren't deserving couldn't enjoy the good things."

Those who felt no quarrel with accepting what they were getting tended also to "be comfortable in give-and-take with other people," McCrimmon said. "They see themselves giving and taking in roughly the same measure," and they are able to meet life head-on without undue concern that somebody is going to take advantage of them.

This was the seed of prosperity psychology, which, in McCrimmon's words, "tries to get [struggling people] to the point that they know who they are, know their value — and have a good sense of their deficits and what can be done to correct these deficits."

Or to put it another way: "I try to get people to the place where they feel that they have control of their lives."

McCrimmon said that one way in which he seeks to accomplish this is by sharing with clients his own struggles — so clients don't feel so alone. Yes, that's right. McCrimmon, like so many of us, has his bad times, too, when the tapes of yesteryear — the little voices — whisper their messages of unworthiness.

"The thing I do to get control is to stop the bad tapes, to force myself to begin to think positive thoughts." If he can't stop the bad tapes that way, he blots them out by "turning on the radio, making contact with friends, doing some work. Whatever I have to do, I do to get away from the negative thoughts." A major force in this, he said, is "building a positive sense of self-worth through contact with friends who can help elevate you."

In a way it's a process that never stops, he said, and good preventive medicine is called for — even when the little voices are silent.

"Before you go to sleep at night, you can review your day, look at 10 or 15 things you've done well and appreciate yourself for doing them. It's a cognitive review of things that you're deserving of praise for doing."

A question that McCrimmon often asks clients in prosperity psychology is this: "What's the nicest thing you've done for somebody in the last week, in the last month, the last year, in your whole life?" Often people are hesitant to respond and insist that they've done nothing for anybody, McCrimmon said, "but I insist that they tell me something. Before long, they come up with a whole parking lot full of wonderful things they've done for others. . . . This is part of the process of helping them to feel deserving."

Here is a page from McCrimmon's casebook to illustrate the art of self- appreciation:

A salesman who had closed two big sales within a month — for $200,000 and $500,000 — was feeling unworthy and uncomfortable. Part of McCrimmon's therapy was to have the salesman examine what purchasing agents are like and the extent to which he functioned so effectively with them. "He began to appreciate himself" for the slick job he was doing, and he stopped feeling guilty about his success.

Some suggestions from McCrimmon:

Use positive words to describe what's going on in your life. "Don't use words like 'but.' Don't say 'Things are going well, but . . .' Don't use words like 'try.' You're not trying; you're doing."

Stand back "from your own picture show and watch it. Realize that this — whatever it is — is what you're doing and it's acceptable."

Help along the self-esteem of somebody who matters to you without being judgmental in your dealings with that person. "This is the magic of making a relationship work. Instead of judging others, it makes more sense to be positive. Most of us already know what's wrong with us. We don't need others always telling us. Being positive makes a substantial contribution to self-esteem."

It's his opinion, McCrimmon said, that the little voices whisper to everybody who will listen to them. "When the voices are not talking, it's because they don't believe they have support for what they're going to say." The way to withdraw support is to feel good enough about yourself to be able to challenge the voices: "If I don't deserve it, who does?"

Although I hadn't heard of prosperity psychology then, that's exactly what my friend primed me to do that day at the Los Angeles airport. I know it works — and in my case it worked quickly.

What about you?

THE ENEMIES OF PASSION
February 6, 1986

The question, said psychologist Thelma Shtasel, has to do with passion — or, more precisely, with the absence of passion in a relationship between a man and a woman.

"When we speak about passion, we describe an agony and an ecstasy. We speak of a fantasy, of an expectation. When we ask, 'Where hath all the passion gone?' we ask, 'Where is that ecstatic agony, that denied expectation? Why was it lost?"

Yes, indeed, where hath all the passion gone?

Most of us, said Shtasel, felt the steamy rush of passion when the relationship was in the early stages, and "maybe it's a fundamental error" to expect passion, by this definition, to continue. "Maybe, like youth, it's a passing phase. . . . My observations disclose a greater sense of satisfaction among couples who accept without regret that high emotions will settle in time to a different, although not necessarily worse, level.

"They expect the passion of the courtship to be time-limited and are not disappointed when the dust settles. They replace the glitter with the real gold: a basis for trust, sexual intimacy, a realistic outlook on the relationship. . . . These relationships are characterized by flexibility, avoidance of routine" in sexual activity, and continuous "open deposits of sexual and other reinforcement" without the expectation of getting something of equal value in return. "Sex is an extension of emotional intimacy and a two-person affair. Invitations for sexual participation are given and received by both, and asking for a raincheck is not interpreted as rejection."

Shtasel, who not long ago presented a paper on lost passion at the eastern meeting of the Society for the Scientific Study of Sex, said in an interview that many factors could cause passion to fade, but that marital discord "probably is highest. . . . Often people don't connect the two. They will say that loss of passion is what caused the discord — and not realize that it's a result, not a cause."

Discord can and often does take place slowly and subtly, said Shtasel. "A wife, say, loses trust in her husband. She thinks that he's squirreling away money without telling her . . . and she begins to look at him in a different way. 'He's not the honorable guy I married.' If this continues, this erosion of confidence, she may not feel very attracted sexually to him" and passion may be on the way out.

But the woman may not understand what's happening — only that she no longer feels the same about her husband. "She may say that it's her fault that passion has been lost. And the partner often is happy to let the other take the responsibility, to say, 'Yeah, you're right; it's your fault. When are you going to get fixed up?' "

For the most part, said Shtasel, loss of passion is a two-way street, and restoring passion is a two-way effort.

"Once we find the problem, what happens then depends on how invested people are in the relationship. I ask how committed they are, how willing they are to change themselves — not the other person — to help the relationship." The prognosis is good if people are willing to look at themselves and to acknowledge and change their role, whatever it is, in the loss of passion.

Shtasel said that the emotional causes of passion lost were found primarily in these three elements:

¶ **Anger.** While anger can stem from any number of sources, it often is tied to marital distress. "While it is true, albeit rarely, that sexual passion may continue while a relationship deteriorates or can be used to make up after a fight, in the majority of cases passion withers" in lockstep with the withering of the relationship. "Most often the desire is to slug — not to seduce. . . . The desire to punish becomes paramount . . . and what better way to punish than not to desire the other, than not to want to feel passion for the other? The loving foreplay that in the past could lead to sensual passion now is eliminated from the behavioral repertoire. Bye-bye, passion."

¶ **Fear.** What is the basis for fear that could wipe out the high-voltage passion that existed in the early excitement of the relationship? It can range from performance anxiety to concern about pregnancy, said Shtasel, and can include ghosts from the past such as incest or rape. But less-tangible fears, such as fear of losing control and fear of closeness or vulnerability, are among "the most common reasons for loss of passion and in some cases of all sexual desire. . . . Each of these has elements of concern for being hurt . . . and a guarding by armoring against potential pain."

¶ **Aversion.** This, like anger and fear, can be tied to many factors, including gender confusion, being raised with "an antisex attitude of religious or parental origin," repeated negative experiences, or pressure from the partner to engage in certain acts that are viewed as repulsive.

Here is an "aversion" example from Shtasel's casebook:

"The young couple courted a year and married three months ago. The woman reported very high passion during the early seductive phase of the relationship when the man was playing hard to get. Excitement was lower" after they were engaged, and sex became a total turnoff after marriage.

The woman "currently is having a passionate extramarital affair. Her background conditioned her to believe that feeling sexual was dirty, disgusting and embarrassing. She requires 'permission' to be sexual by a man she must pursue and who then is very aggressive sexually so that all she can do is relax and enjoy it. Once she was engaged, her husband had become a quiet lover, anxious to please her. The effect of this was a total turnoff . . . and she felt embarrassed even if he saw her in the nude.

"Her mother had instructed her well — nice girls don't."

WHEN A PET DIES
July 7, 1991

The letter was from a woman in mourning. Here is part of what she wrote: "Last week my dog died. My husband and I had him as a family pet for 10 years. He was our 'first' child and, during an anguishingly long period of infertility, he came to represent the family unit we wanted. Our love poured into this animal, and he graciously and constantly loved us back.

"We had a daughter three and a half years ago, and Shane, our golden retriever, became her protector and very best friend. . . .

"Now unexpectedly he is gone, and the loss I feel is so great. It's mixed, however, with a sense of silly privacy. Most of our friends really don't understand why we would mourn a pet. Family members were sympathetic the first day or two, but they don't 'hear' his footsteps or wait for him to bark to come in. . . .

"During his brief illness — he spent the final week of his life in an animal hospital — I actually felt like a helpless parent of a sick child. I called the doctors regularly and got several updates a day. On the day he died, I visited him — the only time they let me do that. . . . I cried so much I thought I couldn't possibly ever have any energy left to cry again. My husband cried, too. He never thought he'd react this way. . . .

"We never gave much thought to the possibility that Shane might die. But now he's gone and we feel almost silly saying we're having a rough time because of his illness and death. People can't believe the money we spent to save him. We never gave it a thought. We trusted our doctors. . . .

"I feel as though I've lost a family member, a child, a friend. It seems that any pain or loss my husband and I experienced throughout our lives has come back — the feelings of sadness, the overwhelming void. . . .

"I know we can get another dog, and he, too, will become important to us. . . . I just needed to write to you about our loss and how we're feeling. Do you think we're strange?"

■

No, I don't think the woman who wrote the letter is strange. To the contrary, I think she and her husband are lucky — lucky to have been able to share the life and love of a pet for 10 years, to mourn their loss, and to talk about that loss in public.

I don't think pets should replace people in our lives, but I do think pets afford those of us who love them a rare opportunity to love and be loved in a way that's different from our relationships with people. Pets are forever dependent on us for just about everything, and they can teach us all about the joy of giving. But pets aren't just takers. They can give back, too, and they can teach us all about the joys of receiving.

I'm partial to cats. I've had cats since I was a young boy, and most of them have lived long, healthy lives — up to 22 years. I like to think it's because they know that they are valued and that their needs always will be taken care of.

Today's cat has been at our house for six years. He was 5 when we got him from an animal shelter — after he was placed there by a divorcing couple. They must have had children because they had named him E.T. Marilyn and I couldn't see how we could have an E.T. cat, but we wanted a name that wouldn't confuse him — so we selected B.G., for Big Gray.

He must have come from a good home. He knows how to give and receive love, how to play, how to ask for what he wants — and demand it if that becomes necessary. He can be ingenious. Since we moved to the country, he spends a lot of time on the screened-in porch, and he learned how to pop open the door — which forced me to wedge it shut. B.G. is an indoor cat, but he doesn't know it.

Like the man who loves him, B.G. suffers from undetermined allergies, and we have to be careful with his diet and with his exposure to pollen at times during the year. Every day we give him three allergy tablets, which he routinely accepts as part of the price for doing business with us.

That I feel closer to him than to any cat I ever shared space with may say more about me than about B.G., although he's remarkable. I've been open to his teaching me about unconditional love, about spontaneity, about rebellion and surrender, about ultimately obeying rules that we don't agree with. During my solitary winter times of work and reflection at the beach, he sometimes has been the only guy I've talked to for days.

Sometimes I get down on the floor with him so I can get a cat's-eye view of the world. Everybody should try that sometime. The perspective is altogether different.

■

Some years ago, I interviewed an English veterinarian who had written a book about pet psychology and who took the position that only "nice" people have pets. He had for Prime Minister Margaret Thatcher a dislike that approached hatred, and he said that he couldn't imagine that anybody as nasty as he thought she was could have a pet. Sure enough, he said, he checked it out, and Margaret Thatcher was petless.

In the column that I wrote based on that interview, I talked about "nice" people and pets, and a reader reminded me angrily that Adolf Hitler had a dog — a German shepherd. Did I regard Hitler as a "nice" person? No, but there are exceptions to every rule, and I still think that, for the most part, unsavory people don't have pets. How could they when they're so bound up in their own misery?

■

I think we need to appropriately mourn the death of a pet — just as we mourn any major loss in life. I think parents do their children a great disservice by telling them to "stop crying, darling, because we're going down to the pet store right now and buy you another dog." This action — while taken for reasons that seem to have the child's best interests at heart — actually deprives the child of learning a valuable lesson: When something sad happens, it's OK to cry and feel bad.

We always can replace a pet. But we can't ever replace the spot that the pet held in our lives, and that loss needs to be felt and honored.

■

A final note:

Five days after I wrote this column, while I was in New Orleans to make a speech, B.G. died in an accident at our home. When I came back, we buried him in a wooded area where rabbits play — in a box with his catnip mouse, a can of his favorite turkey-giblet food, and a note to remind him eternally of how much we loved him. Like the reader who wrote the letter to me, I cried so much I thought I couldn't possibly ever have any energy left to cry again.

WHEN TRUST IS VIOLATED
January 27, 1991

Over lunch, the man was telling me a sad story: After his father died, he thought it made good sense to name his brother, an accountant, to act as unofficial executor of the estate, to look after the money and pay the expenses to keep their mother in a comfortable nursing home.

But along the way, a not-funny-at-all thing happened. The brother became unable to pay the bills because he lost every cent of the money when the stock market tumbled.

"I didn't ask him to invest it; I asked him to take care of it," the man said.

He was troubled, obviously, by the loss of the money. But beyond that, he was shaken by the breach of trust. "If you can't trust your own brother, can you trust anybody?"

■

Over lunch, another man was telling me an equally sad story:

He had decided to invest money — which would be his retirement fund — with a broker who, for many years, had handled money for his friends and who had been highly recommended. But the broker, who was supposed to make only low-risk investments, decided he could make a killing for himself, without anybody ever knowing about it, by putting the money into gold futures.

When the market went crazy a few years ago, he lost all the money. Asked the man: "Can you trust anybody?"

■

The woman acknowledged that her marriage wasn't a 10 on the zero-to-10 scale — realistically it was maybe a 6 — but she wasn't prepared for what she discovered by accident: Her husband of 20 years was keeping on the side a girl-friend and the child he had fathered by her. She was both furious and disillusioned.

"I would have trusted him with my life," she said. "Now I don't know if I'll be able to trust anybody ever again."

■

What does it all mean? Are we living in a world in which trust has become obsolete, something for suckers, for people who don't understand reality . . . and human frailties?

I hope not. I like to think that a healthy attitude is not to extend blind, unquestioned trust but to trust with the knowledge that everybody is capable of disappointing us, of shattering our illusions, and that at some point everybody probably will; that we must expect this and be prepared to pick up the pieces and get on with our lives; that we won't allow it to destroy us; that we'll try not to be bitter and to remain as optimistic as we can.

That's what I think. What about you?

■

I put the question about trust to psychiatrist Jim Hoyme, and asked him what he thought was a reasonable posture for people to take.

Hoyme, who is medical director of the Institute of Pennsylvania Hospital, opened with a question: "What is the need in each of us to trust others?" Then he answered his own question:

"It seems to me that it's a fairly childlike need — because trust, in its strongest form, is based on the belief that others have our best interests at heart, like our parents did, we hope. . . . There is at work a kind of poignant, childlike searching, and this causes us to gravitate toward somebody we see as trustworthy." A lot of the time this trust is misplaced, he said.

A good way to see this acted out, said Hoyme, is to stand around in the business office at a hospital.

"You have the opportunity to see over and over again what people's unexamined beliefs are about medical insurance," he said. "They were sold insurance by a salesperson who told them the advantages, that they wouldn't have to worry, that they'd be secure. Many of them believed that they would be taken care of . . . and they're shocked in the hospital when the fine print is pointed out — that the insurance has a deductible, that they're responsible for 20 percent in cash, that psychiatric treatment may be limited to 10 days in the hospital.

"The point is that most of us go along with an unquestioned assumption of trust. Our insurance company is like an all-protecting parent who is going to take care of us. This is not the case. Insurance is a business that has to make a profit and manage costs."

Hoyme said people tended to approach others in much the same way they approached insurance. "We project into the world a wish to be liked, that others be interested in our welfare. If somebody seems to fill the bill, we're inclined to trust them. Unfortunately, there are people out there — whether criminals, politicians, psychiatrists or writers — who are very good at seeming to be trustworthy." In reality, they are skilled liars — and they can be found in all kinds of places and relationships.

"I don't know any foolproof indicators of trustworthiness in another person," said Hoyme. "Maybe the best indicator is not what somebody says but what somebody does — not for 10 minutes or 10 days but for long periods. It helps to know a lot about behavior over long periods. . . . Still, this is not 100 percent foolproof" — because spouses of 20 years break trust, just like brothers and investment brokers.

"Maybe the price we pay for the inevitable outcome of unconditional trust is modification," Hoyme said. "We scale down our expectations . . . because infantile trust gets damaged, over time, by the turmoil of life, alcohol, anger, dishonesty, gathering indifference."

What about giving people another chance, if they ask for it, after they've broken trust?

"What are they asking for?" he said. "To erase the slate and go back to the way things were? That's not possible. Linda Ronstadt sang about that in 'Heart Like a Wheel.' . . . Once you bend it, you can't mend it.

"You have to readjust your perception of what's possible, based on the new knowledge you now have. But you can't ever feel as safe as you did before.

"It might horrify us to find out how untrustworthy human beings are," Hoyme said.

PHYSICIANS AND CARING
October 5, 1986

The problem with medicine, said George L. Engel, is that it historically has been so hung up on being scientific that it has dismissed the importance of being human — and training physicians to be as tuned in to people as to disease.

Let's listen to Engel, who is professor emeritus of psychiatry and medicine at the University of Rochester School of Medicine and Dentistry and who, at 72, rightfully is regarded as one of the grand old men of medicine:

"The patient comes to the physician for help because he is experiencing something that is strange, different, unusual or alarming and which he does not understand . . . but which he believes — or hopes — the doctor does understand and does know how to handle. The largest part of what is disturbing for the patient is known only to himself . . . and will remain so unless and until communicated.

"For the patient, two considerations loom large in the decision to entrust oneself and one's care to a physician: first, confidence that the physician is competent and, second, the expectation . . . that the physician will be understanding, that he will feel understood by his physician."

What does that mean — to feel understood?

It means more "than just the intellectual understanding of 'what I'm talking about' and more than just an understanding of 'my body and what is wrong with it.'

"Equally important, to feel understood means 'Do my doctors know who I am, who I have been, who I still want to be? Do they understand what I am going through, my suffering, my pain, my distress? Do they understand my hopes and aspirations, my fears and shames, my vulnerabilities and strengths, my needs and yearnings, my values and beliefs, my responsibilities and obligations? Above all, do they sense my personhood and my individuality? Do they acknowledge my humanity?' "

It's true, said Engel, that scientific understanding means getting all the facts and "getting them straight. . . . But every bit as important is that the physician also display the human understanding which is so necessary if the patient is to feel understood. The two are complementary. . . . When expression of human understanding on the part of the physician is not forthcoming and the patient does not feel understood, then trust and confidence may be impaired and with it the patient's capacity and willingness to collaborate," which is critical if the physician's scientific aims are to be accomplished.

How does a physician develop in a patient the feeling of being understood?

Engel told a story:

"As a guest at a medical grand rounds, I was to demonstrate an initial interview with a patient heretofore unknown to me. Wheeled into place in a wheelchair, the patient at once angrily complained that no one had explained the exercise to him, that he had been left unattended in a cold, drafty corridor outside the auditorium, that altogether no one had seemed to care what happened to him. . . .

"He broke eye contact and turned away from me, shrugged indifferently when asked if he would be willing to tell the doctors something about the illness. My 'How have you been feeling?' evoked a sarcastic 'How would you feel?' We were already at an impasse."

Engel struggled to get a dialogue going by asking the man about the illness. "His initial responses were limited to symptoms. He revealed nothing about himself. To broaden our engagement . . . I repeatedly interjected, 'Where were you at the time? What were you doing? Who else was there?' Bit by bit, more personal details began to be included. Then abruptly one item riveted my attention: a vegetable garden. He was tending a vegetable garden when his first symptoms occurred. . . .

"Surely having a vegetable garden in the midst of the squalor and congestion of the urban ghetto where he lived must say something of the man behind the angry facade. My interest was genuine, and he must have felt it — for he at once responded to my echoing query 'You were gardening?' with a willingness until then not evident."

In a few minutes, "quite another human being began to emerge, a man with a life story all his own. Now I was getting to know a former migrant field worker who had successfully established himself as an auto worker in Detroit, only to lose his job in the recession. . . . Insurance lapsed, savings melted away, his home and car were repossessed, and his wife and his children finally went back South to her parents' farm. . . .

"He remained behind, still hoping for re-employment, living alone in a rooming house. The garden he had scratched out in the rubble of a vacant lot was one last effort to sustain his image of himself as self-sufficient and responsible. Falling ill and being hospitalized was the final blow."

As the man's story emerged, said Engel, silence engulfed the room, except "for the patient's now soft voice and my occasional sound or word of concern or encouragement. Finally he fell silent, his head lowered, his eyes moist, his hands resting motionless on his thighs. I knew he was close to tears. . . . I drew my chair closer to his, and I placed my hand on his and squeezed gently, for but an instant. At once, tears began to flow. Still silent, he wiped them away with the tissue I had offered him.

"Then with a faintly apologetic smile, he raised and let fall his hand in the gesture of helplessness, adding, 'What else could I do?' I nodded and said nothing. Nothing needed to be said. We both now knew we understood each other. . . .

"After a brief pause, we resumed the exploration of his illness. In short order, we could be confident that we had all the pertinent facts about his heart attack and about himself. . . . Our total acquaintanceship had spanned but 18 minutes, and when I reluctantly brought the interview to a close, we shook hands. This time it was he who squeezed my hand. 'Thank you, doctor,' he said, though surely he knew we would never meet again."

■

That's how it is done, said Engel in an interview, and there's nothing phony or dishonest about it. If a physician is genuinely interested in understanding a patient, the patient will know — and the patient will respond.

The problem, said Engel, is in getting doctors and doctors-to-be to give this aspect of medicine the attention it deserves . . . and so desperately needs.

Forty years ago, Engel developed at the University of Rochester in New York a program giving students and residents training in how to relate to patients.

"I was working with material that suggested that at least seven diseases — colitis, hypertension, some kinds of ulcers, the so-called 'Holy 7' — could be called psychosomatic because there seemed to be a relationship between certain psychodynamic conflicts and the occurrence of disease. . . . It was not difficult for me to get the hang of how to listen to these patients. . . . When I came to Rochester, my mission was to try to develop a psychosomatic program . . . and the first thing I suggested seemed logical to me but a departure from what had been done elsewhere. What could we learn if we interviewed every patient at random in the same way we interviewed those patients" with psychosomatic illness?

What happened, said Engel, was that physicians quickly built rapport with patients, whose medical progress in many cases was so outstanding that nobody could quite figure it out. Could it be . . . that patients did better if they felt that their doctors understood them? That certainly had to be part of it, said Engel, and before long a formal training program in relating to patients was up and running. The result: Rochester graduates, wherever they went, tended to blaze paths of glory, even though some physicians and some hospitals made fun of them.

Years later, when Engel sent questionnaires to Rochester graduates, he found that they felt that their training had served them well. More than 90 percent who responded said they felt better prepared than other graduates "in all psychosocial aspects of medicine that involved understanding patients."

In whatever areas they felt weak, they said that they caught up within a year. When Engel asked how long it took others to catch them in the psychosocial field, they were virtually unanimous in their response: "Never."

WHEN WAS THE LAST TIME YOU CRIED?
March 13, 1988

In my years as a newspaper editor, I made regular recruiting visits to schools of journalism around the country — and the schools always told me that more students signed up to be interviewed by me than by anybody else.

This made me feel good, because I assumed that students were familiar with my newspaper, admired what we were doing, wanted to become part of it.

One day, at the University of South Carolina, more than 30 students were on my list for interviews — and one of the instructors said that it was "absolutely incredible. Most of the time, we don't get more than 10 or 15."

Well, it was a long day for me, but I met a number of talented people with whom I would stay in touch as graduation time approached. There was one student — a woman who looked more like a model than a journalist — who seemed especially bright, and I asked why she wanted to work for the Charlotte News.

She looked startled for an instant, but recovered quickly. "Oh, I don't want to work for your newspaper. I just wanted to be interviewed by you."

I didn't know what to say, but I managed to croak, "Why?"

"It's because everybody at the school says you ask the most interesting questions and conduct the most unusual interviews. It's fun — and it's great practice."

■

At the time, I wasn't sure that this was a compliment, but, over the years, I've come to believe that it was. What made the interviews so interesting that so many wanted to take part in them? I asked questions that nobody ever asked them before, questions that didn't have anything to do with journalism but that had everything, I thought, to do with being human. I've always been partial to people who are human, even when I was an editor, although, as everybody knows, editors aren't supposed to be concerned with this sort of thing.

Some of the questions I often asked:

¶ If you could change one thing about yourself, what would it be?
¶ On a zero-to-10 scale, how much do you like yourself?
¶ What would it take for you to like yourself more?
¶ What is your idea of a good time?
¶ How would you characterize your relationship with your parents?
¶ If you were going to improve your relationship with your parents, what would you have to do?
¶ When was the last time you cried?
¶ What did you cry about?

Ah, yes, crying. The questions about crying always seemed to stop the students. They'd study their shoes, look at the ceiling, fidget with their fingers. Then the women, for the most part, would say that they had last cried a week or a month or four months ago when they broke up with a boyfriend or quarreled with their parents.

The men, for the most part, would have a difficult time remembering the last time they had cried, and many of them would say something like "I think it was when I was 7 and fell down and skinned my knee."

But occasionally, one of them would surprise me. "I cried last night when I took my dog to the veterinarian. He's old and he's sick, and I'm afraid he's going to die." Over the years, I probably offered a disproportionate number of jobs to people with sick dogs, and they — the owners, not the dogs — usually turned out to be good journalists, because they knew what it meant to be human.

I have a soft spot in my heart for people who aren't afraid to cry — probably because I have learned not to be afraid to cry.

■

I thought about those recruiting years when I was interviewing Richard Lippin, a physician who encourages many of his patients to cry as a way to relieve stress. Researchers have discovered, he said, that the chemical composition of emotional tears is different from the tears we get from peeling onions or facing into a stiff wind. Emotional tears contain more protein, and it is believed that this means that stress hormones actually are being released in these tears.

Lippin has an exercise that, if followed, virtually is guaranteed to make people cry. The exercise involves thinking of something sad — a movie, a song, a story, an event, just about anything — and then relaxing, breathing deeply, giving up control of the defense mechanisms.

I have found that I don't need an exercise to coax me into crying. I cry enough on my own — tears of happiness as well as sadness — and I like to think that it's because I'm in the process of becoming more human, of turning loose of the facade and the games that people are taught to play with themselves and each other.

■

I cried tears of joy last year when I was in San Diego to visit my younger son, Grant, and he got out our old baseball gloves and we went to the beach and played catch. That was an incredibly emotional thing for me, because we'd last played catch a dozen years ago, when I was still married to his mother, before the divorce that, for a time, shattered my relationship with Grant.

It was as if we had turned back the calendar to another age, when he was a boy who shaved once every two weeks, when I was a father who passionately attended every baseball game that he ever pitched, when the world seemed less complicated.

I was glad I cried that day on the beach. Years ago, I'd have thought that it was unmanly. Now I don't think about what it is — except that it's natural.

I cried tears of sadness and frustration a while back, too, when I came face to face with the reality that my older son, Jay, and I are stuck in our relationship, that we can't seem to get where we want to be, that the garbage of our yester-years gets in the way, that at times it seems futile. I felt better after I'd cried, because being so much in touch with my pain seemed somehow to diminish its sharpness. I still didn't know what to do, but things didn't seem quite so futile.

What do you think? When was the last time you cried?

POSITIVE CONFRONTATION
January 22, 1984

Towel on the floor . . . too insignificant to mention. Laughter at my mistake . . .
    not a mountain to climb.
Small disagreement . . . disappointment, hurt feelings.
Moments, days, years . . . of trivial heartache.
Anger mounting, pain developing, division widening.
Gentle feelings turning to rage . . . unsettled, indifferent.
Whispers becoming shouts . . . too late, too much.
Bridges burned by silent fire, smoldering, turning to ash . . . never to be rebuilt.

That poem, from his book *Everything Makes a Difference*, tells it all, Burt Bertram said, because its theme is so familiar to so many of us: We let little things pile up until they become big things, and then we explode.

Bertram is a consultant, and he and his partner, John Curtis, operate in Winter Park, Fla., the firm of Bertram & Curtis, which lists as its primary services human relations, consulting and counseling. As part of what they do, Bertram and Curtis travel around the country to put on business seminars, and not long ago they were in Philadelphia for seminars that included what they call "positive confrontation."

What in the world is that?

Well, they said in an interview, positive confrontation is telling people something that they don't want to hear but need to hear — in a way that is designed to increase the likelihood that they will inventory and then alter their behavior.

Said Bertram: "By our definition, confrontation is not 'chewing' or 'getting even.' It's a deliberate attempt on your part to help another person examine the consequences of some aspect of his or her behavior. It is an invitation to self-examination and productive problem-solving.

The trouble is, however, that many of us can't, or don't, confront those whose behavior drives us up the wall, and, said Curtis, there are two primary reasons for this:

¶ Fear of aggression. "We're afraid the other person will get mad at us," if we say we're sick and tired of the person's blowing cigarette smoke across his or his desk and into our faces.

¶ Fear of rejection. It's possible that the other person won't have anything to do with us anymore if we bring up the subject. For people who clutch onto friendships like life jackets, this possibility is absolutely terrifying — so negative matters are never discussed.

Discomfort about confrontation is widespread, and that is a major reason why Bertram and Curtis incorporated it into their seminars, and it's why the subject is one that they're often asked to present.

"There are things in normal life that we ought to get off our chests," said Bertram. "We need to have our say about it and move on . . . and get rid of our unfinished business," which hogties us not only in business but also in our personal lives. "If it's not talked about, not finished, then a price is paid. Little things pile up, and our psychic energy is absorbed in that and isn't available for tending to the here and now."

Curtis jumped in: "Think of what needs to be resolved in your life. There's usually one person — somebody in the office or a spouse, parent or family member — who is causing a problem for you. . . . Typically in married life, anger and irritation are not discussed. Somebody doesn't balance the checkbook, leaves wet towels on the floor, does the holiday planning to suit the in-laws rather than the spouse. . . . Well, typically the person thinks: 'I can't make waves over something so trivial,' and then benign neglect sets in. The price for that eventually is that the people grow apart."

At the office, said Bertram, a secretary may find that she's irritated not that the boss wants coffee but that the boss hollers, "Coffee!," rather than saying, "Hey, I'd really appreciate a cup of coffee." An employee becomes enraged because the boss is prone to mortgage the employee's time without asking. "The boss will say things like 'Sure, Charlie will come to that meeting,' and, yes, maybe it's only a five-minute meeting and no big deal," but it becomes a big deal when, through repetition, it festers in Charlie's stomach.

How does somebody positively confront somebody else?

Here is the getting-ready blueprint offered by Bertram and Curtis:

First of all, recognize that, while it may be a small issue, it does have impact on your daily life. Give yourself permission to take it seriously.

Consider carefully the fact of life that confrontation will lead to increased involvement with the other person. "Don't confront another person if you don't intend or desire to increase your involvement. Just chew him out or punish him — or whatever."

Remember that the strength and intensity of the confrontation must be geared to the strength of the relationship.

Be certain, when confronting, to present facts as facts, feelings as feelings, opinions as opinions.

Now for the actual mechanics of confrontation. Here are five steps recommended by Bertram and Curtis:

¶ Explain your intent: "I have something I need to talk with you about . . . and I see it as potentially an emotional or difficult issue."

¶ State your observation: "Let me outline what I've noted in my mind about this situation. I have seen . . ."

¶ Disclose the impact upon yourself. "I hope you can see the position I'm in. . . . I'm very uncomfortable, and I find that I'm becoming preoccupied with this."

¶ Define ownership of the problem. "That's how I see it. In my mind I have a problem, you have a problem, so we have a problem. It's important to me that this gets resolved. . . . What do you understand the problem to be? What are you going to do about our problem?"

¶ Clarify and defuse defensiveness. It may be necessary to restate your problem in part or totally. Misunderstandings and defensiveness are inevitable during a confrontation. It may be helpful to say something like: "I know this is difficult to talk about, and I can appreciate that you don't have immediate answers. The first step is an acknowledgement of our mutual problem and a commitment from both of us to find a solution."

Oh, come on now, Bertram and Curtis, would an approach like that really produce change — or a symbolic or even literal punch in the nose?

It's true, they said, that in seminars they operate in a theoretical world, and in real life, the confrontation and the outcome might be less than ideal. But this doesn't diminish the importance of confronting people whose behaviors are troublesome.

It's not likely, they said, that confrontation will produce a punch in the nose, but it's possible — just as it's possible that the secretary who confronts her coffee-screaming boss could get fired. People need to weigh the consequences of confrontation before they act.

It's also possible that confrontation won't produce the change that is sought. But this is no reason to avoid confrontation, said Curtis, because, if nothing else, confrontation can soften a person's "sense of impotence, the feelings of being victimized. . . . If nothing else, the other person knows how you feel," and the unfinished business isn't unfinished any more.

The people who confront most effectively, Curtis said, are those "with a personal sense of security. They can take the time to self-examine, to confront themselves, to ask, 'Hey, what am I doing?' Because they can self-examine, they're able to help others self-examine. . . . Otherwise, the confrontation can become blaming. 'I don't feel good about me, and I'll fix it so you don't feel good about you.' And that ends up nowhere."

IN MEMORY OF A MOTHER
February 26, 1984

It was 4 o'clock in the morning, and lights were on in only one house on the block-long street that clung to the hillside — a sturdy red-brick house with white trim and a full porch, in the classic architecture of the 1920s.

Inside, the man and his wife shuffled from room to room for what they knew would be the last time. They stood in the bedroom in which his parents had slept and loved for so many years, and the man said:

"It looks so empty . . . and so forlorn."

The woman held his hand but said nothing. She pushed shut the closet door to block the sight of dresses, blouses, skirts and coats that hung neatly — clothing that hadn't been claimed by friends, clothing that silently awaited the auctioneer who would appear in a few days and offer it to the highest bidder, along with everything else that remained.

The man and his wife mounted the stairs to the attic for a final look at what they painfully had decided to leave behind because there was no way to take it all back to Philadelphia — the games that a little boy once had played with, the baseballs, the bats, the sports magazines out of the 1940s, the colorful aluminum tumblers in which icy lemonade so many times had been swirled by the tiny grandsons.

"We've got to go now," the man whispered. "It'll take us three hours to get to St. Louis and check in the car at the airport."

"I know," the woman said.

Room by room, they clicked off the lights, and when they reached the front door, the man did a strange thing. He talked to the house. "Goodbye. I hope the next people are good to you. You deserve it."

Then he sealed the keys in an envelope, which he slipped into the mailbox for the real-estate broker to retrieve later in the day.

In heavy silence, they backed the car out of the driveway and lingered for a moment in the street.

"I never knew anything could hurt this much," the man sobbed. "Oh, God, I wish I'd come last week. I wish I'd been here."

The woman cried, kissed the man and said: "I loved your mother, too."

They drove down the hill, and neither looked back.

■

As a boy, I was closer emotionally to my father than to my mother, yet when he died in 1978, my grief, although it was choking, did not equal what I suffered through when my mother died in January.

Why? I've asked myself that many times, and now, as my grief moves toward what I think is its completion, I believe that I have an answer.

When Dad died, I turned much of my concern toward Mom, who had been his companion for 54 years. Could she survive such an injury? Would she even want to survive? What could I do to help her?

170

When Dad died, I still had a parent and a family home, a place to come to at special times. I still had somebody to whom I could write special letters, mail my columns and send funny cards on birthdays and holidays. I still had somebody to whom I was a child and from whom radiated the kind of love that only a parent can offer.

When Mom died, all of that died, too. The connection to childhood now is severed — except in memories — and, as an only child, I sometimes feel terribly alone, even as my wife, Marilyn, and my sons, Jay and Grant, pour out their love to me. For the first time in my life I wish for brothers and sisters.

■

It was late in 1983, and because I had heard complaints from so many people about parents who cling to their adult children, I felt compelled to tell Mom once again how exceptional she and Dad had been. In a letter, I said:

"Lately, I have received many letters from readers about parents who have almost suffocated them with requests for attention and who have primed the guilt pump so that it seems never to run dry. It brings into such sharp focus how fortunate I am to have had you and Pop as parents — because from the both of you I never felt anything but acceptance and encouragement to fly on my own. At the risk of seeming to belabor the point, I want you to know how much I appreciate everything that you both did for me."

In a telephone call not long after that Mom thanked me for sharing my feelings but said: "Honestly, I don't know why you make such a big deal out of it. . . . All we ever did was love you."

But I was determined not to let her off the hook so easily. In my next letter I asked:

"Would you take the time to write down your thoughts on parenting and mail them to me? I'm especially interested in the process of turning loose — and how you and Pop seemed instinctively to know how and when to do that. I'd like to use some of what you say in a column sometime. Who knows? This could be the start of a writing career for you."

After her heart attack, Mom was in the hospital for two weeks and seemed to be about ready to go home before her condition flipped suddenly and she died within a few hours — three days before I was scheduled to fly to Jefferson City, Mo., to spend a week with her.

In what would be our last conversation, 48 hours before she died, Mom seemed in good spirits.

"I've been working on that assignment you gave me — about parenting. I've finished a rough draft, and I'll polish it up as soon as I get home. I hope it's what you want."

Yes, it was what I wanted — her feelings, handwritten on the backside of three calendar pages, surely the last writing of her life. Here is some of what she said:

"We always talked a lot with you when you were a young child. We read a lot to you, and we always let you know that we loved you, that we thought you were very special. . . . You always got along well with your little friends, and you had many. You weren't selfish with your toys, as people might think an only child would be. . . . We just didn't have any problems with you, so what can I say to other parents? I can say that they should try to keep up communication from the time the child can talk — and especially during the teen years. Children need to know that they are loved — no matter what. . . .

"You asked about parents' turning loose of children. This doesn't just happen when the child goes away to college or whatever. The pattern for this happens much earlier, and for me it started when I had to go to work when you were in seventh grade — when we just didn't have enough money. I could have felt sorry for myself and for you. I could have felt guilty about leaving you alone so much of the time. But it was something that had to be done, and we all understood that. . . . So when you went away to college and then into the Army, it wasn't like we were being separated for the first time. . . . What made it bearable was that I knew you loved us and I always felt that you knew how much we loved you. . . .

"Parents who expect something back for all the things they've done for their children are setting themselves up for disappointment. I never expected anything back but love, and you've given me lots of that. . . . It's been hard having you so far away, but I've known you've been happy, and that has made me happy. . . .

"I've been alone for nearly six years since Pop died, and I've learned to be content in whatever state I'm in. God never gives us more than we can bear. Your two letters each week and the telephone calls have kept me going. I love you and Marilyn so very much."

DINING ALONE
September 23, 1986

I both need and enjoy solitude — and I make time to be by myself. Maybe it's because I'm an only child, because only children, if they're lucky, learn that being alone can be a joy rather than something to be dreaded.

Yet there's one part of being alone that I don't enjoy. It is eating out, all by myself. When I'm on the road, or alone at the beach, I almost always order in — or fix something myself — rather than go to a restaurant.

Why? Maybe it's because I associate companionship with food. Without one, the other so often seems to come up short.

What about you? Do you often eat out alone?

∎

In her book *Never Alone*, Phyllis Hobe tells a story that I understand quite well.

"They were eight ordinary women. Any one of them might have been your neighbor. And each of them lived alone, for various reasons. The youngest was 28, the oldest 72. Some worked, and some were thinking about getting a job. . . . They all lived in the neighborhood of a large church, which some of them attended. They were meeting together because the church had invited them to share their concerns with one another. The group was led by a young woman with some counseling experience."

They talked about their dislike of going to the movies alone because they felt "funny sitting in a theater alone." Still, they sometimes went to the theater. They said they weren't enthusiastic about shopping alone, either. Still, they sometimes shopped by themselves. They said that they didn't like to go to restaurants alone, and . . .

At this point the counselor interrupted and turned to one woman: "You mean you've never gone to a restaurant by yourself?" When the woman solemnly shook her head, the counselor asked each of the others. The answer always was the same: No, no, a thousand times no.

Well, said the counselor, "that's your assignment for next week, to go out to dinner — alone."

The response was immediate, unanimous and horrified.

"No, I can't."

"I'd be wondering what people were thinking. 'Why is she here all alone? What's wrong with her?' "

"I'd feel so ashamed. Suppose I saw someone I knew?"

Wrote Hobe: "The counselor couldn't change their minds, and the meeting ended early. The following week there were so many dropouts that the group was disbanded."

■

Hobe, who is twice divorced and who lives alone in the Upper Perkiomen Valley area, about 15 miles west of Quakertown, said during an interview that, like everybody else, she had found dining out alone to be a difficult experience in the beginning, six years ago.

"I always enjoyed eating in restaurants, but I was alone six months before I ate out alone. At first I always called friends and asked them to go with me. . . . Finally I decided that I needed to do it alone, that there would be times when I would want to go out on the spur of the moment or to go to restaurants that my friends might not like. . . . I drove up to the restaurant a couple of times and left. I couldn't make myself go in."

Why not? After all, Hobe is an educated, sophisticated woman with a long history of writing books that are both critically acclaimed and commercially successful.

She was uncomfortable because — well, because she was uncomfortable, that's why.

Finally she forced herself to go to "a crowded place, where they have a fast turnover. I thought, 'Maybe they won't notice me.' It was very neurotic. . . . I expected the hostess to say, 'Sorry, but we don't have any tables for one.' She didn't say that, of course, and so I sat and ate . . . and I kept saying, 'Thank you, thank you' for everything. It was like I was saying, 'Thank you for treating me like a human being.' But at the time it was one of the biggest things I had accomplished in life," eating out by herself.

"Then I started going to favorite restaurants where I had been with friends, and finally to restaurants I'd never been to before. That still intimidates me a little."

Why? Because it just does.

"Being alone is uncomfortable," wrote Hobe. "Try walking into a restaurant and asking for a table for one. You will not get a good table — unless, of course, you learn to ask for one. You will be shown to a table set for two, and the second place setting will be whisked away from you as if you might take offense that it was there in the first place, as if it might remind you of better, more companionable times.

"You will be served quickly, even if solicitously, because what on earth will you do with yourself while you are waiting for your order? By all means bring a magazine or a book to read, if there is sufficient light for such a preoccupation. But count on it — if one other single person, especially one of the opposite sex, walks into the restaurant, he or she will be seated right next to you. Or, better yet, in front of you, so that your eyes must meet at some point during your meal. Both of you are being pitied. Both of you are reminding those around you that they would not want to be sitting in your seat, with your single place setting, with your magazine, with your empty life.

"If you can get past that discomfort, you may then become aware of the space you are taking up. You're sitting at a table for two, eating one meal, using a server who could just as easily carry enough for two and thereby make more of a profit for the restaurant. And more of a tip. Bon appetit!"

LAUGHTER AND TEARS
March 10, 1983

Fat Ethel waddles into the restaurant and tells the waitress that she wants a whole blueberry pie. "Should I cut it into six or eight pieces?" the waitress asks.

Ethel pauses for a moment, then answers, "Make it six. I'm on a diet."

Well, that may be one of history's worst jokes, but it serves the purpose, says Jay Efran, in illustrating the mechanism that produces laughter — and tears also, since the two are like peas in the same pod.

Efran, who is professor of psychology at Temple University, began researching laughter and tears a decade ago, and the first exposure of his work to the outside world came in 1979, when his article, "Why Grown-Ups Cry," was printed in the publication "Motivation and Emotion."

In an interview, Efran said that his research led him to conclude that there are two stages to the physiological process that ultimately produces laughter or tears.

The first stage is arousal, which is activated "by anything that the system can't quite make sense of, anything that knocks the system for a loop, causes us to have to go on alert, anything that's a threat to survival."

The second stage is recovery, and it is in this stage that laughter or tears are produced in response to our letting go of the tension or anxiety that builds during arousal.

What Efran's research strongly suggests is that we don't cry tears of joy or tears of sadness. We just cry — as we emerge from what has triggered joy or sadness. "The tears don't hear who calls them forth," said Efran. "They're just on the job."

Efran used the story about Fat Ethel to make his point because, he said, it's easier to look at humor than sadness. Here's his explanation of why we laughed:

"Until Fat Ethel said why she wanted the pie cut into six pieces rather than eight, everything was fine. Our system was not perturbed. The puzzle was created by her saying that she was on a diet. That didn't make sense to our logic . . . because she was talking about the whole pie, and whether it was cut into six or eight pieces didn't matter. Then we see what Ethel did: She substituted numerosity for quantity. She thought six was less than eight. To get the joke, we have to appreciate that logic, which is a child's logic. We're able to shift perspective — 'Oh, I see . . .' — and shift our logic to Ethel's logic.

"Then it all fits, and this allows the system to shift into recovery. Because it fits, we can let go of it. . . . The laughter is a manifestation of our letting go."

Somebody who didn't get the point wouldn't laugh, Efran said, because he would still be in the arousal stage and trying to figure out what was going on. "The tension of active problem-solving stays, and recovery doesn't begin until somebody lets go."

Efran is suggesting that the same mechanism is at work with tears.

"If a child is lost, he doesn't cry while he's actively problem-solving, trying to figure out what to do. He's tense. But then he sees his mother, relaxes and becomes blubbery. . . . Some lost children, depending on age and background, cry when they see any adult . . . because it means that they can let the problem go and somebody else will take over. But they don't cry — nobody does — while there's a survival problem on their hands."

It's the same process, although infinitely more complex, when we are grieving, Efran said.

"My father died, and I learned about it when I was away at college. I didn't cry then. I went through half a day of travel to get home, and I still didn't cry. I was sad, concerned, worried, but I didn't cry. Then I saw my mother, and she put her arms around me and said 'It'll be OK,' and I cried. Why? Because it was safe for me to let go. I was going off duty."

During grieving, we tend to cry off and on, he said, because "something happens to start the activation again. We cry because there's always something at the pinnacle of the cycle to permit a drift downward. We get ready for another assault on the hill with new resources, perhaps from another perspective."

Another example, Efran said, is this:

We're awaiting the arrival by ocean liner of a friend we haven't seen in ages. We're anxious as the ship comes into view because we don't know if our friend will be as we remembered him. Then we see him, and he's just the same — and we begin to cry.

Tears of joy? Well, that might be what everybody would think, but actually the tears represent nothing more than a release from our cycle of anxiety.

Why are laughter and tears so closely tied together?

That's not a grade-A question, Efran said. A better question is: What makes them different? It's a better question because laughter and tears are products of the same pattern of emotion and recovery. Why, then, do tears come in one instance, laughter in another?

There has not been a lot of work done on that, Efran said. "The best I can come up with is sheer speculation. . . . In both cases, the timing has to be right. If the problem-solving comes over the long haul, we may smile but there'll be no big outburst of laughter." Or we may feel sad, but no tears will flow.

For tears or laughter, there must be an emotional buildup and then a quick release. What may distinguish the two, Efran said, is this:

"If we end up in the same place as before — with the same perspective, as in the Fat Ethel story — then we laugh. We understand the joke and see ourselves as sensible and intelligent. But if we make a shift, if we end up in a different place, then we get tears. The loss of a father, let's say. . . . The cognition is not intact, and we have to restructure our view of the world, taking into account our loss, and we cry."

Tears, said Efran, tend to be a signal that our problem, whatever its identity, is being managed. "We never should block tears. We're told 'tears don't help,' but that's not true . . ." Tears do help in the sense that they signal our turning loose of what's been troubling us.

"A mother is reunited with her lost child in the supermarket. The child begins to cry, and the mother asks 'Why are you crying now?' But it's exactly the right time to cry. The system knows better than we know."

AFTER THE ACCIDENT
October 31, 1982

One recent morning, psychologist Daniel Gottlieb, who became a quadriplegic when his neck was broken in a freak traffic accident three years ago, was driving his modified van from his Cherry Hill home to his job in Philadelphia, and he was approaching the toll plaza on the Benjamin Franklin Bridge.

Paying the toll always was an ordeal, he would say, because it took time for him to set the brake, get the window open, pick up with its slotted handle the bucket that held the coins, empty the bucket into the toll basket, close the window, release the brake and drive through.

"My feeling back then was that it took almost 10 minutes — although it was much less time than that. But the heat's on when the gate goes up. Everybody expects me to go, and they start honking."

That day at the tollgate, Gottlieb was supersensitive to the honking because, after all, he hadn't been driving for very long, and it still was new to him.

He scrambled as best he could to empty the bucket and get moving through the gate, but he was painfully slow, and the honking drummed into his ears. A bridge employee seemed outraged.

"Come on! Move it! The gate's up, and people are waiting. What's wrong with you?"

At the time, Gottlieb would say, he wasn't secure enough to "tell him to go to hell. He intimidated me."

So it wasn't surprising that at the end of that day, he chose another route home — over the Tacony-Palmyra Bridge. He was anxious as he approached the toll plaza, and his thought was: "Oh, hell, here we go again. I'll be slow, and they'll yell at me."

But a bridge employee smiled and asked: "Do you need any help?"

"No, thanks; it just takes a minute."

"That's OK. Take your time."

Gottlieb immediately felt better, but as he tried to empty the bucket that held the coins, he missed the basket, and the coins rattled on the concrete. Frustrated and angry, he said to the bridge employee: "I guess I do need a hand after all."

"Oh, that's no problem. That's why we're here." And the man picked up the toll money and deposited it. He smiled and raised his left arm to doff his hat in a salute to Gottlieb, who was stunned because the man had no left hand.

They smiled at each other, and Gottlieb said: "Thank you."

"Sure."

Gottlieb drove away. "I wanted to hug him," he would say, "because I felt so un-alone."

When he still was at Thomas Jefferson University Hospital, in the months immediately after his injury, Gottlieb was told by a physician that eventually he would be able to drive again. "He was going over the extent of my disabilities, and I assumed that he was lying to make me feel better."

But after he was transferred to Magee Rehabilitation Hospital, "I discovered that I could drive someday. I was excited. . . . I wanted the van. It took a lot of time for it to be modified, but as we came down the homestretch, when it was almost done, I didn't sleep for two weeks.

"It wasn't just anticipation; it was fear, too. Not fear of driving. I'd had lessons. But the van represented a big change in my life, and change is rough. I'd worked so damned hard to get accustomed to where I was, in my wheelchair, and here came a change. It represented more independence, but I had mixed feelings. It was exciting, but it also was scary."

Driving the Ford van, which with hand-control modifications cost Gottlieb's insurance company $25,000, is no picnic, he said. He uses a power lift to get his wheelchair into the driver's position, but "it's a difficult adjustment to drive without body muscles. If I stop too short, I flop forward because I have no stomach muscles. If I make a sharp left turn, I fall against the window."

In many ways, driving is sad because "I remember when it was enjoyment, a way for me to relax, to get away from it all. Now I'm concerned if something is going to break and I'll be stranded. It's a mission to accomplish — and it never was before. I can't have the fantasy of driving the cars I admire. Now there's a big sense of loss that driving is not therapeutic. Before, it was such good therapy for me. It's a hurt — but a palatable hurt. I was without the van for a week when it was being worked on, and I had to be picked up and carried everywhere. I felt even more disabled. It was a regressive experience."

Gottlieb, who is 35 and the father of two children, is busy these days, working half time at Philadelphia Psychiatric Center and dividing the remaining hours between his private practice in Cherry Hill and his clinical work at Crystal Group Associates in Glenside.

"I'm seeing more patients, supervising more students. I'm doing some work with handicapped patients. Once I had a big investment in devoting my career to the handicapped. I don't feel that quite so strongly now, but I do feel a commitment. I feel very deeply that I have something special to give. I can sit with another quadriplegic and talk about how it feels to have a catheter . . . or I can see a couple — one of them is disabled — and when I talk about sexual possibilities, they know I'm not being academic."

But, said Gottlieb, "I don't see myself going into it with blinders on. Something has happened to me since the accident," which left him with no use of his legs and limited use of his arms. "I'm very interested in sharing it with colleagues. It's a kind of sensitivity that I have now. I believe you don't have to break your neck to get that kind of sensitivity. It can be learned," and he'd like to try to teach it to some of his colleagues.

There also exists now a "kind of intensity to my work" that wasn't present before. "I'm not afraid of it. Before, I was afraid of intimacy with my family and patients. But I'm not now. Now I'm afraid of very little. I'm afraid of dying alone. I'm not afraid of dying — but of dying alone."

Gottlieb has sued the manufacturer of the wheel that flew off the truck that he passed that day on the Pennsylvania Turnpike — the wheel that, in the words of his wife, Sandy, struck Gottlieb's sedan with such force that it was "turned into a convertible." As part of the preparation for the trial, Gottlieb's lawyer asked him to participate in the filming of a movie that could show dramatically to the jury what it's like to be a quadriplegic.

"He told me I had a choice, but it immediately made sense to me. Inside, I knew that I had to do it." But the prospect of doing it sent Gottlieb plunging to his emotional basement.

"The first three words I said when I woke up in the hospital after the accident were 'I'm a freak.' It's been a fear that I carry with me all the time. Deep down inside I have the feeling that I'm a freak. . . . When my ego strength is really low, that's how I feel, but usually I'm able to combat it. . . .

"But this movie recognized that I was a freak . . . or else nobody would care how I go to the bathroom. I'd wake up crying — angry and sad. 'I'm a freak! I'm a freak!' At least Elephant Man was dead when they made the movie about him."

The filming, said Gottlieb, was "a nightmare, everything that I feared it would be. We started at 6:30 in the morning and filmed all day. . . . In the bathroom scenes I felt like a cheap whore. The film crew was asking: 'Can we look at this? Can we see that?' The guys were nice, but it was a tough situation. When it was over, I felt numb and exhausted. I didn't feel any sense of accomplishment or mastery. I felt that it was just one more piece of garbage in my life that was past. There's not a finite amount of garbage; it's infinite. And I was past just this one."

Gottlieb did not allow the crew to film the every-morning catheter routine, he said, although he permitted filming of the leg bag attached to the catheter. He did not allow them to film him on the commode, but he did permit filming of him brushing his teeth. "I was in charge. I directed it. I was not a passive participant."

What would a successful outcome of the lawsuit mean to Gottlieb?

"It would eliminate a big source of anxiety about money and guilt. Now I'm not able to support my family the way I used to. It would eliminate that concern. . . . Of all the things I have to worry about, I'd like not to worry about money."

His life at home with Sandy is "incredibly intimate . . . close, secure. We both feel at this moment that the only thing that could jeopardize our marriage is something that jeopardizes life; nothing trivial. We've both had life-threatening times, and what we have now feels really good . . . We constantly renegotiate the marriage contract — how protective of me she needs to be, what ways I can care for her emotionally."

With his daughters, Allison, 9, and Debra, 8, Gottlieb finds the relationship "super, wonderful . . . and typical in many respects. We have the same arguments about bedtime, about behaviors. I feel more intimate with them, and my hunch is that they feel more intimate with me."

But there is a worry, Gottlieb said. "Ten years down the road, will it be more difficult for them to leave when it's time? The three of us go to dinner together, and they cut my meat, open doors. They feel like big girls now. They handle the money. But when they're older, will they worry about who'll do it for me? When it comes to them, I wish I could worry about right now."

WHY MEN NEED MALE FRIENDS
October 6, 1991

He's 43 years old, hard-working, successful, responsible, married with two children. He's also lonely. Two years ago, his best buddy, a guy he'd known since high school, moved 2,000 miles away after a bitter divorce. As painful as it was for him to go through his buddy's divorce, it was even more painful to lose him as a best friend, as his reality check, as somebody he could talk to about the fight with his wife, the problems with his kids, the struggle at the corporation.

To whom would he now turn when he needed the special kind of emotional intimacy one man can provide for another? He didn't know. It was awkward to try to find another best friend. People might laugh at him. Even the thought of it was frightening. Could he ever again be as vulnerable with a man as he'd been with his old buddy? Could he ever again find a man who would understand him so thoroughly, and offer so much support?

No, probably not.

He was becoming, in the words of psychiatrist Richard Moscotti, a "solitary lion," and, said Moscotti, there are hundreds of thousands of these men — men who "yearn to have a buddy but don't know how to go about it. . . . They've lost their navigation system. The light in the lighthouse went out," and they don't know where to go or what to do to get their male intimacy needs met.

"Men need men just as women need women."

To try to compensate, some men drink too much. Others work too much. Still others get hooked into affairs when a woman knowingly or unknowingly taps into their loneliness — and their neediness.

"A man can meet a woman any place — at a restaurant, a bar, a gasoline station. Maybe she's hungry or maybe she's needy, too. Their chemistry seems to match. It's the pleasure-pain principle, and the pain from his neediness may cause him to seek relief. If we're starved, we eat what we can find to eat."

Moscotti, whose practice is at the Institute of Pennsylvania Hospital, said it was difficult for most men "to go up to another man and say, 'I'd like to be your friend.' They may think you're intrusive, weird, homosexual. . . . Even if you find somebody with common interests, he may be so henpecked that he's afraid to go outside the parameters set by his wife. 'Yes, I'd like to play tennis with you after work, but I told my wife I'd be home early.' Men are fearful of rejection," and they'll go to almost any length to avoid the possibility — even to choking on their loneliness.

Moscotti said men were told, "Don't cry; don't be needy," and because they tend to do what they're told, men have five times more ulcers than women. "Some analysts will tell you tears that end up in the stomach instead of the eyes cause ulcers. . . . Men have trouble hugging, crying, asking for what they want. . . . But I'll tell you something: Men who can emote are healthy. They're happy. They live longer. They have warm, dry hands and normal blood pressure and a slower heart rate."

What about overcoming fear of rejection? What can a man do?

"It takes courage to take a shot at making a friend. . . . It's one thing for women to cut down men. We have certain defenses built for that, but it can be devastating for another man to cut us down. . . . Still, I believe that we must live life bravely, take some risks. . . . The more willing you are to brave rejection, the more likely you are to find somebody. . . . 'Say, I like the cut of your jib. Can we meet for a drink after work Friday?' We can diminish fear of rejection when we realize that the price of victory overcomes the price of failure. . . . If you try to make friends with 10 guys and two of them end up as friends, you're marvelously successful."

How many intimate friends does a guy need?

"If you have one or perhaps two really intimate male friends, you can consider yourself very lucky. . . . We have many levels of friends — from people we go to the movies with to people we talk about life with. The higher you go up the ladder toward intimacy the fewer people you find."

What is the obligation an intimate friend must honor to keep the friendship alive?

"You have to be with each other on occasion, to touch base. The more important the guy is to you, the less often you have to touch base, but the more often you want to. You enjoy each other's company. . . . You have to make yourself available, even if it's inconvenient, if the other guy is hurting and needs to talk to you. . . . If you can't do that, you can't have an intimate relationship."

Is anything off limits when two intimate friends get together?

"I think you can share 95 percent of what's going on in your life — money, marriage, sex, affairs, difficulties with your children. There's almost nothing that's out of bounds" when the trust level becomes high enough over time.

I asked Moscotti about wives who discourage, or at least don't support, their husbands in close relationships with other men. What's in it for the wife to have a solitary lion around the house?

"The wife may be threatened by another meaningful person in the husband's life, somebody else to whom the husband may turn and may listen to at certain times. . . . A major task in therapy can be to help the wife understand that if the marriage is healthy enough, the addition of a third party is a plus, an asset. If she's a reasonably healthy woman, she won't see it as a threat."

Another major task in therapy can be finding out why a husband is so hesitant to cross his wife by doing something she doesn't sanction. "Does the man have enough horsepower to countermand his mate? Whose life is it anyway? She calls the tune, and he dances. What kind of relationship is that?"

■

Do most solitary lions have affairs?

"No way," said Moscotti. "There's the guilt and the fear factor — fear of AIDS, fear of the consequences of entanglement, the Fatal Attraction syndrome. Michael Douglas had a tiger by the tail, and this really frightens men. . . . Most lions go through life lonely . . . forever. They sublimate."

But some solitary lions do have affairs, and what happens in the long run is a function of "the psychology of the lion," how needy or maybe how neurotic he is.

Some affairs are short — "a quick fix" — but others lead to long-term relationships and marriage. "Not all affairs are sordid and unworthy. . . . As a psychiatrist, I don't condone or condemn affairs. Each is unique to itself."

THE MEDICINE MAN
May 11, 1982

Without a doubt, Rolling Thunder was saying yesterday, an Indian medicine man is the most independent person in the world. If you come to him sick and needy, he may help you — or he may turn his back on you and walk away.

What the medicine man does hinges on "whether it was meant to be or not. Some are meant to die; some are meant to get an extension of life."

To a medicine man, it quickly is apparent into which camp people fall, said the Cherokee medicine man, who was in Philadelphia for lectures sponsored by the Spiritual Frontiers Fellowship.

"If you have committed a great crime and must pay a penalty, this is not to be interfered with. If your time has run out, this is not to be interfered with, either. There are some people no medicine man will touch and no doctor ever will help. There's a smell about them. We tell them their time has come, and we won't take them. The final judgment is up to me, and I look into it very carefully."

No matter how carefully he looks into it, a cure is not assured.

"I make no claims," said Rolling Thunder. "Some with broken backs have gotten well, but all power belongs to the Great Spirit, what you call God. Some of my enemies — and I have some good ones — say I'm not a medicine man. To them I'm not. Others say I am, and to them I might be. I make no claims."

Rolling Thunder, 67, was the focus of the 1974 book *Rolling Thunder*, written by Doug Boyd, a researcher for the Menninger Foundation in Kansas. In it, Boyd described watching a healing ceremony in which a man's deeply infected leg was cured in full view of an international audience of scientists and doctors. Within an hour, Boyd wrote, the man, who had been bedridden, was jumping and playing table tennis.

Rolling Thunder, who was technical adviser for the two Billy Jack movies, said that, yes, indeed, healing often does take place when the person wants to be healed for the right reasons, which generally center on the person's eagerness to resume his life of help to others.

One thing is certain: A medicine man never needs malpractice insurance. Back in the old days, the family of somebody whom a medicine man tried but failed to heal reserved the right to stone the medicine man to death. "I tell that to my doctor friends, and they don't seem to favor it."

A medicine man also takes his own medicine. "I never give to others anything I don't take first," Rolling Thunder said. "This, also, is unpopular with my doctor friends."

His medicine, he said, generally comes from herbs, but if no herbs are to be found, it's possible to "make medicine out of water. It's something we learned from Eskimos . . . who can take a glass of water and make it boil. It makes a powerful medicine," especially if a blade of grass is added.

Rolling Thunder retired last year after 36 years as a brakeman for the Southern Pacific railroad, where he worked under the name of John Pope. "All Indians are forced to adopt white names. There are no exceptions. Since the early days, we had to adopt white names to be enrolled in school, to hold a job. The general public doesn't know that. The government forced it. It's not our choice — to be called by a foreign name."

The government, he said, has "tried to make all Indians over in [the white man's] image — in language, religion, education. In Indian schools, they forbid Indian kids from talking their native language. It's a brainwashing process."

His two sons, Buffalo Horse and Spotted Eagle, use their Indian names, he said, but "they have other names they use in business." The sons live with him and his wife, Spotted Fawn, in a 262-acre Nevada village called Meta Tantay, an Indian expression meaning "to go in peace." Part of the income from his lectures goes to support the village.

As a young man, Rolling Thunder said, he was called to be a medicine man. And now, he said, one of the sons has the "calling," too.

Dressed in black boots, jeans, striped shirt and multicolored vest, the medicine man said that he had never read Boyd's book about him. "I have no time to read. I think it's probably all right. My family read it and said so. I'm working on my own book, a book that is from the inside out, which is different from the outside in. I think a lot is not included in that [Boyd] book. I want to bring it from behind the Buckskin Curtain. A lot think they know what goes on in the Indian world, and they do not."

There is much, he acknowledged, that he does not understand about "civilized" society. "Although I try, I don't think that I ever will understand. I don't understand unemployment, an economic system that is falling apart, wars. I don't understand."

Rolling Thunder can see on the horizon "one more big war," which will be the end of everything. But it can be avoided, he said, "if enough people put their minds together as one, think about good things and pray. In prayer, we must leave out words like 'I want.' That's no way to pray. . . ."

As he travels around the country, Rolling Thunder said, it is apparent to him that all people want the same things — "security to the extent that they know they can eat, that they can raise their families without fear that a dictator will take their children away. They want the right to worship the Great Spirit in a way they understand. They want the same things that the Constitution provides for, but never fulfills."

GUILT AND SHAME
May 8, 1984

What happened when Mighty Casey struck out? We know that there was no joy in Mudville, but how did Casey feel? Very possibly he was ashamed.

The year was 1980 — a championship season for the Phillies, but a time of misery for Greg Luzinski, whose bat went dead.

"I watched his face during the slump that ended his career in Philadelphia," said psychiatrist Donald L. Nathanson. "His face was a mask" that revealed no emotion whatsoever — not even when fans booed him with an intensity suggesting hatred.

"I asked a pitcher I know if I could get to Luzinski and help treat him. The pitcher said, 'Well, I'll try to talk to him, but when you've been as big a star as Luzinski, you don't talk to anybody.'

"At the time I didn't know what the pitcher meant, but now I do. What he meant was that Luzinski was so shamed by failure that he had become what [psychiatrists] call depersonalized, a condition that mimics depression. He had withdrawn within himself to escape the crushing shame."

Not long after Luzinski had been sold to the Chicago White Sox, Nathanson shared the story with another psychiatrist, who responded:

"There are only two times when suicide is not evidence of psychopathology. One is when you're suffering from the pain of terminal malignancy. The other is when you're a disgraced National Leaguer."

Not long ago, Nathanson treated a woman who was prone to burst into fits of rage, who wore what she called a "mantle of hate" and directed it at the essential people in her life — her children and husband and, as therapy progressed, at Nathanson. "I tried different kinds of therapy, but the problem was that I didn't know where the fits of rage were coming from."

Struggling for an answer, Nathanson asked the woman to keep a journal in which she would record each episode of rage and something about the moments that immediately preceded it. "As near as I could tell, each seemed to involve some sort of guilt. So I asked her, as the next assignment, for journal entries describing each experience of guilt.

"And this is where I began to wake up. She brought in a list, but as she and I examined it, each incident that we previously had considered to be about guilt turned out to be an example of some sort of embarrassment. . . . Suddenly I was seized with a terrible feeling of inadequacy [because] I knew nothing about shame."

The immediate effect of the incident was to send Nathanson scurrying through libraries to bone up on what had been written about shame. What he found was virtually nothing. That's when he began his study of the subject — a study that has led him to conclude that shame must be returned to its "normal, proper place" among the feelings with which psychiatry regularly deals — rather than being denied or considered so trivial as to be unworthy of professional consideration.

In line with all of this, Nathanson has set up a symposium on shame to be held at the American Psychiatric Association's forthcoming annual meeting. Reportedly, it's the first time that a symposium has been devoted entirely to shame — and some of the nation's psychiatric leaders will take part, among them Leon Wurmser, whose book *The Mask of Shame* was reviewed by Nathanson in a recent issue of the American Journal of Psychiatry and which, in Nathanson's opinion, is destined to become a classic work in the field.

In an interview, Nathanson said shame differed from guilt, although the two frequently were confused.

"The content of shame is that 'I am dirty, incompetent, ugly, weak, defective.' Feeling bad about the self is shame. People say, 'I'm so angry at myself.' At first, I didn't understand what they meant. But what they mean . . . is that they are ashamed."

As people become more attuned to shame, they begin to discover shame in every nook and cranny of society — in jokes, in drama, even in commercial nudity, said Nathanson.

"We've become a society of exhibitionists by inverting fear of exposure by exposing ourselves. Look at the pictures of nude women — and men, too — on the newsstands. Look at their faces. What you will see is that while the bodies are nude, the faces are masked as if only one area of privacy remains. This is the mask of shame" — the mask that protected Luzinski during the last months of that awful baseball season.

At the core of shame, said Nathanson, is a feeling of "unlovability." Because the roots run so far down into the soul — about the worst thing that can be said about anybody is that he's unlovable — people spend a lot of time defending against shame and denying shame.

The way to handle shame, he said, is to "find one person you trust . . . and tell that person what embarrassed you. If shame is fear of unlovability, then just being loved, feeling trust can reduce shame. This is why [Alcoholics Anonymous] helps people handle shame — through the fellowship, the feelings of acceptance. There is no way to deal with shame by yourself."

MAKING OUR LIVES MATTER
May 4, 1986

If a tree falls in the forest and there is no ear to hear it, does it make a sound? If a person lives and dies and no one notices, if the world continues as it was, was that person ever really alive? I am convinced that it is not the fear of death . . . that haunts our sleep as much as the fear that our lives will not have mattered, that as far as the world is concerned, we might as well never have lived. What we miss in our lives, no matter how much we have, is that sense of meaning." — From *When All You've Ever Wanted Isn't Enough* by Harold S. Kushner.

Harold Kushner is rabbi of Temple Israel in Natick, Mass., near Boston, and the author of *When Bad Things Happen to Good People*, that blockbuster book of five years ago. He has no formal training in psychology, and he does not pretend to be a therapist. Yet Kushner, through his writing, his preaching and his personal contacts, probably has helped as many struggling human beings as anybody you're likely to meet.

His new book, from which the above quote is taken and which carries the subtitle *The Search for a Life That Matters*, is an important piece of work, and I can't imagine that there is among us anyone who is unable to identify with much of what he writes about.

What is the answer to our eternal question about the meaning of life?

Kushner: "When we stop searching for the Great Answer, the Immortal Deed which will give our lives ongoing meaning, and instead concentrate on filling our individual days with moments that gratify us, then we will find the only possible answer to the question — What is life about?

"It is not about writing great books, amassing great wealth, achieving great power. It is about loving and being loved. It is about enjoying your food and sitting in the sun rather than rushing through lunch and hurrying back to the office. It is about savoring the beauty of the moments that don't last, the sunsets, the leaves turning color, the rare moments of true human communication. It is about savoring them rather than missing out on them because we are so busy and they will not hold still until we get around to them. . . .

"There is no Answer, but there are answers: love and the joy of working, and the simple pleasures of food and fresh clothes, the little things that tend to get lost and trampled in the search for the Grand Solution to the Problem of Life and emerge, like the proverbial bluebird of happiness, only when we have stopped searching."

■

Clearly, said Kushner in an interview, there comes a time when we must throttle back and take time to sniff the roses. But when?

"It was Carl Jung who said that the agenda of life's morning is the agenda of achievement and that the agenda of life's afternoon has to be different," Kushner said. "This is true for men and career-minded women. . . . You spend the first part of life finding out how good you are, how far you can go. But then . . .

"I was speaking to a group in Orange County, Calif., about how power corrupts, isolates, distorts relationships, encourages us to see people as things to be used. The first question from the audience was: 'How can I teach my college-age kids to be less competitive?' My answer was, 'You can't — and you shouldn't.'

"Nothing would happen in the world if young people didn't try hard to succeed. . . . But you've got to get to the point when you say, 'I got it.' Either the dream's true or it's not true. If it's not true, you've got to change dreams. . . .

"If Act 1 of life is goal-oriented — 'How far can I go?' — then Act 2 is 'How can I put it all together and achieve something permanent?' The answer to that has got to involve your connecting with people."

Kushner, who is 50, said that it's not possible and not wise to try to teach this lesson to young people because it's a lesson that can be learned only by traveling the hard road of experience.

"A reporter asked me what I know now that I wish I'd known at 25. I said 'Nothing.' You've got go through it and learn from your mistakes. . . . It's spooky to see a man at 30 with the wisdom of a man at 50. It's like something out of the Twilight Zone, a man with a brain transplant. . . . To young people I would say, 'Don't change. But realize it's a phase you're going through.'

"Take a man of 30 who shelves his family while he succeeds in business. . . . I wouldn't tell him to stop. But I would tell him to realize that there is a time to stop — and a price to be paid while he's ignoring his family. . . . I wish that I had been less self-righteous when I was 30 and ignoring my family. . . . I wish I had thought of it as a need that I had then, rather than telling people to get off my back."

But not all people mellow in midlife and enjoy the little things that make it all worthwhile. What separates those who do from those who don't?

"The people who change are listening to themselves. . . . I wonder sometimes if people are asking the questions to which this book is the answer. . . .

"The earlier book was about bad things and good people. . . . When somebody dies, it's hard not to notice. You've got to confront the question of what it all means. But this book presents a question that's easy to deny, to suppress. You feel blah when you wake up. It's easy to say 'I had too much to eat. . . . Not enough exercise. . . . It's my biorhythm.' You don't admit that life is blah for you. . . .

"The worst pain is the pain we don't know we're suffering. We believe that life is supposed to be smog, traffic jams and high prices. . . . My father was in Lithuania in World War I, and he talked about how people went out in the morning and asked who died last night. . . . People have an ache at the center of their being and no way of knowing it's not supposed to feel like that."

Some people, said Kushner, are pushed into recognition of the pain by trauma — illness, divorce or problems with their children. But others "don't need trauma. They come to midlife and look at time differently, know that life is finite, that they're not going to live forever. . . .

"My father's death at 84 was not trauma. Four years before, he stopped being the man he had been. But his death was a statement of mortality — his and mine. I look in the mirror today and realize how much I resemble my father at 50. It's not trauma, but it puts me in touch with time, teaches me to look at time differently. If you do that, a lot of questions appear on the agenda."

I asked Kushner what he would say to young, bright-eyed career people who are on the way up.

"I would ask them to think of the happiest people they know. They're probably not the people who buy the happiness books and take happiness courses. They're probably not the most famous, the most affluent. The happiest people probably work at being good, honest, reliable neighbors and friends. If the goal of life is to be happy, we can learn a lesson from these people. . . .

"Young business people need to have their eyes on the top rung. But they should know that they will have to pay a price for this . . . and that if all they learn how to do well is to be a good manager or whatever, life will be distorted for them. . . .

"At some point, as Carl Jung said, we have to go back and fill in the spaces we left blank earlier in life."

LESSONS FROM A 'VERY STRANGE MAN'
August 12, 1986

Philadelphia psychiatrist O. Spurgeon English, who is 85, is one of a handful of Americans to have been psychoanalyzed by the famed and controversial Wilhelm Reich during Reich's "best days in Vienna and Berlin" — from 1929 to 1933.

Reich, who had been a pupil of Sigmund Freud's and who at one time was a member of the legendary Viennese Psychoanalytic Group, was the subject of the 1983 biography *Fury on Earth*, which told how he became a communist, lost Freud's favor, encountered disapproval in Scandinavia and eventually moved to the United States, where he died in prison after his conviction in 1956 on what amounted to quackery charges.

In an interview, English said that he felt that he needed to undergo psychoanalysis to advance his medical training and self-understanding, and that he selected Reich as his analyst because "I'd heard so much about him."

In the beginning, analysis was frustrating and disappointing, he said, because Reich, like other analysts, offered absolutely no direction.

"I'd come in daily and lie on the couch and free-associate. . . . I was taking a lot on faith. . . . I wish I had been more active, instead of passively waiting for 'truth.' In my case, it took a hell of a long time for 'truth' to arrive. I kept talking, but everything I said could have been put in a quart bottle. For a long time, there was not much to it."

During analysis, Reich, who was five years older than English, often asked English, "What do you think of me?" It was, English thought, "a strange question. I was flippant and I told him, 'Look, I didn't come here to think of you; I came to think of myself.' He didn't respond to that, but he kept asking what I thought of him. . . . I thought he was pestering me.

"Finally, I said, 'Well, . . . you smoke too much; you talk on the telephone too much on my time; and your skin is too greasy.' He had eczema on his face. But this was all I could muster. He never revealed anything about himself, and I couldn't say anything positive. . . . He sat and smoked and waited for me to talk about myself. . . .

"I was a farm boy from New England, and I later wondered why I didn't say, 'I've had it' and leave. But I wanted the latest and best, and I kept at it."

English recounted a memorable event:

Reich had called and asked if English would change the time of his appointment because it conflicted with something that Reich wanted to do. English said that he didn't want to change because he had a social engagement.

Reich's response: "Do you feel that your social engagement is more important than your session with me?"

English was furious, and when he got to Reich's office, he hollered that Reich was audacious and presumptuous to question the relative importance of the social engagement and analysis. "I went on and on, and he listened patiently. When I finally was finished, he merely said, 'You are perfectly right.'

"That took the wind out of my sails completely. . . . I had the first and perhaps greatest lesson in my life of the fact that a human being may be self-assertive and be given a right to an opinion and not be criticized for it or have acknowledgment given grudgingly."

Another event that stuck forever in English's mind:

"I rarely ever saw Reich outside the analytic hour . . . but one evening I saw him in a restaurant. I didn't say anything to him, and I was surprised at our next session when he asked me why I hadn't come over to him in the restaurant. I said that I had assumed that he wouldn't have wanted this.

"He asked, 'How did you come to that conclusion?' I said, 'You have always been so cold and unfriendly, and I didn't think you gave a damn.' His comment was, 'Well, even though I may have appeared cold and unfriendly in the office, had you felt friendly enough to me to come and speak to me in the social situation, I would have welcomed it.'

"This made me feel that he was a very strange man, because I was obtaining for the first time the idea of the freedom of a person to be what he wishes to be, while he allows the other person to be himself, also."

What did English gain from analysis?

"Finally, I began to realize some things about my parents. . . . Reich taught me that my family was not perfect, that it was not reprehensible to be angry, that sex was not the terrible thing that I'd been taught that it was, that there was something close to pure love that was quite apart from sex. . . . I came to enjoy people more. I was less afraid. I learned that when people paid me a compliment, nine times out of 10 it was genuine. I learned that I was not a liar if I give them a compliment in return. . . . I warmed up. I became much more open, less aloof. Yes, I learned a lot from that silent man."

Something that English didn't learn then still troubles him today, so many years after the fact.

Word went around that Reich, who was living in Maine in the 1940s, had become severely neurotic — even mad — while advancing his notion of an "orgone" energy box that could cure illness, which ultimately was the core of what led to his imprisonment. English wrote Reich and asked if he could visit. Reich's response: "It's fine if you want to come to see me. But if you want to come because you think I need help, you can forget it."

English: "He was cool, and I couldn't deal with it. It took me a long time to become a big-enough person to overlook slights. I wish I had gone to visit him. I'll always regret that I didn't go. This is something that I would do differently today."

A THERAPIST'S NEEDS
December 10, 1985

If you enter therapy, said psychiatrist Carl A. Whitaker, the odds are staggeringly high that you will get what the therapist needs — rather than what you need.

"Where therapy goes is a function of the therapist, not the patient. What the therapist needs to do is what the patient gets. . . . I got into psychiatry to do something about my own craziness. I can't speak for anybody else, but I think this is why many others go into psychiatry, too."

Whitaker, 73, is one of the legends of American psychiatry. He has written or contributed to 70 books, and his *The Roots of Psychotherapy*, published in 1953, has been called "a landmark book . . . and a cornerstone in the development of many psychiatrists."

Whitaker, professor of psychiatry at the University of Wisconsin Medical School, was in Philadelphia to receive from Horsham Clinic the fifth annual O. Spurgeon English award, which honors the former head of psychiatry at Temple University.

What kind of craziness drove Carl Whitaker into psychiatry?

"I still feel like a farmer who just arrived in the big city, and the city slickers are going to get me," he explains. ". . . Insecurity keeps me going. . . . I grew up isolated on a farm [in Raymondville, N.Y.]. One kid came to play with me in 13 years. . . . We lived one mile from school, and half a mile from the next house. Then we moved to Syracuse. I had hayseeds in my hair . . . and I retreated. I was a simple schizophrenic."

He laughed when he said that, but the truth is that Whitaker thinks that everybody is a bit daft and that life's challenge consists of trying to succeed in spite of it. If therapy can't cure us, at least it can help us work around our craziness.

The therapy that Whitaker has dispensed has changed as he has changed, he said, although he didn't figure this out for many years.

At the Kent School of Social Work in Louisville, Ky., during World War II, he worked with small children, and he was amazed how they responded when he held them on his lap, cuddled them, fed them from a bottle "just like mommy."

He moved to the Oak Ridge Hospital in Tennessee, and he cuddled babies there, too. One day a strange thing happened: A manic patient saw Whitaker, the baby and the bottle, and, in Whitaker's words, "the guy went ape. He grabbed the bottle and drained eight ounces of warm milk in about a minute and a half. Then he started beating on his chest and hollering, and he was out of the manic phase."

Whitaker thought he had discovered a revolutionary treatment for mania. "For the next three years anybody who showed up got a baby bottle."

Did it work?

Incredibly, it seemed to work in many cases, but then in a few years, "like all techniques, it disappeared," said Whitaker. Instead of feeding, he turned to fighting. "I had physical fights with almost everybody."

What was going on?

"The baby-bottle technique worked because I think I wanted to be a woman. It worked as long as I needed to bring nurturing and caring to them. . . . But as I got to the place where I could be nourished without this, it lost importance to me — and didn't seem to work anymore. . . . Then I developed fighting with them because I was at a point where I was trying to develop my maleness. I viewed them as little boys, and I wanted to be their father."

When maleness no longer was a burning issue, Whitaker turned to something else, then to something else — and it's possible to trace his development as a person by the kind of therapy that he employed along the way.

Today — as he has for the last 20 years or so — he treats only families, never individual family members, out of his belief that "all problems are family problems. The person is a fragment of the family." When the family can be helped to function reasonably well, he says, the problems of individual family members seem to disappear.

When Whitaker speaks of "family," he means extended family — and this includes parents, grandparents, even former spouses and stepchildren. "It's as if one experience of family reunion sets off a curative process. . . . Logistically it can be difficult — and expensive — to get all of these people together, but . . . their previous failures in therapy motivate them to try this."

What goes on in family therapy, which typically runs intensely for three or four days?

"We goose the hell out of them in ways they don't expect. We invade the unconscious, push them into places they don't expect."

To a husband, Whitaker might say: "Did you ever understand your wife's battle fatigue from raising those two bitches she has as daughters? Or did you try to be her little boy?"

At that point, the wife might jump in: "He never was a responsible father. He never did a damn thing."

The father: "Hell, I was lonely. All she ever did was play with the kids. I could have dropped dead, and she wouldn't have noticed. She only saw me as a paycheck."

Said Whitaker: "I used to worry if it was too tough, but families can take any-thing I can dish out."

Some other comments by Whitaker:

"Schizophrenia is a disease of abnormal integrity. We all have our internal world, but we make believe that it's the same world as everybody else's. We compromise, agree, lie. But the schizophrenic won't do it. He won't violate his sense of how things are."

"If you're in psychotherapy and you're not hurting or bleeding, it's like trying to take out a sick appendix without cutting a hole in the belly. It won't work."

PORNOGRAPHY AND EROTICA
March 23, 1986

Pornography (*por-NOG-ra-fe*) n. The presentation of sexually explicit behavior, as in a photograph, intended to arouse sexual excitement.

erotica (*i-ROT-i-ka*) n. Literature or art intended to arouse sexual desire.

■

There I was — in the lobby of the Latham Hotel in Center City Philadelphia — waiting to have a luncheon interview with two members of the Kensington (Calif.) Ladies' Erotica Society, which, if you haven't heard, has produced what has been called "the irresistible best-seller," a collection of 52 short stories under the title *Ladies' Own Erotica*.

More than 100,000 copies of the paperback have been sold, and the 10 members of the society — middle-aged career women who live in or around Kensington, Calif., near San Francisco Bay — have split up into teams for their promotional tour, which has been marked by their wearing masks during public appearances.

Masks? Yes, of course. In today's society, "respectable" 50-year-old women don't talk about stuff like this, much less write about it. For heaven's sake, some of their stories have titles like "Tantric Sex," "My Gardener," "Moon Bosoms" and "In Praise of Panty Hose."

The women I'm about to meet are Sabina Sedgewick, who founded the organization as something of a lark in 1977, and Rose Solomon, who was instrumental in persuading the women to try to get a publisher interested in the erotic short stories that they had written for their own amusement.

Surely, I thought, Sedgewick and Solomon would appear masked — and I even had brought along my own mask because, after all, it's important for a writer to blend in with the crowd. So there she was, entering the lobby, a woman who was carrying what seemed to be a heart-shaped mask on a stick. She looked too young to be either of them, but maybe, through erotica, she had dipped into the fountain of youth.

"Hi, I'm Darrell Sifford. Are you having lunch with me?"

"You're who?"

"Which one are you — Sedgewick or Solomon?"

"I'm Muriel. Are you really Darrell Sifford? I've read your column for years, and I've always wanted to meet you."

"Ah, but your mask. You're carrying a mask."

"I'm sorry I'm not the woman you're waiting for."

I apologized and then, by a stroke of good fortune, they entered the lobby. Surely they were Sedgewick and Solomon, because they were middle-aged women with a shopping bag full of masks.

I said to Muriel, "See, I wasn't putting you on. Look at their shopping bag." I introduced myself to the real masters of erotica, and Muriel tried on a mask before she departed. Then the three of us, without masks, settled in for lunch, and the interview began.

■

I want you to cry out to me, to expose your secret life to me. I want your lips on my breast, your breath in my ears, all over me. I want soft consonants to rain over my thighs, full-blooded vowels to penetrate my inmost being. I want to taste your lips like exotic fruit. I want to see your words glisten like drops of crystal . . .

Yes, indeed, lovers of erotica, that's a passage straight out of one of the stories written by Sabina Sedgewick, who in real life is a librarian and whose real name is . . . Well, I don't know. All 10 of these folks write under assumed names — for the same reasons that they wear masks.

Sedgewick, 49, pulled "Sabina" out of the air, she said, but "Sedgewick" was stolen from Catharine Sedgwick — never mind the difference in spelling — a 19th-century writer in whose works "men always were sinners and women always were saints."

Solomon, 44, a cartoonist, arrived at her pen name in a different way. "Long ago, in a tender moment, when I and my husband-to-be were still very new to each other, I whispered to him that his ears smelled like roast almonds. Like a man accused, he spun around and cried out, 'Rose Solomon?' Equally alarmed, I demanded, 'Who's she?' Ever since, Rose Solomon has represented that terrible 'other woman,' and it seems only right that she should speak for this other me."

■

I asked Sedgewick and Solomon to distinguish between erotica and pornography, and I mentioned that Gloria Leonard, the former star of X-rated movies, once had told me that the difference was "in the lighting. If you can see what's going on, it's pornography. If you can't quite make it out, it's erotica."

They didn't like that distinction, and suddenly the interview turned serious. Erotica, they said, was fun, harmless, stimulating, the stuff that full-bodied, all-American fantasies were made of. But pornography was . . .

Solomon: "In pornography, people don't care about each other. I think it's dehumanizing . . . and the next step to violence is small. It's dangerous and threatening, because it invites violence."

Sedgewick: "I don't want to sound like a preacher, but sex and violence are linked together like wine and cheese. You can't have one without the other. . . . We don't want to parade around like anti-porn people. . . . Instead of saying what we don't like, we want to say what we do like," which is clean, wholesome erotica in which nobody gets strangled.

Solomon said that her 14-year-old son, after reading the book, said "Mom, you make sex believable." Her 16-year-old daughter "thinks it's gross for her mom to have a sex life, but it's OK for her mom to write about sex. She's my best critic."

Sedgewick, who has a son, 21, and a daughter, 23, said that "in cooking, my kids know my taste. They should know my taste in erotica, too. I'm not ashamed of that. It's a part of communicating between parent and child."

What is erotic by Sedgewick's own definition?

"The attention and focus I get from my partner, the attention and focus I lavish on my partner. It's not just physical, but mental, too. It's knowing what each other likes. . . . Atmosphere is important. The home may be disturbing because of responsibilities. We go away on a lot of camping trips, my husband and I. Nature turns us on. We've had erotic encounters on mountaintops."

Is it possible to separate eroticism from genital sex? Can eroticism exist without sex?

Solomon: "My husband and I were in a restaurant, and a woman at the next table splashed hot consomme on her breast. She was washing it off, and I was practically inside her bra. So was my husband. At the moment our eyes met and we knew that we were enjoying the same thing, we were thrilled. The moment of connecting was almost orgasmic."

How have men reacted to their book?

Sedgewick: "A lot of men think we're frustrated and acting out. . . . Men aren't exactly shocked, but they think we're inappropriate and should have outgrown" our fantasies. In reality, she said, it's healthy to have fantasies, and much sex therapy focuses on giving people permission to have their fantasies.

How is sex different in middle age than at, say, 22?

Solomon: "I thought I was the oldest virgin in the world. . . . I didn't come from a religious home. I had no conscience to stop me. . . . But I just didn't know much about it. I thought the man was the expert. I thought he knew the answers and helped the woman 'succeed' at sex. I thought sex was something that 'happened' to a woman. . . .

"It wasn't until later, much later, that I asked the question: 'What do women want?' I think that's what erotica, the book, the fantasies are all about. . . . Now, at 44, my question is 'How do we grow older sexually without having to live up to youthful standards of performance?' First it was the church that manipulated our sexuality; now it's the media, which pictures all those beautiful, youthful bodies."

Solomon, you might like to know, wrote for the book a short story titled "Queen of the Road," which is about a chocolate-munching fat woman who has a romantic interlude with a truck driver who stops to fix her flat tire.

Erotica is for everybody, said Solomon, not just for the beautiful and the young.

CHAPTER 5

LIFE 101:
THE POLITICS
OF LIVING

Life has a way of presenting us with dilemmas — questions and choices for which there are no clear "right" answers. We are surrounded by illusions of success, illusions about love, illusions about power and authority, illusions about other people, illusions of quick fixes and easy answers to the challenges of life.

Darrell often posed questions of readers encouraging us to think for ourselves, to seek answers from within rather than being overly influenced by the opinions of others, the "shoulds" or the illusions.

The columns in this section provide insights and tools to help us sort through some of the complexities we face. The messages here also ground us in the reality that ultimately each of us is the star of his or her own play and that to achieve our dreams requires the personal commitment, effort and courage to act.

— M.S.

WHAT COLLEGES FAIL TO TEACH
November 17, 1991

The late-night telephone call was from the son of a friend of mine, a third-year student at a big-time university that is known not only for its basketball teams but also — can you believe this? — for its academic programs.

My friend's son is extraordinarily bright and involved in enough extracurricular activities to keep him busy 25 hours a day. His latest project — and the reason he was calling me — was to launch a campus newspaper that would be in competition with the school newspaper, which, in his judgment, has grown fat and lazy. Another voice was needed on campus, he said, and his paper would provide that.

I asked him what kinds of stories he thought that students needed access to — and weren't getting at present.

Well, he said, there hadn't been competitive bidding for pizza franchises awarded by the university, and . . .

I told him that I didn't think students would stand in line to read a story about pizza franchises.

He didn't seem put off by my lack of enthusiasm. He had arranged, he said, to have students who were doing work overseas write some stories about their experiences, and . . .

197

I told him that he was getting warm. Stories about what it's like on the outside, far from the ivy-covered walls, were important. That was the direction in which he needed to take his newspaper, I said, and then I paused and rolled an idea around in my head.

"What I would do, if I were the editor," I said, "would be to contact graduates from three to 10 years ago — maybe even longer — and ask them to write stories about what they never learned in college."

I stopped and waited for his response.

"That's not a bad idea," he said finally.

"It has always been my belief," I said, "that the primary purpose of a college education should be to position people to begin the real process of learning about life. Meaningful education should begin after college, but unfortunately for many people it ends after college."

I could feel myself getting wound up, ready to mount my soapbox. "I'll bet you that people who've been out of college for 10 years could tell students a lot more about living than the best professors on campus." I was breathing hard.

"I think you may be right," he said. Yes, this would be something that he and the other editors would consider. He thanked me for my input. I invited him to call me again anytime that he needed a sounding board.

"Good luck," I said. "You'll need it because starting a new paper is hard work, and keeping it going is even harder work."

We said our goodbyes and hung up. I sat for a long time and thought about the conversation. What would graduates most often identify as the important things they learned after college?

■

I have long believed — and sometimes written — that most colleges do students a terrible disservice by pretending to prepare them for life, when in fact all they're doing is packing them with information that, for the most part, has little or no relevance to the world they will face.

There is, as far as I know, no course that would be equivalent to Life 101. There is, as far as I know, no course that separates idealism from reality without distorting and discounting either. There is, as far as I know, no course that prepares students to deal with adversity that is more likely to fall out of an envelope than to jump from behind a bush.

What do people not learn at college? If I were going to write for the newspaper of my friend's son, what would I say?

Here are some things that come to mind:

Dealing successfully with others is what separates people who grow from people who stagnate. To deal successfully with others, a person has to listen at least as much as he talks. I am aware of many college courses on speaking. I am not aware of many courses on listening.

Most businesses are profit-making — at least that's the expectation — and there is nothing necessarily wrong with making money. I meet an awful lot of young people who in their idealism somehow have linked money with evil and made them one in the same. There's nothing wrong with making money — provided there is time and energy left for other important things, including projects that in some way may make the world a better place.

Whether you are right or wrong often does not matter. Often what does matter is the ability and willingness to compromise, to make tradeoffs. It's better to get part of what you want — rather than none at all, which is what rigid, righteous people often end up with.

The world is not always fair, and might sometimes makes right. This is a hard lesson to learn, and one reason is that a lot of college professors don't understand it — so they can't teach it.

What you learn from books is not necessarily related to what you will learn from life, which can be a splendid teacher if you are open to it.

Integrity is anybody's most important quality — so be careful about cutting corners, even when life seems to demand it.

It's important to say "yes" to many of the things that people ask you to do, but it's also important to say "no." Most people want the approval of others and think that approval is tied to their always doing what others want. This is not necessarily true. Reasonable people respect a person's right to decline.

Don't be too serious too much of the time. Life can be fun, if you're open to the possibility of fun. Ask yourself "What is fun for me?" and "Why don't I do more of it?"

Define success for yourself . . . and give yourself permission to change the definition as life changes you.

■

That's what I would say if I wrote a story about what I didn't learn in college. What about you?

THE ABILENE PARADOX
December 2, 1990

Since the dawn of time, everybody from corporate presidents to heads of households has struggled with a common problem: managing conflict. If you could bring together people with divergent views and passions, you could smooth out the bumps in the road and bring peace. There would be no limit to what could be accomplished.

But what about managing not conflict but agreement? Have you ever thought about that?

Get ready to meet Jerry B. Harvey.

■

It was the mid-1970s, and Harvey, professor of management science at George Washington University, had been invited to speak at a conference of organizational consultants. The topic assigned to him was neurotic organizations, and, said Harvey, "I didn't know what to talk about. I asked myself, 'What is the craziest organization I belong to?' — and my immediate answer was, 'My family.' "

This is the story that Harvey tells:

"My wife's family is in Coleman, Texas, which is 53 miles from Abilene, and it's like the town in the movie *The Last Picture Show*. If you saw that movie, you've been to Coleman. . . . We were visiting her parents. . . . Her dad ran a pool hall and domino parlor right outside town. The Baptists would get upset if he tried to run it in town. . . .

"It was the middle of the summer — 106 degrees, with a dust storm howling — and we were sitting there playing dominoes. Suddenly my father-in-law stood up and blurted out, 'Let's all go to Abilene and eat at the cafeteria.' I thought, 'Man, is that dumb,' but I didn't say anything. My wife said, 'It sounds great, but I don't want to go unless you go, Jerry.' I said, 'I was hoping that somebody would invite me, but I won't go unless your mother goes.' Momma said, 'Of course, I want to go.'

"So we all get into this '58 Buick and drive 53 miles to Abilene, where we have the worst meal you can imagine. Then we drive 53 miles back, and nobody says anything. It takes an hour for us to scrape off the dust. . . .

"I didn't know what to say. Finally, with all the dishonesty I could muster, I said, 'Well, it was a great trip.' My father-in-law responded with an expletive. I said, 'What do you mean by that?' He said, 'Hell, I didn't want to go to Abilene. I was just making conversation, and you all made me ruin my day.' I said, 'I never wanted to go.' My wife said, 'Who would want to drive 106 miles in a dust storm? Not me.' Momma just cried. She didn't want to go either. . . .

"Nobody wanted to go, but we all thought the others wanted to. To avert a fight, nobody was willing to say, 'No, I don't want to go.' And the Abilene Paradox was born."

■

Harvey, who lives in McLean, Va., is a consultant to government and industry and author of the 1988 book *The Abilene Paradox and Other Meditations on Management*, which carries the subtitle *Compassionate Insights Into the Craziness of Organizational Life*.

He is one of the most engaging people I've ever met, and he charmed everybody when he spoke not long ago in Philadelphia at the national conference of the Organization Development Network. No, he didn't talk about the Abilene Paradox — his subject was spirituality in the workplace — but I sought him out and asked if he'd take me on a ride to Abilene.

■

Harvey, trained as a psychologist, said the Abilene Paradox permeated corporate America. Translation: Nobody is very skillful at managing agreement.

"Organizations frequently take action that is contrary to the desires of any of the members . . . and undertake programs that are destined to fail," he said. "It is the inability to cope with agreement that starts organizational insanity. . . . and people end up agreeing to do the opposite of what they want to do."

To avoid getting caught up in the Abilene Paradox, "you have to be willing to run the risk of being rejected. You do this by clearly stating what you want to do at the front end of the trip. The closer you get to Abilene, the harder it is to turn the Buick around. . . . You have to be willing to run the risk of angering others. . . . You have to say, 'This is what I want to do. What do you want to do?' "

■

Harvey truly is a man of a million stories. Here is one he presents — with a straight face — as factual.

"These business executives were working on a research project to make jet fuel out of peanut oil," he said. "They all knew that it wouldn't work and that it would bankrupt the company if they continued, but they were afraid to tell the others. . . .

"I asked the research director about it, and he said, 'The boss would fire me if I say what I really think. The boss is so committed to this.' I asked the boss about it and he said, 'Hell, this won't work, but the research director has staked his future on it. I'm trying to support him.' I asked the financial director, and he said, 'It'll bust us financially, but the other two guys want it so much. The boss keeps telling me that we can do it.'

"Everybody was afraid to state what he wanted. . . . They all took the trip to Abilene. . . . It was like Watergate. Nobody wanted to do it, but everybody thought it was what the others wanted."

I asked Harvey why the boss in the peanut-oil-to-jet-fuel caper didn't blow the whistle. After all, that's what bosses are supposed to do.

"Bosses need as much support as subordinates," Harvey said. "Bosses have few places to get support. They don't want to hack off subordinates."

What is the price that people pay for announcing they don't want to go to Abilene?

Harvey told another story.

■

"This sheriff is standing at the jail door to confront the mob outside," Harvey said. "Somebody in the mob yells, 'That guy you got in the jail killed Maudeen, and we're going to hang him — without waiting for a trial!' The mob surges forward, and the sheriff pulls out his gun and says, 'Hold it! If you come one step closer, I'll blow off some heads!'

"In the movies, when this happens, the crowd always disappears, and people laud the sheriff for his courage. But the sheriff is an agreement manager — not a conflict manager. He can't hold off a mob that really wants to lynch somebody. They have to be in agreement. They don't want to hang the guy, but they're afraid they'll be called cowards if they don't go along.

"Nine times out of 10, when the sheriff confronts the mob, the mob disappears. But the 10th time, the mob surges forward and shoots down the sheriff. . . .

"This is the existential risk of life. If you won't accept a bullet hole in the navel occasionally, you go to Abilene all the time. You've got to risk being shot or you'll let them hang everybody. . . . You've got to be willing to accept the consequences" — and what holds true for the sheriff also holds true for people in corporate life. . . . and everywhere else, too.

"I've seen couples get married when they didn't want to get married," Harvey said, "but they were afraid their parents, relatives, friends would be upset if they didn't get married. I've seen couples who wanted to stay married get divorced — because each thought the other wanted a divorce. . . . But nobody said anything and they checked into the Abilene Motel."

■

I asked Harvey to describe the kind of person who refuses to go to Abilene.

"It's somebody who feels secure," he said. "Generally these people come from families that didn't threaten them with withdrawing support and love if they didn't go along with the program. . . . The negative fantasy is that if we say what we think, others will be mad at us. In reality, we have more friends if we speak up" — because others know where we stand and, even if they don't agree, they respect us for our courage.

"When you're offered a trip to Abilene, you can't blame others if you go."

THE MOST SPECIAL CHRISTMAS
December 9, 1990

It was a Christmas that I remember more than any other, when I was 14 and a freshman in high school. My dad had been wiped out financially in the Great Depression, right before I was born, but he had fought his way back, overcome what doctors then called "a nervous breakdown," found a job that made up in security what it lacked in income.

We lived here and there — at places where the rent was lowest — and in the Christmas of my 14th year, we were in a three-room apartment above a grocery. It had been a tough year for Dad — some of his modest investments had turned sour — and he was tottering on the brink again, despite Mom's salary from her sales job.

There was no money for Christmas. Dad knew it, and he knew that I knew it.

He and I were sitting across from each other in the living room — we decided not to have a tree that year — and he handed me a small sack.

"It's the best I can do," he said.

I opened the sack and found a pair of socks — argyles with gray diamonds on a navy background. "Thanks," I said, and I meant it.

Dad started to cry. "I wish I could do more. . . . I wish things were different." He was crying harder now. "Life can be tough. . . . I'm sorry."

"You don't have anything to feel sorry about," I said, and gave him a hug. But he walked out of the room, a beaten man, I thought, a man who somehow felt that his inability to give his only child a more substantial Christmas present somehow had diminished him as a father.

I don't think I ever felt love so strongly for anybody as I did for him at that moment. Love and sorrow — and maybe some guilt for whatever role I had played in creating in Dad the mind-set that a pair of socks, even in our dire situation, was inadequate.

I kept those argyles for many years, and I cherished them as I had cherished no gift that Dad ever gave me.

That's why Christmas 1945 will always be so special to me.

What about you? Do you have a special Christmas?

■

With tears in my eyes, I told that story to Jim Shelton — that's Pastor James L. Shelton of Messiah Lutheran Church in Newtown Square — and he smiled tightly and said that none of us had to "look very far to find people who don't

202

even get socks" for Christmas.

What we have in this society, he said, is a classic case of the haves and the have-nots, and those who have it would be a lot happier if they shared some of their stuff with those who need it.

But they tend not to share — even at Christmas. Why not? Basically it's greed, he said, and misguided notions of what Christmas is all about.

There was a meeting he was directing to determine what churches in his area could do to help the growing numbers of homeless people. His idea was that churches would bring in people for the holidays, give them food, a gift, and a cot for the night before sending them back to the streets.

One minister said that he couldn't ask his congregation to do that. The members had just paid for a sparkling new building. "Let's wait at least a year or two" before we allow "those people" to dirty it up, the minister said.

Another clergyman said he was "too old and too tired" to get involved with people who didn't bathe regularly and had lice. "Who wants to be around people like that?" he asked.

Pastor Shelton, who was a social activist before the term was invented, shook his head and said that he thought Christ "would be ashamed of what we've done with His birthday."

■

But, said Pastor Shelton, he's been as guilty in past times as anybody when it came to spending too much money on gifts for people who didn't need them or even appreciate them.

He recalled one Christmas when his son, Jimmy, was 6 and sat under the tree and began opening a mountain of boxes — more presents than anybody could ever put to use. Finally, he asked his father, "Do I have to open all of these before I can eat breakfast?"

Said Pastor Shelton: "When your kid asks that, you know that your values are misplaced. I told him to put away some of the stuff for his birthday and to give the rest away. . . . We never did anything like that again. It was a reality check for all of us."

The pastor said that he is not against giving gifts, but that he's in favor of being reasonable.

"Who are the happiest people you know?" Pastor Shelton asked. Then he answered his own question. "The happiest people are those who reach out to help others." But even that can be tricky — and guilt-provoking.

"There was one year," he said, "when I was pastor of another church, when I told the congregation, 'Instead of giving stuff nobody needs, let's put up a big tree in the building early in December and put paper balls on it. We'll give a gift to poor people, and we'll put on the ball the name of the person to whom we'd normally have given a gift.' Well, they agreed, and they seemed happy until about December 20, when they started developing nervous twitches. They hadn't bought their regular gifts. So they went out and bought gifts anyway. There's pressure to do this. . . .

"There's pressure on poor people to buy for their children what they can't afford. I guess your father felt pressure. . . . There's this expectation that has nothing at all to do with what Christmas really is supposed to be. Maybe we should celebrate Christmas quietly, with love and joy, and then create another holiday — call it Seasonal Greetings — in January or February and give gifts then."

■

Jim Shelton grew up poor, too. He didn't even have an indoor toilet until he was 12. "I always had a perfect attendance record at school," he said. "People thought it was because I loved school. Actually, I wanted to use an indoor toilet. . . .

"I always was taught to share whatever I had. My father said, 'No matter how bad you think you have it, there always are people who are worse off.' He was right, you know. . . . But we get caught up in our rising expectations, and we don't remember what life should be. Our vision is blurred by the sparkle of the lights, and we become so content that we don't help others."

Since the death of his mother in the summer, said Pastor Shelton, he has come to believe more strongly than ever that he can't fill his life "with stuff from under the tree." He can fill his life only by helping others.

"Most of us have everything anyway," he said. "That's why they invent gifts for people who have everything — like soap on a rope and machines that blow away leaves. . . . I don't blame the merchants. They make half of their year's income off Christmas. I do blame our greed. We have become a nation of greedy people — 6 percent of the world's population consuming 50 percent of the world's goods — and we're always wanting more."

■

Pastor Shelton said that he is for "anything that brings the family closer together. . . . You can buy two gifts — one for somebody in the family and one for somebody who really needs it. We can make things to give — cakes, cookies, paintings, flowers, caps . . . or we can give things that are fun."

Fun?

"When I was a kid, I wanted a pair of spurs, like a real cowboy, and one Christmas, my mother bought them for me," he said. "I promptly climbed on the sofa and spurred it to shreds. Mom took them away from me. . . . I told the story to my congregation one Christmas, and guess what? They gave me a pair of spurs. That was wonderful."

He walked across his office, reached up on the wall, took down the spurs from their permanent display place and said, "Now here's a perfect gift."

I told him that I liked navy-and-gray argyles better. He said that he couldn't argue with that.

THE WISDOM OF A STONE
September 25, 1990

The story is written by Samuel, the pen name of a Philadelphia-area man, and it makes the point that . . . Well, read along and find out. Here is the story:

Once, before mankind or any other form of life existed, two stones rested near each other on the primeval land.

One stone looked at the other and said: "You know what would be great, Louie?"

"What?"

"Now, I know it's impossible — and I'm wasting my time thinking about it — but it would be fantastic!"

"Get on with it, Arthur. What?"

"Now, you're not going to believe this, because I know it's impossible. But bear with me, Louie. Let your imagination soar. You know what would be really great? If we could have arms and legs, play handball, listen to Beethoven, experience love, look into the eyes of children, and contribute to our fellow stones."

"You're out of your mind."

"I know. But if it could happen, I would greet each morning sun with such thankfulness and living that the Creator who gave me that life would look down and say, 'Now there's a stone that knows how to use a gift.' "

"Fat chance."

"I know."

This impossible miracle, wrote Samuel, actually has happened to us all, but the vast majority of people don't see its beauty and choose, instead, to wallow in their troubles, think small and feel cheated. How can one be cheated by a miracle? Auntie Mame said it beautifully: "Life's a banquet — and most poor suckers are starving to death."

■

The point really needs little explanation or elaboration. We don't recognize the tools that we have been given, and, as a result, we don't make good-enough use of them.

It brings to mind something that Norman Cousins told me: We don't take the time — or we lack the inclination — to inventory our lives, and this brings on a kind of darkness that makes it impossible for us to realize that in many ways we have been pursued relentlessly by good fortune. If we knew how lucky we are, we'd be more eager to climb to the sky and claim a piece of it.

When I interviewed Bill Case, who wrote the book *Life Begins at Sixty*, he told a story that I've since used many times in speeches to make the point that each of us needs to recognize and develop our assets — rather than make excuses for why we haven't succeeded at this or that. The story:

Winston Churchill forever is being held up as the example of somebody who came about as close to self-actualization as is reasonably possible. He ran a government in wartime; he was a husband and father; he wrote books; he painted pictures; he grew flowers, and he built gardens to enhance those flowers. He was a man of many interests — and many talents.

But whenever Churchill's accomplishments are mentioned, somebody in the audience invariably laments that "If I had Churchill's name, his family connections, his education, his wealth, his political savvy, I could have been just as great. I could have gone down in history, too."

But on Judgment Day, God is not going to ask, "Why weren't you Winston Churchill?" Rather, God is going to ask, "Why didn't you make the most of what I gave you? Why weren't you the best that you could be?"

One of psychiatrist Dick Moscotti's favorite lines is, "To give yourself the best chance of getting what you want, you have to risk losing it." This should be chiseled in everybody's memory because, for the most part, it holds the answer to why, for so many people, dreams seldom come true. We are unwilling to take reasonable-enough risks, and, as a result, nothing much happens in our lives.

It's easier for us to complain about what we don't have and what's going wrong than it is for us to take responsibility for our lives by drafting a plan and risking implementation of it to get what we want.

When we take a risk — any risk — we take a chance. The chance is that we may fail, and the fear of failure is so strong that some of us would rather live lives that are turning brown from dullness.

If we can blame other people for our misery — spouse, parent, boss, teacher, friend, enemy — we can construct the illusion that we're off the hook. "Don't you see? It's not my fault. I'm helpless." But we haven't escaped the hook at all.

We stay in jobs that are boring, even demeaning, because they're safe. We stick in marriages that died years ago because we fear the alternatives.

We refuse heart surgery because something might go wrong — and continue to trudge through lives that are severely limited.

We pass up opportunity because it doesn't come with a money-back guarantee.

We play the game of life not to win but to keep from losing, and the outcome is almost predestined: We lose.

Judith Viorst, who wrote the acclaimed book *Necessary Losses*, was telling me about the philosophical message that she frequently delivered when her three now-grown sons were little:

"We all are going to fall down at times. We can't live life to avoid falling down. That would be an unexciting, unproductive life. The trick is to know how to pick yourself up, dust off and go on your way. What you have to try for is to get up after the fall — not to avoid the fall."

It's hard to say it with any more clarity than that. If we're lucky, we all fall at times — because that's what it means to be alive.

To repeat Auntie Mame: Life's a banquet. Arthur, the stone, knew that. He was way ahead of his time, and, unfortunately, still is.

(The story of the stones is from the book *Rehab Diary* and is reprinted by permission of Libra Publishers Inc. of San Diego.)

THE MYTH OF ROMANTIC LOVE
September 8, 1986

In his book *Marital Myths*, psychologist Arnold A. Lazarus lists 24 "mistaken beliefs" that can lead to all kinds of grief — and sometimes to the end of a marriage.

Of all the myths, said Lazarus in an interview, the one that probably damns more marriages than any other is the myth that romantic love should last forever and ever.

"In search of romantic marriage . . . people often end up in romantic — or not so romantic — divorce. Men and women who expect to find marriage a continuation of the ecstasy of courtship are in for an enormous disappointment. . . . Romance thrives on barriers, frustrations, separation and delays. . . . Remove these . . . and replace them with the intimacy and everyday contact of married life, and the ecstatic passions fade. The thrills and chills of romance are doomed in the face of day-to-day proximity."

Lazarus, who is professor of psychology at Rutgers University, said that in the early months and years of marriage, partners "inevitably discover that their spouses do not have the attributes of their dream heroes and heroines. Most are able to adjust to this reality, but extreme romantics are unable to do so. The male romantic idealist searches fruitlessly for a mate who will provide the tenderness, the security and the solicitude of the ideal mother, as well as the ecstatic sexual joys of a fantasy sweetheart. . . .

"The romantic woman wants her man to be the ideal father, husband, caretaker, companion and lover, all rolled into one. Viewed from a clinical perspective, these perceptions are decidedly abnormal. . . . While we balk at the idea of abandoning our romantic idealism, much emotional pain would be spared if more people knew how to replace romantic love with conjugal affection as the basis for a truly successful marriage. . . . The affection that enables a marriage to endure is something finer, deeper and more rewarding than the romantic love of the story books."

And how does Lazarus define conjugal affection?

It is affection that is built around what he calls "mutual evidence" of kindness, consideration, communication, harmonious adjustment to each other's habits, joint participation in some activities, consensus on important values and issues, reciprocity rather than coercion, clear-cut respect for each other.

Lazarus: "Married couples must adjust to daily routines of dressing, eating, working, sleeping and similar habits that call for synchronous schedules . . . and countless activities that become conditioned to each other. The aim is to build up a common capital of acts, habits and experiences that result in a profound acceptance of each other, without the false hopes and impossible illusions of the romantic ideal."

Lazarus said that the very night before this interview, he had met with a couple, and . . . "there was nothing wrong with their relationship, but each had the feeling that it should be more romantic." It's an old, old story that plays and replays in so many marriages.

"Romantics keep on wanting it always to be as it was in courtship, when there was the deep and passionate yearning to see each other. But remove the obstacles to seeing each other . . . and romance changes. There's no longer the rush that one gets when the other appears. After 10 years — or maybe even after a few years — they don't feel the way they did in courtship, and they feel that love is dead. . . . Again and again, I see it — a perfectly good marriage, but it's not 'romantic,' " and this mindset causes many to end marriages that fundamentally are healthy.

These are the people, the romantics, said Lazarus, who "go for divorce, who marry and remarry. . . . I was on a TV show a while back on remarriage. On the show with me was a guy with his 10th wife . . . and a woman who had been divorced nine times. What had happened to each of them was the romantic illusion, which doomed their marriages to end up in divorce court again and again — until they got older and came to their senses."

The way out of the romantic myth, said Lazarus, is for people to realize that falling in love is "not an instinct or automatic process. . . . People have to be taught to fall in love," through exposure to and acceptance of the other person, but, unfortunately, that's not the kind of teaching most of us get.

Why not?

Because our education about romance tends to come from popular songs, television, books and magazines, all of which "emphasize rapture as the index of a successful marriage. The love bond becomes idealized and the partners worship each other. . . .

"This mythical romantic tradition has a number of allies. Love at first sight is one of the prominent romantic themes. Anyone who understands the meaning of love will realize that this complex emotion requires the passage of time for its development. . . . Infatuation or physical attraction is certainly possible at first sight, but love comes from the discovery of qualities that are lovable, and from a shared togetherness that lends fulfillment and mutual enrichment."

But "real love" is no guarantee of success in marriage, Lazarus said. Even people who bear no false romantic expectations can grow apart "instead of growing together. People do evolve . . . at different rates and maybe in different directions . . . and 10 or 15 years later they don't have enough in common to make a marriage.

People can audit their marriage, he said, by examining how they view their problems. Do they meet them head-on? Or do they rationalize?

"People who say, 'Our troubles are because of the new house and the big mortgage' or 'It's the stresses of the business' are rationalizing. This is one of the danger signs in marriage — blaming external factors for what's going wrong between them. . . . In good marriages, external factors don't create a wedge; they bring people together."

THE TRUTH ABOUT LYING
March 14, 1982

Today's history lesson, rewritten: Little George takes out his hatchet and begins to hack relentlessly on the cherry tree. Hearing the commotion, his mother charges outside in time to see the tree topple. Standing among the branches is her son, hatchet still in hand, and it is there that she confronts him:

"George, did you chop down the cherry tree?"

Without a pause George answers: "Who, me?"

Today's reality, unvarnished:

The young man is fresh out of college with a degree in accounting, and he squares himself to face the interviewer, who represents a small certified public accounting firm in the South.

"Tell me what you'd like to do," the interviewer asks.

"I'd really like to work here. I think this would be a good place for me to start. I want to learn, and I think I could learn a lot in this company."

The interviewer smiles, then proceeds: "And what about going on to get your CPA? How do you feel about that?"

The young man does not hesitate: "Yes, I hope someday to get my CPA, but that's not the most important thing for me right now. There are some other things I'd like to do."

The smile is gone, and in two minutes the interviewer has terminated the conversation — and left the young man nursing his wounds.

Later the young man says to his father: "He wanted me to tell him that accounting and getting my CPA are the most important things in my life. I know what he wanted to hear, but accounting never is going to be the biggest thing in my life. I couldn't lie to him, could I?"

No, the father says, he couldn't lie to him. He had done the right thing.

The young man was Grant, my son, and the story he told me was so similar to what I heard from my older boy, Jay, not long before. Jay had applied for a job as a management trainee for a national company, and the interviewer seemed quite interested until this exchange:

"Tell me, Jay, where do you see yourself in five years?"

"Well, I'll have finished Bible school by then, and I'll be preaching or doing something. . . ."

That was too bad, the interviewer said, because he needed somebody who would commit body and soul to the corporation for at least five years. Sorry, but . . .

Jay seemed to understand. "I had to tell him the truth."

Yes, I said, it's always best to tell the truth.

I told those stories the other day — the stories about Grant and Jay, not about little George — when I interviewed psychiatrist Harold A. Rashkis, who is in private practice in suburban Elkins Park, who is attending psychiatrist at the Institute of Pennsylvania Hospital and who is author of a new book, *Caring for Aging Parents*.

My sons had been penalized, occupationally at least, for their honesty, I told Rashkis. Is there a lesson to be learned from this? Could he imagine a circumstance in which it would be OK to tell a lie?

Rashkis grinned. "OK? It's not only OK; it's what we have to teach young people."

Teach people to lie?

No, said Rashkis, teach them to engage in "the politics of living" — and that's far removed from lying, if you're able to look at it in what Rashkis called the context of the moment.

Little children, he said, grow up afraid to lie to their parents — not because they necessarily think lying is wrong but because they believe that their parents are omnipotent and immediately will be able to nail them in their lies. "One of the things a child has to learn is to be able to stonewall it," to bluff and fake, because "this is part of defining the limits of our parents . . . learning that parents don't know it all. Yes, it's a disappointment, but it's also the beginning of reality."

Rashkis, 62, who is the father of three children, acknowledged that "lying is one of my favorite topics," and over the years he has prepared papers on lying for presentation at psychiatric meetings.

When somebody can't lie in an important job interview, Rashkis said, it's probably because he feels that the interviewer is omnipotent and will see right through him. But interviewers are no more omnipotent than parents, he said, and the beginning of reality in the job market is to put yourself first and go after what you want.

"You need a good ego, and a good ego is to feel that you can sell yourself, that you are credible. Some say it's wrong to lie, but I don't think it's wrong. What is wrong and bad for us and our children is to lie out of weakness."

Does that mean that Rashkis thinks it's all right to lie from strength?

Yes, he said, that's exactly what he thinks.

"We lie from weakness when we lie defensively, when we're backing out of a situation. Example: A child asks his mother: 'Why don't we have a big house like Johnny?' And the mother answers: 'We could have even a bigger house, but your father was cheated in business by his brother.' That's a lie to protect parental power, and it doesn't give the kid any strength."

It's OK, said Rashkis, for parents to lie "to further their ends. A parent tells a child: 'Don't smoke cigarettes because they'll stunt your growth. Well, nobody could get away with that today, but they could back then, and to me this is an acceptable lie. It represents a believable argument . . . and it's aimed at discouragi the child from doing something undesirable — or encouraging him to do something desirable."

So is Rashkis saying that it's OK to blow smoke all over job interviewers?

"If I'd been Grant, I would have looked straight into his lying eyes with my lying eyes and told him: 'Sir, there is nothing I could want more than to get my CPA and eventually become a senior partner in your firm.' "

Actually, it's not lying at all, Rashkis said. "You have a right to your goals. Maybe you want to be a guitar player, but you need this job. You want this job. And you're willing to do all you can to get this job. That is the truth . . . and that's what is important. To thine own self be true. In a minor context it's a lie, but in the major context it's the truth."

Besides that, Rashkis said, nobody is being damaged. "The interviewer is thinking: 'Gee, here's a guy who really wants a job. He's going to work his tail off to be successful.' The interviewer has no concern about Grant's ultimate destiny on earth. He just wants to hire somebody who's going to work."

In reality, he said, this is not too far removed from the emissaries and the potentate.

Oh, how's that?

"The emissaries bring gifts to the potentate, but only so the potentate won't destroy them. The potentate and the emissaries all know that, but the emissaries say that they're bringing the gifts out of love. The potentate wants the gifts, and he likes to think that the emissaries love him. It pleases him to equate gifts with love, and he won't destroy the emissaries as long as they keep bringing gifts."

This, too, Rashkis said, is a classic example of "the politics of living . . . which is very complex and very interesting."

Truth, he said, has to be defined in the context in which it is spoken. In a different context, it well may sound like a lie.

What do you think?

TORN BETWEEN HUSBAND AND LOVER
unpublished

The letter was from a woman in South Carolina with a dilemma: She is torn between her husband and her lover. Here is part of what she wrote: "I'm 33, attractive, intelligent, and I'm married to a good man who is a wonderful father to our four children. He absolutely adores me. . . . I love him and never would I want to hurt him. However, something is missing in our relationship — the emotional spark that makes me feel like a woman. . . .

"For several years, I tried to compensate by burying myself in the things that wives and mothers are supposed to do, respectable things like carpooling, sewing, taking piano lessons — but I can tell you that they don't fill the void. . . .

"A while back, I met a man, and we quickly crossed the line that separates innocent flirting from things that aren't so innocent. Now I'm madly in love with him. I mean *real* love. It feels so wonderful. I can't give it up. I don't want to give it up . . .

"I was at the point of leaving my husband and children to live with this man, but he wouldn't let me do it. He said that he had been through a divorce and that it was so terrible that he didn't want me to suffer through the same thing. He said that he didn't want the breakup of another family on his conscience. . . .

"I said that he didn't love me enough — or else he'd have welcomed me into his house. He said that he loved me so much that he couldn't let me make what I later might regard as a big mistake. . . . We still see each other — and our time together is wonderful — and I'm hoping that one of these days he'll change his mind and want me always to be with him. . . .

"I guess I just don't understand men. Why is it that a woman will go to the ends of the earth for her man, while the man is more cautious, less willing to announce where he stands and what he wants to do? Does the woman act solely out of emotion? Does the man use the left-brain approach and consider the consequences more thoroughly? Or is the man simply afraid of change and commitment?

"I know I'm not the only woman in your audience who is struggling through something like this. What are the other women doing? The divorced women I know all tell me that if they had it to do over again, they would stay married and do what they needed to survive — keep a lover on the side. . . . This is what I'm doing now — because he won't let me move in with him — but the duplicity is killing me. Sometimes I can pull it off, but sometimes I can't. My husband knows something is wrong, but he hasn't yet figured out what. . . .

"My heart is pulled in two directions — for the husband with whom I have 13 years and four children and for the lover who lights up my life. I get sad and depressed when I think about giving up my lover . . . but I don't feel good about what my leaving would do to my husband, who is doing the best he can do. . . . Is something wrong with me? Am I expecting too much? Am I unrealistic? Should I try to be happy with what I've got?"

■

Well, what do you think?

What I think is that people sometimes get blinded by the blitz that comes from a new relationship — blinded to the point that they enhance the relationship into something that it is not and probably never could be.

When people have been married for a while — seven years, 13 years, or whatever — they can get set in their routines, to the point of boredom, and this is what can turn their lives brown with atrophy. Anything — yes, *anything* — would bring change, excitement, a new dimension, and when it comes along, usually in the form of another person, there can be a tendency to leap before looking.

It seems to me that the trick — if you can call it that — is to try to bring change, excitement, and new dimension to the existing relationship rather than to turn to something, or somebody, on the outside. Does this require some effort? Yes, it does, but in the long run less effort than living with constant deception and, perhaps eventually, tearing up lives and starting over.

Doris Wild Helmering, the psychotherapist from St. Louis, Mo., gets on her soapbox when she preaches about the need to put at least as much energy into marriage as we would put into extramarital relationships. If we tried as hard to please spouse as we try to please lover, we might find that remarkable changes were taking place at home — changes that possibly foreshadowed a renewal of the marriage.

I'm a great believer in trying. Even if nothing comes from it, we at least have the peace of mind that comes from knowing that we made the effort, that we didn't just pack our bags and slip away into the night. And there's much to be said for peace of mind.

■

Are women more emotional, as the letter writer wonders, when it comes to relationships? Are men more intellectual? I don't think that it has anything to do with gender. Some *people* give more consideration than others to consequences.

But as I re-read the woman's letter, I wasn't swept up with the feeling that her lover was trying to protect her from herself, that he wanted to spare her the agony that comes from breaking up a family. What I felt — and maybe it comes from my interviewing over the years so many people who felt cheated or deceived — was that he was trying to look out for himself, that he wasn't ready for the closeness that she wanted but that he wanted to keep the relationship alive. He had a good thing going, and he didn't want to mess it up by having her move in with him. That would be like marriage, and he wasn't in the market for marriage — not yet, anyway.

I hope the woman finds the emotional spark that she needs from her husband. But she won't find it unless she looks in the right place.

THE FUNNY GUY IN THE IVORY TOWER
November 12, 1989

I was in Minneapolis, walking across the campus of the University of Minnesota and wondering why colleges don't teach courses on how to live.

Instead of classes in the French literature of the 16th century, how about Living 101 — to be followed by Living 202, then 303 and, at the graduate level, 404?

Students could learn how to get a job, what to do when the boss hassles them, how to rebound from disappointment, when it's reasonable to change jobs, how to be responsible citizens, how to ask for what they want — and what to do if they don't get it, which they probably won't.

Students could learn about emotional involvement, love, getting married and staying married, becoming parents — and about being divorced and guarding their health, and growing into middle age and beyond.

If people took — and passed — courses on living, they surely would be better prepared for the real world out there than many of them now seem to be. Some of them even could go ahead and graduate — and not go through the endless graduate programs that can protect them for many years from the real world.

Why don't colleges teach courses on how to live?

In a flash, I had what I thought was an answer — not because of a blinding insight but because of what approached me on the sidewalk.

He had to be a professor. He just had to be. He wore a funny cap, a funny jacket and funny shoes, and he carried a funny knapsack. He sported a funny beard, and he had a funny look in his eyes — as if he'd just awakened and wasn't sure what country he was in. On just about every campus I've ever been on, including that of my own school, the University of Missouri, I've seen this guy — a faculty member who represents the lower end of higher education, a fumbler, a bumbler who, incredibly, is entrusted with the task of expanding young minds.

Colleges can't teach courses on how to live until they have enough teachers who know how to live, who have experienced the real world, who have laughed, cried, shed blood, made love, battled, won some and lost some. The problem with the funny guys is that they've never lived — this is my bias — and, as a result, they can't help anybody who wants to know what it's like off campus.

Some of these funny guys went to their schools as undergraduates, took their graduate work there, then remained as faculty members. Some of them even live in the same rooms they occupied as students. Have they stayed around because they're convinced that this is where they can make their greatest contributions? No, not the funny guys I've talked to. They've stayed around because they're scared to leave. Their world has shrunk — and so have they. They know what Plato said to Aristotle, but they don't know how to live.

I got shoulder to shoulder with the funny guy at Minnesota and, out of orneriness, said: "Minneapolis. You're in Minneapolis." He mumbled something that sounded like "T'ank you." I turned and watched him shuffle away, toward some ivory tower, and then, for reasons that escape me, I asked myself what I could learn from him and other funny guys — if I opened myself to the possibility that they knew something that could benefit me in the real world.

What might they know?

My inner voice supplied the answer: "Idealism. The funny guys can teach you about idealism."

Yes, indeed, idealism. We all had it — at least, many of us — in those early years. We were going to change the world, right the wrongs, help bad guys become good guys. We were going to deal honorably with those who tried to chisel us. We were going to open doors for people, smile and wish them a good day, stand in line without complaint, step to the back of the elevator — just like we were supposed to.

But something happened in the years that followed. We were wounded more than a few times, and the scar tissue got thick, then ugly, and we stopped opening doors and, instead, joined the crowd — pushing, shoving, elbowing, complaining. Our behavior became the behavior we once had railed against.

We had joined the real world. We had put our idealism in mothballs, and if we ever took it out, it was to ridicule it. ("Boy, was I dumb then.")

I wondered if the funny guy in the ivory tower ever felt dumb.

Is it possible to be both realist and idealist?

It's a question that I've thought about a lot lately. If we somehow could temper our hard-nosed realism with the softness of idealism, we might live longer, accomplish more, feel better, squeeze more juice from the grapes of joy. If the funny guys somehow could dilute their idealism with a dollop of realism, they might increase their sphere of influence. At the very least, they would seem less funny.

Is it possible to be both realist and idealist?

The more I think about it, the more I am convinced that we must have healthy amounts of realism and idealism if we are to have any chance at all to become the best that we can be.

A corporate executive can't win if he's such a realist that he believes with all his heart, based on experience, that people are no good, that they aren't willing to do a day's work for a day's pay, that they're only out for what they can get. A writer can't be effective if he sees only ugliness and loses the ability to appreciate the quiet beauty that surrounds him. A parent can't really parent without an idealistic view of children. A painter can't paint, a speaker can't speak, a manager can't manage without enough idealism — just as a teacher can't teach and a philosopher can't make sense without enough realism.

As I've mulled how to mix realism and idealism, I've talked with some of the best minds I could find, and I have discovered, to my surprise, that they are very much in agreement.

Take idealism as the basic stance, they say. Expect the best from people; expect the sun to shine every day; anticipate sweetness, courtesy, competence. But — and this is the key — understand and accept that, at times, you surely will be disappointed. People from whom you expect the best will deliver the worst; rain will fall on your parade; incompetence, greed, rage will compete to try to convince you that they dominate the world.

So how do you keep idealism from being tarnished when so many bad things are happening to so many good people all around us?

I think we have to be like Tug McGraw. We gotta believe. We have to believe that good ultimately will prevail over bad, beauty over ugliness, order over chaos.

Not long ago, I talked with an old-time executive who explained to me, with a great deal of pride, his corporation's old-time approach to business:

"We believe that, if you do the right thing long enough, eventually, something good happens."

That's what it takes — belief. Belief that is strong enough to withstand the firestorms of disillusionment and hard times.

If we believe, eventually something good will happen.

Do you suppose the funny guy in the ivory tower knew this all along?

IS SUCCESS MAKING MONKEYS OF US?
September 30, 1982

A long time ago, when he was 18, Ashley Montagu was riding on top of a double-deck bus in London, and "seated across from me were two cockney girls who were talking about their friend Harry. One of them said: 'Oh, yes, Harry, he knows everything about everything — except what it's for.' I wish I'd had the courage to get up and embrace her because what she'd said was so profound, and it was a tremendous help to me later on."

The reason it was so profound, said Montagu, was that it placed in perfect perspective what's wrong with modern education. "We're in danger of becoming educated about everything — except what it's for. We have people who are trained as Ph.D.s, but they don't know what it's for."

Montagu, 76, is a British-born anthropologist who for 31 years has lived in Princeton, N.J., and taught at Princeton University. He is the author of more than 40 books, the most recent of which is *Growing Young*, which aims to show us how to regain, as adults, our child qualities of curiosity, zest for life, hunger for knowledge — and lots more.

In an interview, Montagu said it was possible today for somebody with a fresh doctoral degree in mathematics or physics to start at $52,000 a year. While that sounds rosy, the truth is, he says, that such a graduate has been seduced by the success syndrome and mostly "he ends up looking at dials. With all his calculus, all his training in organic chemistry — or whatever — he doesn't know what it's for.

"We're taught that a successful human is one who makes a success of himself.

What is success? Well, we're told that it's getting all A's in schools; it's winning. We're taught that winning is everything, that we shouldn't play for fun. And this is reinforced when we see a chap who hardly can read or write but he becomes a hero and signs a contract for $8 million to play ball."

The success syndrome is making monkeys of many of us, Montagu said.

"Not long ago, I was driving along a Los Angeles freeway with a chap who lives there, and I said to him: 'This is tangible insanity.' The chap didn't understand what I meant. He drives daily in the traffic — like all those other people . . . about 150 miles a day in a car that looks like a success. This is why every American car falls to pieces — because it's got to look like a success.

"We're told by the Ivy League copywriters for ad agencies that if we have this or that car, when we drive to a neighbor's house he won't ask whom we are — because he'll know. Success is measured by external validation   . . . and it doesn't make [any difference] whom you are. We have been taught to worship before the bitch-goddess success . . . and our schools are turning out instructed barbarians who don't know what humans are for."

The problem with modern education, he said, is that it really isn't education at all; it's instruction. "We're given answers. We're not encouraged to ask questions and to question answers. Our schools are like our armies. We're told what to do. But the purpose of education ought to be to teach us how to be human beings, warm and loving. If we're not warm and loving, we become the most dangerous creatures on earth — to ourselves and others — and this is why we're the most self-endangered species ever to inhabit this planet."

In school, Montagu said, we're taught facts, which we "memorize and regurgitate during exams. We don't think; we just give answers . . . and the student with the highest regurgitative capacity is considered the brightest and best. This is one reason why at universities students die intellectually and spiritually by degrees. They emerge as scientists who split the atom and then make atom bombs. . . ."

At Princeton, he said, he teaches a course that has as its main thrust helping students to use their brains.

"I tell them that we're going to revalue their values, that I'm going to rush into their minds and make shambles . . . and then help them put their minds together again. I tell them that I will help them develop one critical trait of the child — being critical. They should accept nothing any authority says without challenging it. They should challenge me, check the evidence for themselves.

"Many of them are seniors, people who've had four years of philosophy, but they don't have the faintest idea of 'causes.' I tell them that in the South there's a problem with pellagra and I ask them: What is the cause? They come back with their answer: Doctors found pellagra is due to poor nutrition, due to the lack of riboflavin, Vitamin B-12. People are given B-12, and the disease is eliminated. Yes, they say, the cause is poor nutrition.

"But I say 'no.' The cause is the socio-economic structure of the society in which people live. Cause always is made up of a number of life conditions . . . that, when taken separately, don't make a cause but that, when taken together, create a significant condition. B-12 is one of the conditions of pellagra."

While Montagu enjoys college students, he enjoys children even more, he said. "I love to talk with children, and I always have. In my home I have skulls of gorillas and chimpanzees . . . and for 30 years children from the neighborhood have been coming in and bringing their friends with them. They've been here so many times, some of them, that they can give guided tours to their friends. They'll go to the attic and see all the books, and they'll be in awe: 'Oh, my God, so many books.' Then the leader of the group will explain the gorilla skull.

"They don't call before they come. They just appear and knock on the door, and I'm always happy to see them. I find great pleasure in talking with them because of their open, inquiring minds. The thing that distinguishes me from other adults to them, I think, is that I don't talk down to them. I don't use big words."

If his home has been open to children for 30 years, a lot of traffic must have come through.

Yes, that's right, and Montagu said he liked to think that his receptivity to the traffic had been in part responsible for the neighborhood's producing one anthropologist, one archeologist and one geneticist. It's the way education ought to be — stimulating rather than deadening. The children who come to his home end up knowing "what it's for."

FEELERS, THINKERS AND DECISIONS
April 7, 1985

What do you do when you're faced with a major decision? Do you sweat about it, stew, toss and turn — and hope that it somehow will resolve itself or that somebody else will make the decision for you?

Do you shoot from the hip — the "ready, fire, aim" strategy — on the assumption that getting the decision behind you is the most important thing?

Are you ruled by what your head tells you? Or do you listen more attentively to your stomach?

Let me tell you how I approach major decisions. I draw a line down the middle of a sheet of paper, and on the left side I write everything that would constitute a plus if I exercised option X. On the right side I write the minuses.

Then I do the same thing with option Y and option Z — and with other options, too, if I recognize them. I study the options, sometimes soliciting reaction from people whose judgments I respect. And then I discount everything and follow my stomach — because it feels right, even if it's in conflict with my head, which it sometimes is.

I am, you see, a "feeler," not a "thinker," when it comes to decision-making, and over the years my stomach has established a track record with which I cannot quarrel.

What do you think about that, Theodore Isaac Rubin?

Well, said Rubin, what he thinks is that he's not at all surprised, because a lot of people are like that — the feelers, who look as if they're operating differently from the thinkers, but "I don't think they are. The thinker is more conscious of the [decision-making] process than the feeler. That may be the distinction. But I think they — thinkers and feelers alike — go through the same process."

That process is the theme of Rubin's new book, *Overcoming Indecisiveness*, which offers what Rubin calls "the eight stages of effective decision-making." The book is the 25th by Rubin, a psychiatrist, and, like most of his others, it presents a down-to-earth road map for reaching higher ground in our emotional lives.

During an interview, Rubin, who lives in New York and who is president of the American Institute for Psychoanalysis, said that a major block to decision-making was "loss of touch with one's own feelings. . . . You've been indecisive for so long without awareness that you depend on others to make decisions for you . . . and you no longer know what you feel about anything. You try to tap into feelings but nothing comes through."

When people don't feel, they don't get hurt, said Rubin, and they don't suffer from anxiety, anger or disappointment. But it's a losing proposition because "this kind of defensive maneuver also removes us from our potential for joys of any kind, as well as for self-realization. And it is very damaging to decision-making."

Often people who are out of touch with their feelings come from families in which nobody felt much of anything. "It's promoted from one generation to another. People are buffeted about without ever taking charge. Occasionally there's a reaction to this, and somebody moves in the other direction and takes charge — but only rarely."

The way to establish contact with feelings sounds relatively simple, but it can be agonizingly difficult because it may involve overcoming a lifetime of learning. "When we really make the effort to discover our preferences and priorities, we initiate the process of knowing what we feel. We can begin to own ourselves," said Rubin.

Other blocks to decision-making, he said, include inappropriate dependency on others, "option blindness," anxiety and perfectionism.

Ah, yes, perfectionism. If we insist that every decision always must be perfect — to guarantee a perfect outcome — then we can't ever make a decision, because perfection is an illusion that is kept intact only through inaction. Once we decide to do anything, the illusion is shattered, said Rubin, and so the perfectionists never decide. For them, illusion is preferable to reality.

Here are Rubin's eight stages of decision-making:

1. Listing and observing all the possibilities, options or choices involved in the issue. It's important to let the mind roam and to consider everything, no matter how absurd it may seem.

2. Sustaining a free flow of feelings and thoughts about each of the possible choices.

3. Paying attention to these feelings and thoughts and determining what they are trying to tell you.

4. Relating choices to established priorities. Are the choices in sync with what's really important in the personal value system?

5. Coming to a conclusion by designating one choice and discarding the others.

218

6. Registering the decision. This involves nothing more than "sitting with it for a while, feeling it out, letting it sink in and become part of yourself."

7. Investing the decision with committed feelings, thoughts, time and energy.

8. Translating the decision into optimistic action.

What is important to remember, said Rubin, is that "in very few instances is one decision actually better than another. In 99 percent of the cases, almost any choice can be converted into a constructive decision" if the person is committed to making it work.

"If you believe it's the right option, it generally is — because it becomes a self-fulfilling prophecy. . . . Even in medicine, the dedication to choice is more important than the actual choice."

Rubin said that over the years, his decision-making process had been refined. "It's easier now, with my having made peace with the realities of living — that to gain something, you have to pay a price, that you can't have it all. . . .

"If you grow and change in healthy ways as you get older, you learn more of what it is to be a human being, your assets and limitations. You get big doses of humility without humiliation. This aids in the decision-making process. . . . An enemy of decision-making is lack of self-esteem and the reaction to lack of it," which he said was often a projected kind of grandiosity that shuts off a realistic view of oneself and the world.

What has been the hardest decision that Rubin and his wife, Ellie, have made?

"Whether to stay in New York or live in a quieter place. We tried a lot of things, experimented. A lot of considerations went into it . . . but now it's resolved. We're still in New York."

What can parents do to help their children become comfortable decision-makers?

"Anything that increases self-esteem helps enormously. Parents who love each other and show it . . . always are way ahead of the game. Mutual respect rubs off. Kids are glad to be human beings because they see up close how human beings are treated. . . .

"Anything that helps kids feel a sense of reality is helpful — understanding how the real world is, that priorities exist, that a price has to be paid. . . . Anything that enhances children's awareness of feelings — so they can make use of feelings."

Parents can help their children by showing "willingness to make decisions early on . . . and to get the children involved in decision-making, when appropriate. They can encourage the children to make decisions. Overprotection is harmful to the decision-making process."

STYLES OF DECISION-MAKING
October 19, 1986

A long time ago, when I was drafted into the Army right after college, I was thrown together with — and became quite fond of — an old master sergeant who wore impatience on his sleeve, right along with his stripes.

If there ever was a person who couldn't tolerate indecision, it was Sarge, who almost hourly bellowed at everybody: "Do something, even if it's wrong!"

Why did I like him so much?

I didn't know it at the time, but it probably was because in Sarge I found somebody who shared my philosophy. For much of my life, in one way or another, I've been telling myself and those around me to "do something, even if it's wrong." Without a doubt, I am action-oriented, and it drives me wild when something important is at stake and people can't pull the trigger. They seem to be saying, "Ready, aim . . . ready, aim . . . ready, aim . . ." The problem with not acting is that the opportunity may be lost, forever.

On the other hand, some of these people have told me over the years that I drive them wild, too, with a philosophy that seems to be "Ready, fire, aim." The problem with doing something, even if it's wrong, is that sometimes it is wrong.

Isn't there a middle ground?

■

I put that question to psychologist Nathan W. Turner, who last year wrote for the Journal of Psychotherapy & the Family an article titled "Dynamics of Decision Therapy."

Turner's answer: Yes, indeed, there is a middle ground — but it's not easily found by a lot of people, some of whom need professional help to learn how to pull the trigger . . . or how to stop pulling the trigger.

Turner, who is assistant professor of psychiatry and human behavior at Thomas Jefferson University, is in private practice in Bryn Mawr. In an interview, he said that decision-making is related to how we think and somehow connected to our mental wiring, which differs from person to person.

The two most common decision-making styles, said Turner, are those at the extreme ends of the spectrum:

¶ Those who "think in terms of the larger picture and generalize" and are quite deliberate. Carl Jung, when he typed personalities, called these people "intuitors." A more common term today is "visionaries" — also known in some quarters as "airheads."

¶ Those who are "more detail-oriented . . . and who feel that the decision should be made right away." In Jung's terminology, these people are "sensors." A more common term today is "cowboys" — because they shoot from the hip.

It is absolutely amazing, said Turner, how often intuitors and sensors marry each other. A reason may be that "intuitively we know what the other has to offer." But often it's a basis for conflict, with one person, usually the sensor, haranguing the other to change styles.

When he gets these people in therapy, as he often does, Turner teaches what he calls the rule of "no fault," which he explains this way: "A lot of people want to find fault with the spouse, but . . . we have no control over how we are wired. To assign blame misses the point," which is that each can benefit from the other, that one is not right and one is not wrong.

"We need to realize that we need both types to make superior decisions," and therapy tends to pound away at the need to compromise, to work as a team, to try to maximize the strengths and minimize the weaknesses.

The intuitors, said Turner, tend to do a better job in the first half of the decision-making process, which involves defining the problem and listing and examining the alternatives. The sensors tend to do a better job in the second half, which involves selecting and implementing an alternative.

A problem in marriage, said Turner, is that "neither understands that the other has something to offer," and instead of being teammates they work against each other. "Most married couples I see are all over each other's case."

Why is the "wiring" different in people?

Nobody knows for sure, said Turner, but some of it probably is learned, while some probably is genetic "or something else." While the wiring can't be changed, people can learn to "change the messages we send over the wiring."

Turner said that he teaches people to negotiate and to try to learn from each other. Sometimes he finds that a power struggle is at the root of it all, and he tries to defuse that by explaining that because each has something to offer, each has equal power. "They usually are unaware of that."

One way in which Turner works is to try to speed up the intuitor and slow down the sensor. This is done by "assigning time limits for decision-making. The fast one must take twice the normal amount of time, while the slow one must act in half the time."

Decision-makers can be found at all points on the spectrum, Turner said, and some are able to be deliberate when it is appropriate and be speedy when it's necessary. "They are more flexible." They also are relatively rare, and they are not among those who typically come to therapy.

Is it possible for people to change their actions, even though they can't change their wiring?

Turner: "When people are in a crunch, it's amazing what they can do."

A case history: "I was a consultant to a business group, and these guys had been struggling for months over a decision about a $2 million addition to a building. . . . My remedy was rather old-fashioned. I asked them to go along with me in a 10-minute experiment . . . and I told them to pretend that the building was on fire and they had to make a decision before they could get out the fire exit, which would be blocked by fire in 10 minutes. . . . They made their decision in three minutes, and everybody seemed satisfied with it."

What happened? What broke their deadlock?

"They were a mixture of different types [of decision-makers] and they had been blocking each other. . . . What I did was create a larger goal — their survival." This eliminated the blockage by getting them to work together for a common cause.

■

Being deliberate is a plus, said Turner, when it brings into play the consideration of many options and their consequences. It becomes a minus when "nondecision becomes a decision because the deadline for action has passed. It's a minus when others are constantly complaining" about the lack of decisions. People who are slow to decide may be fearful that they will be wrong — and they want to postpone it as long as possible.

Being quick on the trigger is a plus when the time is short and action is necessary. But it's a minus in the sense that the decisions can end up full of errors. There's often "a bit of regret," said Turner, because more options or the ramifications weren't considered.

Sensors often tend to "have a real need for closure . . . so that the level of anxiety can be reduced. They want to get it done. The feeling of achievement is what is sought" rather than the best possible decision.

Intuitors tend to be "quite comfortable with anxiety. . . . They have a tremendous ability to handle ambiguity . . . and this can drive the other type bonkers."

WHY IS COMMON SENSE SO UNCOMMON?
April 26, 1982

A fter almost every speech I make, when questions are invited from the audience, somebody wants to know where story ideas come from. The question usually is framed something like this:

"How on earth do you keep from going dry and running out of things to write about?"

My answer always is that readers are a constant and dependable source of suggestions and that most of their suggestions are seriously considered — whether or not I eventually follow through and write something. Take today's column, for example. It was generated from a letter that read in part:

"If possible, would you do an article on common sense? So many seem to lack it and others surprisingly have it. How is it acquired? Apparently college does not guarantee it . . . What lifestyle, if any, tends to develop it? Is it prevalent in one sex as opposed to the other? How can common sense be obtained? And, finally, what is common sense?"

I thanked that reader for what surely is one of the brightest ideas I've heard in a long time, and then I arranged an interview with somebody who over the years has impressed me as having a high level of common sense — psychiatrist Erwin Smarr, a past president of the Philadelphia Psychiatric Society and president-elect of the Pennsylvania Psychiatric Society.

Smarr, who is clinical director of Horsham Clinic, a private psychiatric hospital near Ambler, Pa., seemed as intrigued by the questions as I was and said that in his whole life nobody before ever had asked him about common sense, its origin and development.

So join us now — won't you? — for a common-sense look at a subject that Smarr described this way: "The most common thing about common sense is that it's so uncommon."

A strong case could be made for this definition of common sense, Smarr said: "It's those things that people believe in a practical sense are true about everyday life and affairs, including relationships. By and large people believe that most who are sensible and reasonable have common sense."

A second definition that is closely related to the first holds that common sense consists of "beliefs and attitudes that are held in common by people of a community, region or time — arising from commonality of circumstances and environment."

Yes, said Smarr, all of that amounts to quite a mouthful — and the question must be asked: Is any of it true?

The presumption, he said, is that a person who "grows up under average, expectable conditions will get to know practical things of ordinary life in a pretty common way. The general expectation then is that if this person is faced with a situation or problem, he will have certain ways of viewing it . . . and this will constitute a common-sense approach. Everybody who deviates very much will be seen as lacking in common sense."

Some of that might have been true a long time ago, when life was less complicated and the culture was more uniform, Smarr said, but it's less likely to "prevail from the mid-20th century on . . . because of the rapidity of cultural and societal change. It becomes less possible for people to have a common sense about things . . . and this is part of the problem of youth in growing up: Their parents don't know what to model for them because they don't know what their children's lives will be like. . . .

"We used to take common sense for granted . . . because of expectable circumstances of life, but we can't do it now. The more differentiated people become as humans, the more their lives differ. . . . Or the less developed toward maturity they become, the less possible it is for them to have a sense in common about things and to think alike."

It's apparent, Smarr said, that common sense has virtually nothing to do with high intelligence, although a certain amount of average intelligence is needed. In fact, super-high intelligence could be a barrier to common sense because "it might lead one to be so different from average as to see things quite differently . . . or to become over-intellectualized and with insufficient experience in common, practical reality."

What are the components of common sense? "A firm grasp on reality, intuition and an empathetic sense of other human beings," Smarr said. "Judgment is fairly good."

How is common sense acquired?

"The best prescription is for parents to have a good bit of it themselves. Children learn by example, by their exposure to everyday attitudes. If they can't do that, then it's not too likely to happen."

Another way to develop common sense, Smarr said, is having "healthy relationships with social peers through childhood. You take healthy kids in a healthy neighborhood . . . and this is how you learn about people and life. It's in the peer group that kids develop consensus of attitudes about reality things. You learn about people that way . . . and how to evaluate the attitudes and reactions of others. If you're isolated in books, you don't learn it in the same way. Maybe you learn it only secondhand through literature," and that's not the same as absorbing it through real-life experiences.

It's possible, Smarr said, that some people may be predisposed neurologically to better common sense than others, but "this is an area in which very little can be said . . . because there's a lot we don't know about innate factors in cognitive development of the brain and mind. Some people may be predisposed to perceive and appraise experiences differently from others."

Are there sexual differences that relate to common sense?

Smarr: "It's traditional for each sex to tend to regard the other as lacking common sense," and this is based generally not on reality but on the different experiences that males and females have in "growing up and training in different roles. . . . The sense that men and women develop about their worlds of reality tends to be different, and there is difficulty in appreciating and understanding these differences."

The result: A lot of finger-pointing and name-calling. "Hey, you don't have enough sense to know when the buttons are falling off your shirts." . . . "Oh, yeah? If you're so smart, how come you're always running out of gas?"

If common sense isn't tied to high intelligence, then it obviously has nothing to do with formal education. Right?

That's correct, Smarr said. Common sense doesn't come "from education per se. . . . It runs through a lot of uneducated segments of society, among people who know life from having to struggle with its direct experience. These people develop a wisdom . . . and they know an awful lot about the practicality of basic living and survival. They're not so dependent on a lot of money. . . . Life teaches it best that way."

ARE SOUTHERNERS DIFFERENT
FROM EVERYBODY ELSE?
May 2, 1985

William T. Carpenter, who is director of the Maryland Psychiatric Research Center in Baltimore, grew up in Rutherfordton, N.C., did his undergraduate work at Wofford College in Spartanburg, S.C., and attended Bowman Gray School of Medicine in Winston-Salem, N.C.

To this day, his Southern heritage remains, and it's obvious when he speaks and when he . . .

Well, let's listen as he talks about it:

"To the dismay of my colleagues and my secretary, I'm willing to speak on the telephone to anybody who calls. It's so ingrained in me — if somebody calls, you talk. That's what you're supposed to do, and that's what I do. I don't know how to put up reasonable barriers. It's a liability sometimes, but that's the way I was brought up."

■

Are Southerners different from everybody else? Are they more friendly and less defended?

I'm not sure — even though I lived the first 45 years of my life in the South. After eight years in the Northeast I'm still not sure, but I'm in a better position now to appreciate the contrasts that Southerners offer in their behavior. I don't take it for granted anymore because I'm not part of it anymore.

Not long ago, I was back in North Carolina, where I lived for a decade, to do some medical stories at Duke University. In the weeklong visit, I encountered some unusual things:

A physician with whom I didn't have an appointment agreed to make time to talk to me — while he was shaving. Then when he finished shaving, he invited me to accompany him to a reception that honored Duke's 1959 medical school class, which was back for its 25th reunion.

I was wandering around in the rental agency parking lot, looking for the car I'd just rented, and an employee rushed to my aid. He apologized because the car wasn't where it was supposed to be. The reason: It had just been returned, and it still was being washed. But, he said, "come on inside and have a cup of coffee and then, when the car's ready, I'll load your luggage and you'll be on your way."

The driver of the bus that took me to the airport terminal said: "I hope y'all had a successful trip, and please do hurry back and visit us again."

A service-station attendant not only cleaned my windshield, checked under the hood and asked if he could check the tires, but he also wanted to know all about the Buick Skylark I was driving. He was thinking about buying one, he said — and then he told me about his wife and two daughters — and showed me their pictures.

A clerk in a state-run liquor store watched as I marched in front of the cognac display, and then he approached me and said: "I'm not supposed to recommend brands, but if you'd like to try something that's really good and not too expensive, you might like . . ." He was right. It was not too expensive — and it was really good.

The man behind the counter in a golf pro shop, when he didn't have the orange knit club covers that I was looking for, seemed on the verge of tears. "This is really unusual. I can't remember the last time we couldn't give a customer what he wanted. But you will come back and try us again, won't you?"

■

What about it, Layton McCurdy? Are Southerners different?

McCurdy is in a position to have an opinion because he is a Southerner, and until he came to Philadelphia a year or so ago he'd lived almost his whole life in South Carolina — in Florence and Charleston.

McCurdy, who is director of psychiatry at Pennsylvania Hospital, said he didn't know "if the differences are real, but I recognize that some things are different. In the South, people walk on the street and speak, acknowledge others, nod. They don't do this [in the North]. People here are friendly, but nobody speaks."

Why?

"I think in the South there's a little less interpersonal uneasiness. There's more fear here. . . . I go into somebody's house, and there are six locks on the door. It's a reaction to crime, and the fear is almost as bad" as being a victim of crime because "it's malignant. It makes you not trust people . . . and you lose the capacity for easy intimacy."

In Philadelphia, he said, "I hardly ever find a cabdriver who is not willing to communicate. But that's not true in New York. The driver's behind a barricade . . . and this makes me uneasy. He's scared of me . . . and I feel that I have reason to be scared of him."

McCurdy's wife grew up in Marion, S.C., and "there was no key to her grand-mother's house. Nobody worried about locking up a house. . . . I don't know if the crime rate is any different — certainly there's crime in the South — but it's more easy to trust." A reason for that, said McCurdy, may be that in the South, people are brought up with what amounts to a presumption of trust rather than a presumption of distrust. Basically this orientation remains with them as adults — although it may be modified if they leave the South.

Are Southerners different — in a moral sense? Well, said McCurdy, the answer is yes . . . and no. As a little boy, he said, he was preached to constantly about the virtues of honesty. "I was taught that if you lie, people will catch you — and you'll be known as a liar. This is morally wrong . . . and it also compli-cates doing business with people."

Psychiatrist Carpenter, who was in Philadelphia to receive an award for his research into the treatment of schizophrenia, said that he sensed in the North a "hustler aspect" of behavior that tends not to be so obvious in the South.

"It's almost as if you see what you can get out of people in the first few min-utes. In the South people are less eager . . . and this may be a subtle form of seduction. . . . Southerners tend to be less intimidating in the initial encounter. Maybe that means we hide our greed better."

Carpenter said — and I personally think he's right on target with this — that the differences may be less a matter of geography than of size.

Generally speaking, Southern living tends to be rural living, and "part of our rural heritage is that you know everybody, and so you have to face the conse-quences of your lack of civility. In the Northeast, you can go to a lot of parties before you meet somebody you insulted earlier," because of the anonymity of big cities. "There are more social sanctions in the South," and this, as much as any-thing, may influence behavior.

There also tends to be a certain amount of what might be called phoniness in the South, said Carpenter.

Phoniness?

"It's not humble to think that you're Christlike, but it's important to have friends who view you that way."

What do you think?

THE SUPPORT OF FRIENDS
January 29, 1981

The more I see of life, the more I am convinced that one of the essential ingre-dients of success is persistence. Yes, you have to be talented. Yes, you have to harness and direct your energies. Yes, you even may have to be a little lucky, too, and stumble into the right place at the right time.

But somewhere along the way you also need the steel in your spine and the hope in your soul that enable you to overcome setbacks — and heartbreaks. You have to be willing to keep plugging along when anybody else with common sense would call it quits.

A few years ago, I did an interview on that very subject with Howard Head, who struggled for years before he developed the snow ski that ultimately would revolutionize the sport and turn him into a millionaire.

There were times, Head told me, when first one design of the ski and then another failed, and when he tottered on the brink of total disillusionment. Maybe what he was trying to do just wasn't possible. But each time, a few people whose opinions he valued cheered him on. Eventually he would design the ski, they told him, if he didn't give up.

It was their encouragement, he said, that made it possible for him to reject the 35th version and go on to the 36th — and the 37th — and the . . .

As long as somebody is getting positive feedback, he said, there is hope. "But if nobody tells you that you're on the right track, the chances are that you're not." That would be the time to quit, Head said. That's when he would have bailed out.

I knew an artist who persisted in his dream for years — without very many encouraging words, but with tons of confidence in himself. His name was Jim Childress, and he was a draftsman when I hired him as a cartoonist for the newspaper of which I was executive editor.

Childress had a comic strip that he drew on the side — a strip named *Conchy*, which was a collection of Pogo-like humor that appealed to intellectuals but that, I often felt, left many readers scratching their heads and asking each other what the point was.

I suggested to him that the strip needed to broaden its appeal. Somehow he didn't seem to hear me. When I offered the suggestion again, he reminded me that I was the editor who had canceled *Doonesbury* because I was convinced that not enough readers understood it, either.

Childress plodded on, self-syndicating his strip and turning away all suggestions for change. "I believe in it. I know it will succeed. It's just a matter of time," he often said.

He rejected offers from syndicates that wanted him to reshape the focus of the strip and even move *Conchy* off the beach and into the blue-collar work world. But finally his perseverance won out. A major syndicate agreed to take the strip as it was, and before long *Conchy* was in newspapers from coast to coast and Childress was on the verge of collecting big money.

Shortly before his death, in one of the last letters that we exchanged after I came to Philadelphia, Childress wrote: "Nobody ever can tell me that it doesn't pay to stick to your guns."

I thought about Childress and Howard Head the other day when I interviewed another man with a success story — Jim Everroad, author of the best-selling *How to Flatten Your Stomach* and two other exercise books, whose earnings last year from his books exceeded $100,000. That's more than he was paid during the nine years that he taught school in Indiana, before he started to write.

But before he hit the jackpot with a California publishing company, Everroad twice went broke trying to publish and market the stomach book on his own. The heartbreak was enough to make him want to surrender. Almost. But he kept plugging away, convinced that the book ultimately would succeed because people who had bought it wrote letters and thanked him for showing them the way to flatter stomachs.

"I knew it filled a need. I knew there was enormous audience interest. That's why I stayed with it. There wasn't much encouragement from anybody else. Many of the people who knew me thought that I had gone off the deep end, that I was squirrelly" to·resign a teaching job and devote fulltime to promoting the book. "Those people weren't against me, but they just didn't believe that I would be successful."

His background in athletics also gave him the tenacity to hang in there when the wolf was at the door, he said.

"I was influenced by terrific coaches. They believed in me . . . from the very beginning. In high school, I weighed 110 pounds, and the coach gave me a shot at playing halfback. . . . Everywhere I turned — at Indiana University, too, somebody was telling me that I could do it, whatever it was, and encouraging me. I remember the time when . . ."

At that moment, Jim Everroad's eyes watered and his voice cracked. He began to cry, and I stopped asking questions, and we sat in silence for perhaps 15 seconds. Then he said: "I'm sorry . . . but it really got to me . . . when I started thinking about all the people who've done so much for me. Without them, I don't know what I'd be doing today."

We ended the interview not long after that, and, when we parted, Everroad thanked me for funneling our discussion into the yesteryears and reminding him of those who had dug the footings that supported his life.

I thanked him — because the interview had given me reason to go back and inventory the important people in my life.

Has that ever happened to you?

THE FLASHBACKS AND FALLOUT OF WAR
June 30, 1981

George Ewalt grew up in Upper Darby Township and graduated from Monsignor Bonner High School in Drexel Hill. His first job was operating an addressing machine for Curtis Publishing Co. and then, for more money, he labored in a foundry. He hunted a little, small game mostly, and he owned a shotgun. On his 19th birthday — September 14, 1966 — he was drafted into the Army, and he went quietly because "it was the thing to do."

All of the men in his family had served in the military. His father and his uncles were in World War II, and an uncle was killed in Korea. "I didn't give it much thought, being drafted. There was no peace movement then. Everybody went when his time came."

Less than six months later, George Ewalt was in Vietnam with the First Infantry Division. He was there for 365 days, and on the morning that he left, a rocket smashed into the air base and killed 20 soldiers who were headed for home.

He doesn't discuss some of the things that happened in Vietnam, he said. But as he sat in Scanlon's Saloon with his ever-full glass of ginger ale he began to let some of it out. In a voice so soft that it sometimes was difficult to hear over the din of the jukebox, he offered this introduction to horror:

"It was commonplace for kids to set things off on people. Old ladies made bombs. You couldn't trust anybody. . . . I didn't think about what was happening to me. I was too busy trying to keep myself alive. . . . One night I was shot in the mouth, almost crucified. We were out on a listening post, which is sort of an early-warning system, and two new guys were with me. I told them that the way it worked was that they would watch while I slept for an hour, and then I'd take over. They had a radio in case they saw the enemy coming in — so they could warn the rest of the company.

"The new guys screwed me up. I woke up, heard movement, and there was a squad of Vietcong, moving in on us, trying to circle us and capture us. We had to fight our way out. When I started running, the Vietcong were 15 or 20 feet from me . . . and everybody was shooting at everybody. We threw 10 hand grenades, but only three went off. The rest were duds. We got out . . . I don't know how. Then we were in a bunker, and I was sitting over in a corner. The medics were looking at the other two guys, who seemed OK, and then they came over to me, and one of them cried: 'Jesus Christ, it's all over you!' I felt my face, and it was all blood. Now it was hurting — a burning sensation — but there was no sensation when I got nailed. The bullet split my lower lip. . . . I got up, and they were going to send me out again in a couple of hours with two other guys, but I raised hell and I didn't have to go. . . .

"The Army didn't punish people in the field. Nobody was court-martialed. Instead they sent you out into the night on ambush. I went out three weeks straight . . . because at the time I was very vocal. But after three weeks, I was conditioned to going out at night. If anybody was going out, I saddled up and went along on ambush. We'd set up a position along an ox-cart trail or any place where we expected people to move. We'd lie there all night, in the rain, and wait for somebody to come down the road, and then we popped them. We set up so that all the fire was interlocking   . . . and it created a kill zone. It was like hunting at night . . . I was conditioned to it. It boiled down to survival. . . .

"But they did it to us, too. The NVA [North Vietnamese Army] had a $50 bounty on us. They'd kill us, take our dogtags and unit markings and get $50. That's why a lot of war prisoners were killed, done in right away. They were excess baggage and worth money . . .

"We had little incentives to kill, too, little incentives to get the body count up. They wanted numbers. The thing about cutting off ears and getting a three-day pass was common knowledge. We didn't do that where I was, but everybody knew about it. Once they offered a three-day pass to anybody who brought in a live one. We brought in two. . . .

"The Army was spraying a lot of Agent Orange then . . . but they never told us anything about it. They just poured it in on top of us. We'd set up in a rice paddy or in the jungle, and late at night they'd fly over and spray, and the next morning all the leaves would be off the trees and the elephant grass would be dying . . . in a matter of a few hours."

It now seems apparent, George Ewalt said, that Dioxin, the Agent Orange poison, is at the root of most of his physical problems. He has had half a dozen cancerous growths removed from his body and throat, and his hands tremble constantly because of nerve damage in his arms.

The skin cancers, he said, "start out as small pimples. Then they go flat and start growing. . . . They grow down toward the bone, instead of up. They get about the size of a fingernail."

His surgery has been paid for by his own insurance, he said, because the government "is trying to run away and hide . . . and has refused to acknowledge that there is a correlation between my problems and Agent Orange."

Ewalt has become a member of Agent Orange Victims International, which has filed a class-action lawsuit against the government and the chemical companies that produced Agent Orange. The suit, according to the organization's newsletter, is "the largest . . . in the history of the United States. . . . Essentially we are asking the courts to award a percentage of the chemical companies' profits to a court-administered public trust fund that will be used to repair the damage done to our children, compensate those who have been disabled and fund research into proper medical treatment for Dioxin poisoning."

Ewalt, who joined the suit by forwarding his records to the organization, said that "doing something" had minimized some of the bitterness that he feels toward the government for "ignoring us."

His daughter "was born sick" and has had continuing medical problems, Ewalt said, and he believes that this is a direct result of "my genes being scrambled" by exposure to Agent Orange.

In the beginning, Ewalt wouldn't go to the hospital to visit his daughter, and his wife was furious. But, she said, "I came to understand that he wouldn't go because he was afraid she was going to die — like everybody else he ever loved."

Sheila Ewalt said that "times are better now" between her and George. "We couldn't continue to live together and sleep together and not know what was going on. But now I know what's going on."

Daughter Tara, 9, has been to therapy, too, and has learned to stand up for herself when her father storms at her. Said Sheila Ewalt, "She now says, 'Please don't scream at me, Daddy. I don't deserve that kind of treatment.'

And that really brings George out of it."

Ewalt still suffers nightmares, still gets flashbacks to when he was in Vietnam, killing and trying to keep from being killed. "The only way I can describe it is that it's like you're watching a TV show and somebody behind you with a remote control switches to another show. . . . I'll be sitting somewhere and then I'll be in battle in Nam. I can smell the jungle and taste the gunpowder."

Once he and Sheila were watching TV, and somebody fell out of a helicopter. Ewalt went berserk. Sheila didn't know why until later — when she found out that a battle-crazed soldier sitting next to Ewalt in a helicopter had leaped to his death, rather than fight any more.

The flashbacks, Ewalt said, are "happening to my friends, too, the Nam veterans, many of them. They're just like I am."

Most of his friends were in the war, he said. "I can pick out a Nam vet in a crowd. . . . It's something about the look in their eyes. We tend to hang together. The normal relationships that people have . . . well, ours are mainly with other veterans. I guess we don't trust anybody else."

People don't talk to Ewalt much about the war any more, and that's the way he wants it. Right after he came back, a lot of people, including a Catholic priest who was a family friend, wanted to know how many he had killed. Even Sheila wanted to know.

"I can't believe that I asked — but I did," she said. "I think that for those of us who weren't there, it seemed like an adventure. But it doesn't any more."

HAPPINESS IN 10 EASY STEPS?
September 12, 1991

In a year's time, I read two or three dozen books and skim through maybe a hundred more to find out what's between the covers. Because I'm a writer, I'm interested in books, and sometimes I wander into bookstores not to buy but to see what people are buying.

This is an experience that tends to depress me. What people are buying, and what bookstores and publicists are pushing, are books that all too often tell us that life can be a bowl of cherries if we do this or that, if we try harder, if we don't give up hope, if we're willing to experiment with new things.

There are books about one-hour orgasms, making love all the time, marrying the person of our dreams, getting the perfect job, winning the cherished promotion, bringing up world-class children, becoming beautiful, making life-long friends, being eternally popular.

Now all of these are worthwhile goals, I suppose — maybe if you screen out the one-hour orgasm — but what these books have in common is what makes me feel depressed. The commonality: a simple-minded view of how life works. If readers commit to the easy-to-follow 10-step program, they will be rewarded. Their dreams will be fulfilled and they will live happily ever after.

That's rubbish — and everybody knows it, except the people who buy the books.

Seldom do I come across a book that describes life in what I consider realistic terms — that it's sometimes hard as a rock, with serious problems that perhaps can be resolved over time with dedication, blood, sweat, tears and luck. There aren't many books that take this viewpoint because they wouldn't likely be commercially successful. Who wants to pay $18.95 to find out how tough life can be? Answer: almost nobody.

Somewhere along the line we were sold a bill of goods — a lot of us — and we've never been able to shake the belief that life always should be easy.

Psychiatrist Leo Madow, in an interview with me a while back on anger, spoke to this point: "There is a high level of expectation that things will go our way. Television would have you believe that we're all entitled to a mansion and a

Cadillac. . . . It's a kind of promise in this country, where everybody can grow up to be president or a millionaire. But it doesn't work out that way for most of us most of the time" — and when it doesn't, we're angry because we didn't get what we thought we were entitled to.

So some of us run out and buy another book that offers a 1-2-3 approach to success or happiness or whatever.

We want easy solutions.

The people who develop and promote diet programs understand this. That's why they tell us we can lose weight without hunger or exercise. That we buy so many of their books stating eloquently our distaste for anything that's in the least bit difficult. But the truth is, and always has been, that the best way for most people to lose weight is to go to bed hungry once in a while and to exercise as much as their doctor will allow.

Do you think a book advising occasional hunger and regular exercise to lose weight would draw long lines to bookstores?

The people who write books about career success understand about making it easy. It's mostly in how we dress, smile, play political games. Isn't that what the books tell us? But the truth is, and for the most part always has been, that the best way for most people to be successful in their careers is to work long, hard and smart, to find out what the organization needs and develop a way to meet that need.

There aren't many shortcuts to being successful — and few books I am aware of that tell exactly how much toil and how many sleepless nights are necessary to climb the mountain.

The people who write books about successful marriage seldom preach the gospel of compromise, of biting our tongues, of doing some things we'd rather not do. Rather, too many of these people give us 10 rules to follow, rules that will revitalize our marriage and keep us forever in love. Successful marriage is hard work, but would anybody pay $18.95 for that startling revelation? No thanks, but how about those 10 rules?

It's the same way with books about health. It's hard for many of us to stay healthy, to resist the foods, lifestyles and habits that can contribute to the erosion of health. We'd rather not work that hard. So many of us buy rule books. Easy. Simple. Quick. Also phony, but . . .

This summer, my golf game deteriorated to the point that it wasn't fun to play anymore — and I'm certain it also wasn't fun for the people who played with me, watching me hack around and miss shots that a few years ago I would have nailed.

It got so bad that I took lessons, which were enormously helpful in enabling me to identify the bad habits I'd fallen into. But what I learned that was even more important was that there is no easy way to play good-enough golf — unless you happen to be one of those relatively few people who are blessed with lots of natural ability. For the rest of us it comes down to practice, practice, practice.

We stand out on the driving range in boiling heat and we hit balls. We sweat, and we hit balls. We think our fingers can't hold the club any longer, and we hit balls. Then we go home and think about hitting balls.

In this way, golf is about the best metaphor for life that I know. If we want to make things better, we have to pay the price, and the price, more often than not, is hard work requiring commitment that at times can approach obsession.

Symbolically, and sometimes literally, we have to hit golf balls when we'd rather not, if we want things to be better in our lives.

How do we get ourselves into the frame of mind to do this?

Maybe the Nike shoe commercials have the answer: "Just do it."

It's not easy, but it surely increases our chances of getting what we want.

'LOBSTERING' AS ADULTS
December 29, 1986

Eda LeShan, family counselor and at one time moderator of the Emmy-nominated public television series *How Do Your Children Grow?*, was describing something that happened to her years ago, when she was writing the book *The Wonderful Crisis of Middle Age*:

"I was having trouble crystallizing the idea of the necessity for continual growth and change at every phase of one's life. We were invited to a dinner party where I was seated next to a marine biologist. . . . I asked this man about his work . . . and at one point he asked me if I knew how a lobster could possibly grow when it had such a hard shell. . . .

"He explained that when a lobster begins to feel crowded in, let's say, a one-pound shell, by natural instinct it knows the hard shell must be discarded and a new, bigger shell formed. The lobster is in great danger during this process, which . . . takes about 48 hours. It can be eaten by other fish while it is completely naked and vulnerable, it can get tossed against a coral reef and badly damaged. But there is no alternative. If the hard shell is not given up, there can be no growth. The risk is essential.

"I couldn't get this imagery out of my head — I even dreamed about it — and when I mentioned it to the therapist I was seeing at the time to try to overcome my writer's block, she pointed out quite accurately that this was the symbolic, metaphoric theme of the book I was trying to write about middle age — a time for change, a time for growing. . . .

"It was absolutely true. . . . The problem for human beings is that, unlike the infallible, instinctual lobster, we don't always know when it is time to 'de-shell,' to take risks, to make room for new growth. And sometimes even when we recognize the symptoms — migraine headaches, marital crises, losing three jobs in a row, hitting a child — we don't have as much courage as the lobster. We cling to the life we are leading, terrible as it may be, in terror of facing the unknown."

■

The lobster story is recounted in LeShan's new book, *Oh, To Be 50 Again!*, and when I read it, I was stopped in my tracks. I first heard the story many years ago from a guy who was, I thought, the originator of it. Then the story turned up in the script of a made-for-television movie in which I was involved a few years ago. I've used the story in many of my speeches, and audiences always respond to it — because the analogy of the lobster's plight and our growth dilemma is so easy to picture in the mind's eye.

Was it possible that this unnamed marine biologist really created the story? I couldn't wait to ask LeShan about it when I interviewed her. What was his name, and where could I contact him?

Well, said LeShan, that really wouldn't be necessary. She and she alone had thought up the story, and when the marine biologist told it to her, it was "the second time around." The idea had come to her some years before, she said, when she saw a film about lobsters as she was doing her homework for a children's program that she was putting together.

So if I wanted to thank somebody, I should thank her, she said, smiling.

Thank you, Eda.

■

LeShan and her husband, Larry, a psychologist, were returning from Europe on the Queen Elizabeth 2, and she decided to attend in the ship's theater a one-woman show about midlife crisis.

"I sat there, and I was speechless. The woman's show was right out of my book *The Wonderful Crisis of Middle Age*. The stories were exactly the same. She was reading my material, almost word for word. I wasn't angry; I was proud. It was wonderful to hear somebody recite my work. . . .

"After the show I went up to her, and she recognized me . . . and we talked. She asked me if I would write an original one-woman show for her. That's a very exciting possibility for me, and it's going to be my next project. It's going to be the way in which I'm going to lobster."

■

LeShan, who is 63, talks a lot about lobstering. In fact, she does more than just talk about it. Not long ago she had a jeweler make up a batch of lobster pins — that's right, little pins shaped like lobsters — and she gives them out to people who have lobstered, people who have taken that frightening step into the unknown, who have dared to grow.

Would she send me a lobster pin? After all, I am the greatest fan of her lobster story, and I have helped spread it far and wide.

How about a pin, Eda?

Fine, she said, she would see that I got a pin — if I was certain that I qualified. What sort of lobstering had I done recently?

Well, I'd filmed some pilot shows for public television, and . . .

That was enough, she said. A lobster pin would be on the way to me shortly.

■

The key to aging in grand style, said LeShan, is to "go on exploring life, go on learning. The most bitter people are those who are not fulfilled, who never lived out their dreams. They spent their lives doing for others and denying themselves. . . .

"My message to young people is, 'Don't let this happen to you. For God's sake, get to it. Live your life. Don't get caught in the quiet despair of a well-paying job you hate. Don't devote your whole life to caring for others. If you do, you'll hate your life — and other people. . . . You can be helpful to somebody else only if your own life is worth living.' "

LeShan told this story:

"The woman in the hospital knew that she was dying. She was weeping, and the physician was trying to comfort her. She said, 'Doctor, you don't understand. I'm crying not because I'm dying but because I never lived.'

"The secret is to live. We have a choice. We can grow old, or we can be old and growing."

LESSONS LEARNED FROM COUNTRY MUSIC
February 6, 1984

The rental car bounced through southwestern Missouri on into northeastern Oklahoma, and the radio blared out a steady beat of country music — not because that's what I wanted to hear, but because that's all I could get, even on the powerful stations out of Kansas City.

I've never been a country-music fan, although some years ago I did have memorable interviews with Roy Clark and Merle Haggard — memorable because Clark and Haggard were so candid about their personal lives that their words were like solvent in a society in which the aim of the game seems to be to coat yourself with as many layers of disguising paint as possible.

So I sat back, reminisced and listened to the words of song after song. First I heard: *Some people never die; some people never live . . .*

Then there was: *You're the wind under my wings . . .*

And then: *You'll have a good time at my farewell party, but, please, act as if you love me. . . .*

Finally something like: *Thank God and Greyhound, you're gone. . . .*

Suddenly I bolted out of what had become a trance and said to my mother, who was making the six-hour ride to Tulsa with me: "Good grief, the guys who write the words to country music all must have doctoral degrees in philosophy — or something."

"What do you mean?" Mom still was in her trance, cradled there by the monotonous hum of tires against pavement.

"You listen to the words, and it's like you're getting a lesson on what it takes to be happy. It's a blueprint for living a rich life, for being real."

Mom said it sounded like plain old country music to her — the kind that she'd grown up with and been surrounded by her entire life. What was the big deal about it?

Some people never die. . . .

Those of us who never die are the real people. We like ourselves enough to be ourselves — not cheap imitations of others — and we never die in the sense that some part of our genuine selves rubs off on others, who learn from us something about becoming genuine, too. Perhaps, it rubs off on those who matter most to us, those in our families. But maybe it also rubs off on some people we never know, people who brush against us in the course of living and who forever are changed by something we say or do.

To me, this is our legacy, our immortality, the part of us that always lives. It's the good that we leave behind, the good that is not buried with our bones.

Some people never live. . . .

Those of us who never live are those of us who've never been ourselves — because we don't know ourselves. Often that's because we've devoted our lives to conforming to what we thought was expected of us, and in our misery, when we allowed ourselves to acknowledge misery, we cried out and asked why the landscape of our existence was so barren.

When I interviewed John Ehrlichman a few years ago, I was prepared to dislike him thoroughly — because of my memories of the austere, cold, haughty person who had lied into the television cameras during the Watergate investigation. But I found instead a warm, humble fellow who now understood, he said, what it meant to be resurrected from the grave of selling his soul to the highest bidder.

He has survived the soul-bending agony of personal and professional disgrace, he said, by deciding that he had to live his life by what he — not society — thought was important. "I have a different idea of what is important now. What do I think is important now? Will string beans climb cornstalks or not? That's what I'm trying to find out in my garden, and it's very important to me. What is very unimportant to me is what other people think of me."

There are two kinds of people, Ehrlichman said:

Those who "care enough about life to figure out what is important to them and who go and claim these things."

Those who "never come to grips with the question and who let others supply the answers and tell them how to live and what is important."

Eventually, some in this second group "may realize that they are unhappy and that they have an opportunity to change. The others are miserable, and they never know why. Society continues to tell them how to live."

The result: They never really live.

You're the wind beneath my wings. . . .

The psychiatrist had told me on the golf course one day that the people who made it big in life — in that they were happy and fulfilled — were those without too much unfinished business.

To a great extent, this means telling people who matter to you that they, indeed, do matter, that you love them, that you appreciate them. This was brought home to me with staggering force when Dad died in 1978, when I stood beside the casket for the final time and thanked God that I'd mended my fences with the man who so indelibly shaped my life, that I'd told him so many times that I loved him.

If there is victory for the living, it is for those who have said what they felt in their hearts. If there is hell on earth, it is for those who are left to cry: "Oh, God, if I'd only told him how much I loved him, but now it's too late."

You'll have a good time at my farewell party, but, please, act as if you love me. . . .

The fellow knows that funeral time is approaching for him, and he's asking the woman to make one final, supreme effort at being something she is not —

somebody who loves him.

It's a plea for pretense, no doubt about that. But it sounds like more than that to me. It sounds like a statement of self-pity from somebody who thinks that his life and even his death are hinged totally on another person, that he is a hapless and helpless victim of fate, too frail to make it on his own. Too silly to be true? To the contrary, it's a classic road map followed by people who never live.

Thank God and Greyhound you're gone. . . .

It was Roy Clark's voice — so easily recognizable — and he sang about the beauty of the black smoke that curled up around the license plate as the bus chugged away with the woman to whom he'd been chained for ever so long. No, lamented Clark, he was sick and tired of acting, of pretending that he felt things he didn't feel. It was time to say what he felt and to live the way he wanted to live. It was a mandate for honesty, a classic road map followed by people who never die.

When Mom and I pulled into Tulsa, I didn't feel tired; I felt invigorated. Mom said she felt good, too.

It would be the last trip that she and I ever would take together. On January 13, she suffered a heart attack, and in the early-morning hours of January 28, she slipped into her final sleep and died at age 74. But some people never really die — and Mom is among them.

IMPRESSIONS OF 'UNCLE SIGI'
February 9, 1986

The year was 1913, and Edward L. Bernays, the ink still fresh on his diploma from Cornell University, did what was expected of all "proper" young Americans: He went to Europe for the summer to absorb some culture.

But for Bernays, who had come to America from Vienna with his parents in 1892, it was more than a summer of culture. Rather, it was a summer that in some ways would fundamentally influence his life — because Bernays spent much of the time with his uncle, Sigmund Freud.

"He treated me as a contemporary . . . although he was 57 and I was 22," Bernays recalled. "His manner toward me reflected deep intimacy — of the kind that might be expected of two close friends who exchanged confidences after a long absence. . . . When we walked and talked, he revealed modesty, warmth, friendliness, affection — everything contrary to the image that often is given him by biographers, some of whom made him appear as tough and ego-centered. It taught me one thing: You can't always believe what biographers write."

For reasons that he doesn't understand, Bernays remembers vividly two trivial incidents from that summer. Let's listen:

"He'd taken me to a little restaurant in a house by the side of a brook. The restaurant's specialty was brook trout, which were caught in the brook and put in an aquarium, where they swam around — and you could pick out the one you wanted. . . . Uncle Sigi — that's what everybody in the family called him — stood with me at the aquarium and said, 'There are the fish, swimming in the order of their price range.' "

Another time, at another restaurant, a fly landed on their table. "At home I'd been taught to swat a fly on the table at mealtime, and so I was ready to swat this fly, but Uncle Sigi said, 'Oh, let the fly enjoy his promenade on the high plane.' So I didn't swat it."

■

Bernays, 94, who is called the father of public relations and who still is active as a consultant, is a double nephew of Freud, the legendary figure who founded psychoanalysis and who to a great extent shaped psychiatry. Freud was the older brother of Bernays' mother, and Freud married the sister of Bernays' father.

Freud's daughter, Anna, who carried on Freud's work after his death in 1939 at age 83, once told Bernays that at 21 she had been in love with him. Bernays replied: "If I had married you, it would have been the nearest thing to incest that the law permits" — because they had common grandparents.

Anna's response, said Bernays, was: "You did much better." And, indeed, Bernays always felt that he had done much better. His wife, Doris Fleischman, who died five years ago, was a writer for the New York Herald-Tribune, the author of many books and articles, and an outspoken feminist before anybody knew what a feminist was. "We had a wonderful life together," he said.

Bernays lives in Cambridge, Mass., on tree-lined Lowell Street near Mount Auburn Hospital. He talks with enthusiasm about Freud and about his support for international efforts to raise $2 million to restore Freud's London house and turn it into a world-class museum. After being whisked out of Austria to escape Nazi persecution, Freud lived the last two years of his life at 20 Maresfield Gardens. It is the house — complete with Freud's famous couch, his library and his sculpture collection — where Anna Freud remained for 44 years and founded the field of child psychiatry.

The primary fund-raising event in the United States will be a forthcoming concert in Philadelphia — "The Music of Freud's Vienna." Psychiatrists Donald L. Nathanson and Layton McCurdy are co-chairmen of the program and members of the executive committee of the International Campaign for the Freud Museum. Nathanson said that "Freud and Einstein were the two dominant intellects of the 20th century, and while Einstein has been honored everywhere, Freud still is regarded with suspicion in some circles. I believe that Freud deserves his museum and that it should be in London. Why London? Because he was happy there, and because the Freud family never lost its mistrust of Vienna" and feared an upsurge of anti-Semitism.

■

The year was 1919, and Bernays was in France at the Versailles peace conference, as a member of the U.S. Committee on Public Information. One day, he walked past a state-run tobacco store and, recalling Freud's passion for cigars, he bought and sent a box of cigars to his uncle in Vienna. Freud responded by sending not only a note of profound appreciation but also copies of lectures that he had given on psychoanalysis from 1915 to 1917 at the University of Vienna.

Bernays returned to New York to set up what was the nation's first public-relations office, and his first client was Horace Liveright of the publishing house of Boni & Liveright. Not handicapped by shyness, Bernays asked whether Liveright would consider publishing "my uncle's papers" as a book. Yes, said Liveright, he would be interested — if Freud agreed and didn't expect any advance payment. Freud gave the go-ahead, and the book, *Introductory Lectures in Psychoanalysis*, was published in 1920 at a retail price of $4, from which Freud received 15 percent.

It was this 15 percent royalty that carried Freud and his family through the depression that had made the Austrian crown virtually worthless, that had wiped out Freud's $29,000 in savings and $20,000 in life insurance, that had haunted Freud with concerns about dying before his wife and leaving her without means. Bernays regularly mailed royalty checks to Freud, and Freud always registered his appreciation by return mail. Here is the text of one of Freud's letters to Bernays:

"I am deeply touched by your unselfish zeal in this matter, which can have brought no profit of any kind to you and simply meant a kind desire of yours to assist me, your uncle, in these hard times. In truth, you are the only one of my relatives who has ever, or at least since many years, done me any service."

A few years later, the head librarian of the J.P. Morgan Library asked Bernays if she could buy some of Freud's manuscripts. Freud's response to Bernays:

"I would not object at all. I can't imagine what the value of such manuscripts might be, and I am quite willing to turn them into tangible assets, should a connoisseur turn up. But, of course, it would have to be worthwhile, if only for the sake of prestige."

Today, a Freud letter is worth about $8,000, Bernays said, but back then the going rate was . . . well, he doesn't remember the financial arrangements that eventually were reached.

In 1929, publisher Liveright approached Bernays to find out whether Freud would consider writing an autobiography — for an advance of $5,000, which, Bernays reckoned, would translate to $100,000 in today's money. Freud's response is contained in a classic letter, which is one of 52 in Bernays' possession. Wrote Freud:

"The proposal is, of course, an impossible one. An autobiography is justified only on two conditions. In the first place, if the person in question has had a share in interesting events important to all. Secondly, as a psychological study. Outwardly, my life has transpired quietly and without content and can be dismissed with a few dates. A psychologically complete and sincere life recital would, however, demand so many indiscreet revelations about family, friends, adversaries (most of them still alive) and about me that this is precluded from the very outset. What makes all autobiography worthless is, in fact, its lying.

"Besides, it is really an example of your American editor's naivete to believe he could get a hitherto decent man to commit such an outrageous act for $5,000. Temptation would begin for me at a sum a hundred times as great and even then the offer would be rejected after half an hour."

When Bernays' trailblazing book, *Crystallizing Public Opinion*, was published in 1923, he dispatched a copy to Freud and hoped for a more expansive response than he received. Wrote Freud: "I have received your book. As a truly American product, it interested me greatly."

But Freud had more to say about Bernays' second book, *Propaganda,* in 1928: "I picked up your new book not without misgivings that it might prove too American for my taste. However, I found it so clear, clever and comprehensible that I can read it with pleasure."

What did Freud mean by "truly American" and "too American"?

Bernays: "I think he meant that in my first book I maybe was too conscious that I was sure of what I was writing about. 'Who is this guy to say that he can bring about change in public attitudes?' The certainty with which I presented myself as an authority, Freud regarded as 'truly American' or 'too American,' which to him was exaggerated, overstated, semi-brash. . . .

"Cooking raw meat on a grill . . . . To Freud, that was *echt* American, true American. What cultured person cooked raw meat out in the open and then ate what he cooked? Uncle Sigi never understood that."

Was Freud fully aware of the impact that he had made on psychiatry? If he returned in 1986, would he be surprised by the honor in which he is held by so many?

"He would be surprised, I think. He did feel very devoted to his field, but he never thought of it as Einstein thought of his work — or the way Thomas Edison did. . . . I would say that Freud underestimated the idea of his importance in the world. He felt that he was into a new field of medicine, the way the first orthopedist might have felt. . . .

"If Freud came back today, he'd start trying to psychoanalyze the people of the world to try to find out why he was such a big deal. . . . He had no idea of the impact of what he'd done. . . .

"In 1931, we had a party at the Ritz-Carlton Hotel to observe Freud's 75th birthday. . . . Clarence Darrow and Theodore Dreiser were among the guests. William Allen White was the principal speaker and he called Freud 'the intrepid explorer who discovered the submerged continents of the ego and gave new orientation to science and life.' White had a much better idea of what Freud had accomplished than Freud did."

Was Freud happy?

Bernays: "I think he was warm rather than happy. When I'm talking to you now, I'm happy. When Freud talked to me, he didn't exude joy — but he was warm. He was very warm."